Jñānagarbha's Commentary on the Distinction Between the Two Truths

SUNY Series in Buddhist Studies

Kenneth K. Inada, Editor

Jñānagarbha's Commentary on the Distinction between the Two Truths

An Eighth Century Handbook of Madhyamaka Philosophy

MALCOLM DAVID ECKEL

State University of New York Press

Published by
State University of New York Press, Albany

Printed in the United States of America

For information, address State University of New York
Press, State University Plaza, Albany, N.Y., 12246

Library of Congress Cataloging in Publication Data

Jñānagarbha, 8th cent.
Jñānagarbha's commentary on the distinction
between the two truths.

(SUNY series in Buddhist studies)
Includes index.
Mādhyamika (Buddhism)—Early works to 1800.
2. Truth (Buddhism)—Early works to 1800. I. Eckel,
Malcolm David, 1946- . II. Title. III. Title:
Commentary on the distinction between the two truths.
IV Series.
BQ7460.J63 1986 181'.043 86-5695
ISBN 0-88706-301-2 (hc)
ISBN 0-88706-302-0 (pbk.)

10 9 8 7 6 5 4 3 2 1

Buddhas rely on two truths when they teach the Dharma: ordinary relative truth and ultimate truth.

To ignore the distinction between these two truths is to ignore the profound meaning of the Buddhas' teaching.

Without relying on conventional usage, it is impossible to teach the ultimate, and without understanding the ultimate, it is impossible to attain nirvana.

— —Nāgārjuna

Conventional truth is the means and ultimate truth is the end. False concepts lead anyone astray who ignores the distinction between them.

— —Candrakīrti

Here [the object] that is capable of effective action is said to be ultimately real and the other relatively real.

— —Dharmakīrti

What is ultimate for one is relative for another, just as one person's mother is another person's wife.

— —Jñānagarbha

. . . the purpose of asking a question may be twofold. One may ask a question for the purpose of obtaining an answer containing the desired content, so that the more one questions, the deeper and more meaningful becomes the answer; or one may ask a question, not in the interest of obtaining an answer, but to suck out the apparent content with a question and leave only an emptiness remaining. The first method naturally presupposes a content, the second an emptiness; the first is the speculative, the second the ironic.

— —Søren Kierkegaard

. . . The past, since it cannot really be destroyed, because its destruction leads to silence, must be revisited: but with irony, not innocently.

— —Umberto Eco

All genuinely ultimate projects of consciousness eventually become projects for the unraveling of thought itself.

— —Susan Sontag

Contents

Abbreviations

AAA	*Abhisamayālaṃkārālokā of Haribhadra*
AO	*Acta Orientalia*
IIJ	*Indo-Iranian Journal*
JAOS	*Journal of the American Oriental Society*
JIABS	*Journal of the International Association of Buddhist Studies*
JIP	*Journal of Indian Philosophy*
JRAS	*Journal of the Royal Asiatic Society*
MMK	*Mūlamadhyamakakārikā of Nāgārjuna*
PEW	*Philosophy East and West*
PTT	*Peking Tibetan Tripiṭaka*
WZKS	*Wiener Zeitschrift für die Kunde Südasiens*
WZKM	*Wiener Zeitschrift für die Kunde des Morgenlandes*

Preface

This study of the philosopher Jñānagarbha grows out of my earlier work on the formation of the Svātantrika Madhyamaka tradition in the works of Bhāvaviveka. Jñānagarbha is Bhāvaviveka's heir and helps carry Bhāvaviveka's philosophical innovations into the period when Madhyamaka thought first took root in Tibet. For someone whose focus is Tibetan Buddhism, this book could be understood as a study of one formative element in the tradition that eventually came to dominate the intellectual life of Tibet. But it would be wrong to think of Jñānagarbha and his Mādhyamika contemporaries only as a means to understand the origin of the Tibetan tradition. As I have studied the works of Jñānagarbha and come to appreciate his subtle combination of different points of view, drawn from sources as different as Nāgārjuna, Bhāvaviveka, Candrakīrti, the Yogācāra, and the Buddhist logicians, I have come to think of Jñānagarbha's thought as an example of something very dynamic in the Madhyamaka tradition. Jñānagarbha's work on the two truths records his struggle to adapt Madhyamaka thought to the philosophical innovations of his contemporaries without losing what is distinctive in his own past. What began as a study of one small part of a larger tradition has become a study of the flexibility and liveliness of the tradition itself.

Of all the forces that modified and shaped Madhyamaka thought in the period between the time of Bhāvaviveka and the time of Atiśa, the most important may very well have been the Buddhist logical tradition of Dignāga and Dharmakīrti. In spite of Jñānagarbha's clear identification with the Madhyamaka tradition, the ideas of

Dignāga and Dharmakīrti permeate his text. A poem attributed to Dharmakīrti seems to lament the absence of any worthy successor, but Jñānagarbha shows that Dharmakīrti's influence extended well beyond the narrow limits of his own lineage. One of the most important challenges still ahead in the study of Indian Buddhist philosophy is to make clear just how far Dharmakīrti's influence actually extended. The relationships between Buddhist thinkers in the eighth century and beyond are much more complicated than our textbook categories suggest. Jñānagarbha gives a good picture of the way the boundary between schools was crossed, but he also shows how much work lies ahead before we can really claim to understand the evolution of Buddhist thought in its most mature phase in India.

In the course of a study such as this, one incurs many debts. It is a great pleasure finally to acknowledge the help of those who have made this project possible. My pilgrimage through Svātantrika literature has brought me into contact with a number of Tibetan scholars who speak in eloquent ways for the living Madhyamaka tradition. Doboom Tulku, Director of Tibet House in Delhi, helped introduce me several years ago to the works of Bhāvaviveka. Palden Dragpa, Librarian of Tibet House, and Geshe Lobsang of Sera Je monastery helped me read portions of Jñānagarbha's text. Among Tibetan scholars I am particularly indebted to Tsultrim Gyatso, Abbot of Go-mang, whose restless intelligence and mastery of the Madhyamaka tradition brought many of Jñānagarbha's arguments to life. Donald Lopez of Middlebury College and Christian Lindtner of the University of Copenhagen were kind enough to read early drafts of this book and allow me to benefit from their knowledge of the Svātantrika tradition.

Finally, I would like to express my particular gratitude to Professor Masatoshi Nagatomi of Harvard University, who as my advisor and colleague has encouraged my study of the Madhyamaka tradition and made clear, through his own work on Dharmakīrti, how much the later Madhyamaka tradition owes to the tradition of Buddhist logic.

Introduction

If the volume of new literature is any measure, the Madhyamaka school of Buddhist thought has lost none of its power to attract attention and tantalize the mind. Madhyamaka thought still seems to draw students and critics the way a circus draws a crowd of five-year-olds. It even seems to exude the same sense of controlled danger and imaginative play. When a Madhyamaka author steps out on the wire of an argument, denying the ultimate validity of a concept and then denying the validity of its opposite, it is hard not to wonder how he will get home. The danger of falling into extremes always lurks under foot, and the step back onto solid ground evokes a palpable sense of relief. Meanwhile there are the distractions of the rest of the show. Philosophy is so closely related to Buddhahood that even the tightest arguments bring to mind the powers and attainments of crowds of Buddhas and bodhisattvas. Madhyamaka thought seems to be infused with what Stcherbatsky called "the solemn and exuberant catholicism" of the Mahāyāna tradition.[1]

But in all that has been written about the Madhyamaka tradition, there are still few places to turn to understand the development of the tradition in India in its later stages. Historians have let their instincts lead them elsewhere. The tradition has been approached most often through the works of its founder, Nāgārjuna.[2] When a second opinion seemed necessary, the natural place to turn was the commentator Candrakīrti, since Candrakīrti's work was available in Sanskrit and had the support of the dominant tradition of Madhyamaka interpretation in Tibet.[3] Historians have helped catalog the disputes that split the school in its later stages,[4] but the substantive study of

Madhyamaka thought has not moved far beyond the works of a few well-known authors. For someone who comes to Madhyamaka literature to understand how the philosophers formulated the great questions of Mahāyāna thought, there have been few options other than Nāgārjuna and Candrakīrti. The rest of the tradition, with all its variety and detail, has been left to philologists and specialists in the history of Buddhist thought.

This book is meant to help fill the gap. It is a translation of and commentary on a late Madhyamaka work, *The Commentary on the Distinction between the Two Truths* by the eighth-century philosopher Jñānagarbha. For specialists it is meant to add another piece to the puzzle of Madhyamaka history. For non-specialists it is meant to give a fresh and in some ways quite novel view of the basic problems of Madhyamaka thought. For both specialists and non-specialists it is meant to raise a series of questions that cannot be raised by concentrating only on the earliest or dominant expressions of the Madhyamaka tradition. Someone familiar only with Nāgārjuna or Candrakīrti will find Jñānagarbha a surprising change. The real fascination of Jñānagarbha's work, however, does not lie in the occasional new comparison or odd argument that casts the tradition in a new light, although there are enough peculiarities in the text to satisfy the most avid philologist. What is fascinating in the text is the sense of dynamism that comes from seeing a neglected author grope to express the tradition in new ways. Whether he finally succeeded or failed is almost beside the point. What is important is that his efforts show the problems and constraints that forced new generations of Mādhyamikas to express the tradition in new ways, and at the same time to channel changes in certain predictable directions. The problems are just as visible in the works of the founder as they are in the products of a late author like Jñānagarbha, but they only come to the surface when different approaches to the same questions can be held side by side. As Max Müller said, he who knows one knows none.[5] A work like Jñānagarbha's is the stimulus that forces a genuinely comparative and historical understanding of Madhyamaka thought.

Among the many virtues of Jñānagarbha's text is its size. Better known works in the Madhyamaka tradition, such as Candrakīrti's *Prasannapadā* or Bhāvaviveka's *Madhyamakahṛdayakārikā*, are too large to be dealt with completely in a single volume. When parts of their argument are extracted for special treatment, it is easy to lose sight of the pattern or structure of the work as a whole. Jñānagarbha's text is short enough to be read in a single sitting, and it allows a reader to concentrate not just on single arguments, but on the way arguments are related to the structure of the whole. The text also has distinctive historical value. It comes from the beginning of the eighth century when Madhyamaka thought was entering one of its most creative periods. The Madhyamaka tradition was then five or six hundred years old and had been criticized not just by its Hindu opponents,[6] but by a series of sophisticated critics within the Buddhist community itself. The Yogācāra commentators of the sixth and seventh centuries, Sthiramati and Dharmapāla, had each written commentaries on Madhyamaka works and objected to elements of Madhyamaka thought.[7] The tradition of Buddhist logic, stemming originally from Vasubandhu, but given definitive shape by Dignāga and Dharmakīrti, had also become powerful enough to affect the way any Buddhist philosopher shaped arguments and posed questions.[8] Jñānagarbha stood at a point in the history of Madhyamaka when Madhyamaka authors were asked to respond to Yogācāra critics while making a subtle accommodation to the style of the Buddhist logicians. And all this had to be done in a form consistent with the convictions of the Madhyamaka tradition itself.

Apparently the Mādhyamikas succeeded, at least if the stature of the eighth-century representatives of the school is any measure. Śāntarakṣita and Kamalaśīla, two major eighth-century successors of Jñānagarbha, wrote works in both the Madhyamaka tradition and the tradition of Buddhist logic. (Or perhaps it would be better to say that they wrote in a single tradition recognizing the authority of both Nāgārjuna and Dignāga.) Tibetan sources tell us that Śāntarakṣita was the monastic advisor responsible for the founding of the first Tibetan monastery at bSam-yas and that Kamalaśīla won a debate securing the dominance of Indian Buddhism in Tibet.[9] It is hard to know even today whether they are more justly venerated as logicians, Mādhyamikas, or precursors of the long line of successful missionaries to the land beyond the Himalayas.

Jñānagarbha is mentioned in Tibetan sources as Śāntarakṣita's teacher.[10] Compared to Śāntarakṣita, his works are quite brief. They lack the encyclopedic character of the *Tattvasaṃgraha*, Śāntarakṣita's compendium of Indian logic, and they do not even have the breadth of Śāntarakṣita's *Madhyamakālaṃkāra*.[11] But Jñānagarbha's position at the start of the eighth century gives *The Commentary on the Distinction between the Two Truths* significance out of proportion to its size. In a sense the text is a snapshot of Madhyamaka at a point of transition. There are features in Jñānagarbha's text that tie it more closely to the work of Jñānagarbha's sixth-century predecessor Bhāvaviveka than to the work of Śāntarakṣita. But these features exist side by side with arguments that could only be developed at a time when the terminology of Dharmakīrti had been absorbed into the Madhyamaka tradition and flowed as naturally from Madhyamaka pens as the words of Nāgārjuna. Jñānagarbha gives us a precious dose of historical specificity. He not only shows us a distinctive phase in the development of Madhyamaka thought. He shows us how the development actually occurred.

This book is designed to give a reader the tools to reconstruct Jñānagarbha's role in the changing intellectual scene at the beginning of the eighth century. Such intellectual reconstruction is complex, and it is not made any easier by the blending of otherwise divergent traditions that takes place in Jñānagarbha's work. To understand the argument of the text itself a reader might begin with chapter 3 of Part I on "The Structure of the Argument." The chapters on "Jñānagarbha's Madhyamaka Background" and "Jñānagarbha's Debt to Dharmakīrti" then can be used to identify the two main streams of influence in Jñānagarbha's thought. The next step is to read the text itself with the help of the selections from the subcommentary and notes that appear after the translation.

The notes to the translation are meant to give a detailed view of the relationship between Jñānagarbha and his intellectual background, and to assemble a cross section of the references, allusions, arguments, and terms that a contemporary of Jñānagarbha would have used to understand the meaning of the text. Anyone who has studied a similar text will know that the reconstruction of Jñānagarbha's intention goes through several stages. First, when there is no available Sanskrit text, the Tibetan translation has to be made to yield as much of the Sanskrit original as possible in order to understand Jñānagarbha in his original idiom. This does not necessarily mean reconstructing the Sanskrit text, a process of which scholars are now justly skeptical. But it does mean discerning the original Sanskrit terminology wherever possible and visualizing the structure of the original Sanskrit prose. With an image of the original modes of expression, it is possible to retrieve the substance of the argument itself. To do this, however, sometimes requires more resources than the text itself provides. Sanskrit philosophical style prizes elliptical expression. A master of philosophical prose in the eighth century omitted as much from the written formulation of the argument as he could while still making his point. It is often said that the Sanskrit grammarians rejoiced at saving a fraction of a syllable as much as at the birth of a son.[12] Eighth-century Mādhyamikas were perhaps not quite so parsimonious, but they shared the same stylistic values. Brevity was much to be sought, and the reader was left to fill in the gaps in the text from a store of common allusions, from the implication of the text itself, or from oral or written commentaries. The style was meant for an insider who was educated in the language of the learned few and had access to a tradition of oral explanation. Now, when the store of allusions has become obscure and the tradition of interpretation has been broken, reconstruction of the meaning of the text is an exhausting detective process.

The sources for this reconstruction reach out in a series of widening circles from Jñānagarbha's own work. The first source for interpreting an ambiguous argument is the text itself. Sometimes the meaning of an argument can be fixed by a comparable argument elsewhere in the text. Sometimes the meaning of an argument is made clear by the position it holds in the structure of the text. It is much easier to understand what Jñānagarbha means, for example, by his argument against "self-cognition" (*svasaṃvedana*) if the argument is read as part of his analysis of the "inexpressible ultimate" (*aparyāya-paramārtha*). It is not an argument about relative truth, but about the nature of the ultimate.

The next source for interpretation is the subcommentary. As I explain in the discussion of Jñānagarbha's works, the subcommentator seems to depart only rarely from the intention of Jñānagarbha himself. In some passages Jñānagarbha's text is so elliptical that it could not be interpreted without the subcommentary. In the argument against "self-cognition," for example, Jñānagarbha sometimes does not indicate whether he is talking about *self*-cognition or cognition in general. The subcommentator comes to the rescue by filling in the gaps. The only flaw in the subcommentary from the perspective of a modern reader is that it is only a *pañjikā* (a commentary on difficult passages) rather than a commentary on every word. In some places the subcommentator finds the argument so transparent that it needs no explanation, sometimes because it involves a maxim or proverb whose meaning was clear in Jñānagarbha's day, but now is lost. In such places we are left to struggle as best we can.

The next circle of sources is the body of Madhyamaka literature that deals with similar issues in a similar style. The Madhyamaka writers of Jñānagarbha's own day, such as Śrīgupta and Śāntarakṣita, are helpful for interpreting the significance of certain arguments. Another valuable source is Haribhadra's *Abhisamayālaṃkārālokā*. Haribhadra quotes several key verses from Jñānagarbha in the Sanskrit original and gives an expanded version of the important "one and many" argument against real causation. Slightly farther afield are the works of Bhāvaviveka and Candrakīrti. Bhāvaviveka gives earlier versions of several key arguments against the Yogācāra, and Candrakīrti's *Prasannapadā* is the source of the Sanskrit version of a number of important scriptural quotations. Outside the Madhyamaka are further circles of sources, the most important of which are Dharmakīrti's *Pramāṇavārttika* and *Pramāṇaviniścaya*. Jñānagarbha also presupposes several generations of Yogācāra thought embodied in the works of Asaṅga, Vasubandhu, Sthiramati, and Dharmapāla.

These works provide the vast majority of the textual resources for the interpretation of Jñānagarbha. Beyond this interpretive core the sources become rather vague and ill-defined. Some arguments are best illuminated by reference to works of the Abhidharma or the Hindu philosophical schools, but I have made no attempt to survey these works exhaustively for parallels to Jñānagarbha 's ideas. They are cited only when Jñānagarbha makes use of an argument that is clearly pan-Buddhist or pan-Indian in character.

Finally, there is the question of Tibetan sources. With the vast body of Tibetan exegetical literature now becoming available in the West, there is considerable temptation to interpret Indian Madhyamaka sources through Tibetan eyes. The Tibetan tradition has had the benefit of nearly a thousand years of sustained study of the Madhyamaka corpus and has the added cachet of a living connection through oral tradition with the words of the Indian masters. In this work I have attempted to incorporate the insights of the dGe-lugs-pa exegetical tradition reflected in the works of Tsong-kha-pa and lCang-skya and in the wise counsel of a number of living Tibetan scholars. But I have not attempted to survey the vast body of Tibetan literature for other references to the text, nor have I attempted to tailor my commentary or explanation to Tibetan categories. I do this quite consciously to focus attention on the interpretive resources available within the Indian tradition itself. With the presence of so much fine Tibetan analysis of Madhyamaka materials, it is easy to make the anachronistic error of thinking that Tibetan categories, worked out in another language and five centuries after the fact, define the meaning of the Indian original. In many ways Tibetan philosophers perceived the implications of Madhyamaka arguments better than their Indian predecessors. But the Indian tradition is understood most accurately in a historical sense if it is read against the Indian philosophical and linguistic background in which it first acquired its meaning.

Reconstructing the substance of an argument, of course, is only the beginning. There still is the problem of making that argument accessible to a reader in another language and another culture. There is now so much difference of opinion about how Buddhist literature should be translated that I should say a word about the principles that govern my own translation. By "translation" I mean what Dryden had in mind when he said of his own translation, "I have endeavor'd to make Virgil speak such English as he would himself have spoken, if he had been born in England, and in this present age."[13] Richard Gombrich made a similar point when he called literal translation "an intellectual fallacy and an aesthetic monstrosity."[14] For a translation to be *accurate* (as opposed to literal) it has to produce an effect on the reader that is similar to the effect it would have produced on an informed reader in the original language. If the original is meant to be obscure, the translation should be obscure. If the original is meant to be clear, the translation should be clear. The problem for the translator is that clarity in one language is not necessarily clarity in another.

The elliptical quality of Sanskrit prose poses problems in English. A vigorous Sanskrit prose style omits anything that is unnecessary or can be inferred from the context. In English it is almost impossible to be vigorous and clear without identifying parts of the sentence that would be omitted in Sanskrit. This means that a translation from Sanskrit will be littered with words inserted in brackets. In most cases these are words that the Sanskrit author can omit from the text and expect an informed reader to supply from the context. A good example of such omission occurs in verses 9–11. Verse 9cd reads: "If there is no object of negation, it is clear that in

Reality there can be no negation." Verse 10ab then reads: "If *it* is imagined, its negation must also be imagined." "*It*" in the beginning of 10ab refers to "object of negation" in the previous verse. A reader of the Sanskrit would be expected to carry the term down from the preceding verse in spite of the intervening commentary. To make this relationship clear in English, "object of negation" has to be inserted in brackets in verse 10ab. In some instances I have also used brackets to introduce short explanatory phrases rather than terms presupposed by the context, but I have tried to keep the explanatory usage to a minimum.

Sanskrit philosophical prose also favors passive constructions, in part because the passive sometimes makes it possible to omit the subject of the sentence. To produce an appropriate effect in English, I have often changed passive constructions to active. In many cases this means identifying a subject that is omitted in the Sanskrit, and in the process losing some of the conciseness of the original. In other cases it is possible to be even more concise in English than in Sanskrit. Sanskrit philosophical prose makes frequent use of abstract suffixes in order to treat abstract nouns as properties of other nouns. Mādhyamikas might say, for example, "of all things [there is] non-arising-ness" (*sarveṣāṃ bhāvānām anutpādatā*). Unless the context requires a more literal rendering of the Sanskrit, this comes across best in English as "nothing arises."[15] On the question of terminology I have tended to be conservative rather than revolutionary. For good or ill, there is an established tradition for the translation of Buddhist terms in English. Accepted terminology is rarely perfect, but I find translations most intelligible when they follow the paths charted in the earlier generation by someone like Edward Conze rather than someone like Herbert Guenther.[16] Within this broad category it is possible to make incremental changes that bring the translations more up to date.

In the end, the sad truth is that translations of Indian Madhyamaka works cannot and probably should not read with the lucidity of the best English philosophical prose. They were originally meant to use a condensed form of expression and require a reader to squeeze every word for its meaning. To simplify too much is probably to mistranslate. The final hope of a translator is to provide enough commentary and explanation for attentive readers to penetrate the meaning of the text for themselves. The size of Jñānagarbha's text helps bring that goal within reach. I hope only that my translation and notes have provided the signs and clues necessary for a reader to bring this distinctive moment in the history of Madhyamaka back to life.

Notes To The Introduction

1. Stcherbatsky's comment is found in *Madhyānta-vibhaṅga: Discourse on Discrimination between Middle and Extremes* (reprint ed., Calcutta: Indian Studies Past and Present, 1971), p. 7.

2. On the life and works of Nāgārjuna see Étienne Lamotte, "Der Verfasser des Upadeśa und seine Quellen," *Nachrichten der Akademie der Wissenschaften in Göttingen* (1973), pp. 3–49; David Seyfort Ruegg, *The Literature of the Madhyamaka School of Philosophy in India*, A History of Indian Literature, vol. 7, fasc. 1 (Wiesbaden: Otto Harrassowitz, 1981); and Chr. Lindtner, *Nagarjuniana: Studies in the Writings and Philosophy of Nāgārjuna* (Copenhagen: Akademisk Forlag, 1982).

3. For a recent summary of works on Candrakīrti see Helmut Tauscher, *Candrakīrti: Madhyamakāvatāraḥ und Madhyamakāvatārabhāṣyam* (*Kapitel VI, Vers 166–226*), Wiener Studien zur Tibetologie und Buddhismuskunde, vol. 5 (Vienna: Arbeitskreis für Tibetische und Buddhistische Studien Universität Wien, 1981). Candrakīrti's role in Tibetan interpretation of Madhyamaka can be seen in such works as Robert A. F. Thurman, *Tsong Khapa's Speech of Gold in the Essence of True Eloquence: Reason and Enlightenment in the Central Philosophy of Tibet* (Princeton: Princeton University Press, 1984); and Jeffrey Hopkins, *Meditation on Emptiness* (London: Wisdom Publications, 1983).

4. Especially in Ruegg's *Literature of the Madhyamaka School.*

5. Max Müller, *Introduction to the Science of Religion* (1873), p. 16.

6. For an example of the treatment of Madhyamaka in a brahmanical text see Daniel H. H. Ingalls, "Śaṅkara's Arguments against the Buddhists," *Philosophy East and West* 3 (1954). Mādhyamikas also could respond in kind, as, for example, in the chapter on Vedānta in Bhāvaviveka's *Tarkajvālā* (Derge Tibetan Tripiṭaka, Tohoku #3856). For brief excerpts from Bhāvaviveka's argument see V. V. Gokhale, "The Vedānta-Philosophy Described by Bhavya in his *Madhyamaka-hṛdaya*," *IIJ* 2 (1958), pp. 165–80; and "Masters of Buddhism Adore the Brahman through Non-adoration," *IIJ* 5 (1961–2), pp. 271–5.

7. Sthiramati's commentary on Nāgārjuna's *Madhyamakakārikās* and Dharmapāla's commentary on Āryadeva's *Catuḥśataka* survive only in Chinese translation. On the criticism of Madhyamaka found in these texts see Yuichi Kajiyama, "Bhāvaviveka, Sthiramati, and Dharmapāla," *WZKSO* 12–13 (1968–9), pp. 193–203.

8. The works of Dignāga are discussed in Masaaki Hattori, *Dignāga, On Perception*, Harvard Oriental Series, vol. 47 (Cambridge, Mass.: Harvard University Press, 1968). Jñānagarbha's relation to other Buddhist logicians, such as Dharmakīrti and Devendrabuddhi, will be discussed later in the introduction.

9. Paul Demiéville, *Le concile de Lhasa* (Paris: Imprimerie Nationale de France, 1952).

10. As in the ordination lineage found in George N. Roerich, *The Blue Annals* (Calcutta, 1949; reprinted Delhi: Motilal Banarsidass, 1976), p. 34.

11. *Tattvasaṅgraha of Śāntarakṣita With the Commentary of Kamalaśīla*, ed. E. Krishnamacharya, Gaekwad's Oriental Series, vol. 30 (Baroda: Central Library, 1926). The *Madhyamakālaṃkāra* is preserved only in Tibetan translation (Derge Tibetan Tripiṭaka: Tohoku #3884). The bibliography of works on Śāntarakṣita should be expanded to include Masamichi Ichigo, *Madhyamakālaṃkāra of Śāntarakṣita* (in Japanese) (Kyoto: Buneido, 1985), which unfortunately arrived too late to be considered in this book.

12. *Ardhamātralāghavena putrotsavaṃ manyante vaiyākaraṇāḥ: The Paribhāṣenduśekhara of Nāgojibhaṭṭa*, Part 1, ed. K. V. Abhyankar (Poona: Bhandarkar Oriental Research Institute, 1962), p. 198.

13. "Dedication of the Aeneis," in *The Poetical Works of Dryden*, ed. George R. Noyes (Cambridge, Mass.: The Riverside Press, 1950), p. 516.

14. Richard Gombrich, *On Being Sanskritic* (Oxford: Clarendon Press, 1978), p. 27.

15. Much more could be said about the peculiarities of Sanskrit nominal style. Those interested should consult Hermann Jacobi, "Über den nominalen Stil des wissenschaftlichen Sanskrits," *Indogermanische Forschungen* 14 (1903), pp. 236–51.

16. A useful compendium of Edward Conze's translation terminology is *Materials for a Dictionary of the Prajñāpāramitā Literature* (Tokyo: Suzuki Research Foundation, 1973). One of Herbert Guenther's more effective translations is *The Jewel Ornament of Liberation* (Berkeley: Shambhala, 1971).

Part One

Jñānagarbha and the Growth of the Madhyamaka Tradition

CHAPTER 1

Jñānagarbha's Madhyamaka Background

Tibetan tradition unfortunately tells us very little about the Jñānagarbha responsible for *The Commentary on the Distinction Between the Two Truths*. The few brief references to Jñānagarbha in Tibetan historical literature associate him with eastern India and with the philosophical circle of Śāntarakṣita.[1] Tāranātha describes Jñānagarbha as a member of the Madhyamaka lineage of Bhāvaviveka and indicates that he received instruction from a teacher named Śrīgupta in Bhaṃgala (Bengal).[2] An ordination lineage recorded in *The Blue Annals* also lists Śrīgupta as the teacher of Jñānagarbha and names Jñānagarbha as the teacher of Śāntarakṣita.[3] The historical accounts linking Jñānagarbha to Śāntarakṣita gain circumstantial support from the tradition of classifying Jñānagarbha's *Commentary* with Śāntarakṣita's *Madhyamakālaṃkāra* and Kamalaśīla's *Madhyamakāloka* as one of the three chief works (the so-called *rang-rgyud-shar-gsum*) of Svātantrika-Madhyamaka.[4] But, as with so many important movements in Indian thought, the sketchy information offered by the historians forces us back into the philosophical literature to reconstruct the intellectual background. To learn more about Jñānagarbha we turn specifically to the branch of the Madhyamaka tradition known as Svātantrika.

The origin of the Svātantrika lineage is traced to the sixth-century philosopher Bhāvaviveka. This loose lineage, which ties together thinkers as different as Kamalaśīla, Avalokitavrata, and Haribhadra, is called "Svātantrika" (*rang-rgyud-pa*) in the Tibetan tradition on the basis of a style of argument (the *svatantra anumāna*) that particularly characterized Bhāvaviveka's works. Bhāvaviveka's reputation has suffered until only recently from the enormous shadow cast by Candrakīrti over modern Madhyamaka studies. For most of this century the only access to his thought in western languages has been through translations of Candrakīrti's *Prasannapadā*, where Candrakīrti treats Bhāvaviveka's style of argument as a distortion of the method of Nāgārjuna:

> When the Master [Nāgārjuna] commented on the *Vigrahavyāvartanī*, he did not state syllogisms (*prayoga-vākya*). [Bhāvaviveka] wants to show nothing more than his excessive skill in logic (*tarka-śāstra*). Even though he accepts the Madhyamaka viewpoint, this logician's statement of independent (*svatantra*) syllogisms is immediately characterized by the appearance of numerous problems.[6]

Edward Conze must have had such passages in mind when he made the comment that until recently epitomized the modern understanding of Bhāvaviveka: "Bhāvaviveka's Svātantrika system . . . seems to have upheld the well-nigh incredible thesis that in Madhyamaka logic valid positive statements can be made."[7] Now that Bhāvaviveka's own writings are being translated from Tibetan sources, it is possible to have a more balanced, and even a more sympathetic understanding of his thought.

Bhāvaviveka's works show an author who not only had an innovative grasp of logical method, as Candrakīrti's comments suggest, but had a truly encyclopedic imagination. He wrote one of the first comprehensive compendia of Indian philosophy. In his *Madhyamaka-hṛdayakārikās* with their autocommentary, the *Tarkajvālā*, he outlines his own position, then compares it systematically to the positions of his opponents, ranging all the way from the Disciples (*śrāvakas*) to the Jains.[8] His description of other schools is faithful enough to give us important information about systems such as the Vedānta whose early history is obscure.[9] But he also has a satirical eye that enlivens what otherwise might be just a mechanical listing of different philosophical views. In his chapter on the Disciples, for example, he records the caricature of a Mahāyānist as someone who prattles mantras, bathes in sacred rivers, and is no better than a brahmin.[10] The philosophical landscape changed substantially in the two centuries that separated Jñānagarbha from Bhāvaviveka, but the tradition that stems from Bhāvaviveka never really lost either his fascination with the doctrines of other schools or his concern for logical procedure. It was natural for Jñānagarbha to treat the major philosophical figures of a later time, such as the Yogācāra commentators Sthiramati and Dharmapāla, and the logicians Dharmakīrti and Devendrabuddhi, as a reason to reevaluate and adapt the procedures of his own school.

Bhāvaviveka's major works, at least those whose authorship is not in doubt, show that he only partially anticipated the direction of this change. By the middle of the eighth century Madhyamaka works show signs of a more explicit attempt to include Yogācāra elements in a Madhyamaka synthesis. Śāntarakṣita, for example, uses a metaphor that gives equal weight to the Yogācāra doctrine of mind-only (*citta-mātra*):

> On the basis of mind-only one understands that there are no external objects, and on the basis of this [Madhyamaka] teaching, one understands that everything is empty.
>
> Riding the chariot of these two systems [i.e., the Yogācāra and the Madhyamaka] and holding the reins of reason, one attains the Mahāyāna that is their goal.[11]

His verses are reminiscent of the stages of meditation on mind-only in the *Laṅkāvatāra Sūtra*.[12] They also are reminiscent, in a different way, of Bhāvaviveka's verses on the ladder that ties the study of conventional reality to knowledge of the ultimate:

> It is impossible to climb to the top of the palace of truth without the ladder of correct relative [truth]. Thus one should first focus one's mind on relative truth and be very certain about the general and specific character of things.[13]

The metaphor of the ladder seems to allow Bhāvaviveka to include a wide range of positions as preliminary stages in the study of emptiness. But Bhāvaviveka's attitude toward the study of mind-only, at least in his formal analysis of the Yogācāra system, was much less compromising than the image suggests. He did not treat it as a necessary step in the ascent to a higher level of understanding, as it would be if it were a rung on a ladder. Nor did he treat it as one of two equal vehicles. To him it was like mud that had to be washed away before someone could move on to the correct understanding of ultimate truth:

> [Verse:] If you think that another argument is used to refute this [idea that external objects are nothing but consciousness], it would be better to stay away from the mud and not to touch it than to wash it away.
>
> [Commentary:] If you think that external objects actually do not exist, why consider them part of consciousness? If you think that someone first treats them as part of consciousness, then uses another argument, other than [the argument] that they are part of consciousness, to refute [the idea that they are part of consciousness], it would be better to stay away from the mud and not to touch it than to wash it away. . . . It is as if a certain fool were to leave a clean road and enter an unclean, muddy river. Others might then ask him, "Why did you leave the clean road and enter the mud?" If he said, "So that I can wash it off," the others would say, "You fool! If you have to wash it off, you should stay away from the mud and not touch it in the first place."[14]

The form of Śāntarakṣita's compromise was anticipated by Bhāvaviveka's image of gradual study, but the substance of the compromise seems to be a significant departure from Bhāvaviveka's own position.

It is important to say "seems" at this point until the status of the *Madhyamakaratnapradīpa* is finally settled. The *Madhyamakaratnapradīpa* is attributed to Bhāvaviveka in the Tibetan canon, and the text refers to itself as having been written by the author of the *Tarkajvālā*. But the fact that the text quotes from Candrakīrti and Dharmakīrti and shows other differences from the content of Bhāvaviveka's other works has tended to cast the traditional view of its authorship in doubt. Without getting into the question of authorship, which I think can only be settled when we examine the contents of the work as a whole, it is important to recognize that the doctrine of mind-only does appear in the *Madhyamakaratnapradīpa* as part of a graded system of meditation (*bhāvanā*). The text quotes two verses from the *Laṅkāvatāra Sūtra* that describe a form of meditation on mind-only.[15] There are a number of ways to explain the difference. It is possible that Bhāvaviveka's other works deal only with the stage of the path concerned with *darśana* ("insight" or "philosophy"), while the *Madhyamakaratnapradīpa* explicitly takes up the stage of *bhāvanā* ("meditation" or "practice"). If so, Bhāvaviveka was more inclusive in practice than he was on the level of philosophical analysis. Regardless of how we resolve the question of authorship, the text is a reminder that we still know very little about the background of the Mahāyāna philosophical tradition. Our knowledge is particularly thin when it comes to the relationship between "philosophy" and "practice." Many of the accepted ideas of the relationships between philosophers may have to be revised when we understand more fully how the philosophical literature is related to questions of practice.

It is Śāntarakṣita's formula for the use of mind-only that led the Tibetan tradition to treat his position as a second, distinctive variety of Svātantrika thought. In the work of Bu-ston, Śāntarakṣita is classified as a Yogācāra-Mādhyamika and Bhāvaviveka as a Sautrāntika-Mādhyamika.[16] Later, dGe-lugs-pa scholars adopted the terminology now used in western studies of the school: Śāntarakṣita was called a Yogācāra-Svātantrika-Mādhyamika and Bhāvaviveka a Sautrāntika-Svātantrika-Mādhyamika.[17] The difference between the two forms of Svātantrika, as mKhas-grub-rje explains it, comes from their treatment of external objects:

> There are two [forms] of Svātantrika: Ācāryas Bhāvaviveka and Jñānagarbha, among others, hold that form (*rūpa*), sound (*śabda*), and so forth are inert, external objects (*bāhyārtha*) other than mind (*citta*). Ācārya Śāntarakṣita and his followers hold that form, sound, and so forth are not objects other than mind and that neither external objects nor an inert basis [of cognition] exist.[18]

The problem with this classification for our purposes is the position of Jñānagarbha. The philosophical criterion, namely the way he treats the existence of external objects, seems to link him to the sixth century rather than to the eighth, but the historical evidence places him in the circle of Śāntarakṣita in the eighth century.

Before relegating Jñānagarbha to the position of a philosophical anomaly, it is worth looking at the sources to see how the dGe-lugs-pa tradition developed its system of classification. In Tsong-kha-pa's *Legs-bshad-snying-po*, discussion of the Svātantrika approach to conventional objects begins with a key passage in the 25th chapter of Bhāvaviveka's *Prajñāpradīpa*:

> Imagined nature consists of mental and spoken utterances such as "form," and to claim that this [imagined nature] does not exist is a denial (*apavāda*) of entities (*vastu*), since it is a denial of mental and spoken utterances. You may say that what do not exist are the objects of [mental and spoken utterances] that someone imagines [to exist], like the snake [that is imagined] in place of a rope. But [we reply that] imagined [objects] are not non-existent. [The rope] is not the object [the snake] that a mind confused by similarity imagines it to be. But conventionally it is not the case that a coiled snake is not [a snake]. To say that a coiled snake is not even a snake conventionally is to contradict common sense.[19]

In its original context, the argument is meant to be an attack on a Yogācāra position rather than a positive assertion of a Madhyamaka position, but it can be made to yield a positive statement of what Bhāvaviveka accepts as conventionally real. According to a verse quoted by Bhāvaviveka earlier in the argument, Yogācāra philosophers took the position that imagined reality (*parikalpita-svabhāva*), or the duality of subject and object, does not exist at all. To Bhāvaviveka this is an improper denial (*apavāda*) of things that do exist in a relative sense (*saṃvṛtyā*). The passage is loaded with weighty terminology, but it can be squeezed to yield a simple result. All we need to do is ignore Bhāvaviveka's studied double negative ("It is not the case that. . . is not. . .") and take it as an assertion of what he thinks exists conventionally. The parallel passage in Jñānagarbha occurs in the commentary on verse 24ab:

> [Yogācāra objection:] But [imagined nature] does not depend on anything because it does not exist.
>
> [Jñānagarbha's reply:] This contradicts perception (*pratyakṣa*). Subject and object are of imagined nature (*parikalpita-svabhāva*), but both are generally accepted (*prasiddha*) as perceptible.

The argument is more abbreviated than Bhāvaviveka's, but it clearly makes the same point.

In the *Madhyamakālaṃkāra* Śāntarakṣita handles the existence of external objects quite differently.

> Those who want to answer all false criticism should investigate relative (*sāṃvṛta*) things. Are they merely mind and mental phenomena, or are they external? Some take the latter position and say that the scriptural statements of mind-only are meant to deny that there is an agent or enjoyer. Others think:
>
> > Cause and effect are nothing but cognition. Whatever exists in its own right exists as cognition.[20]

The first approach to the doctrine of mind-only (introduced by the phrase "Some take. . .") is the one taken by Bhāvaviveka in the twenty-fifth chapter of the *Prajñāpradīpa*. The second approach (beginning with "Others think. . . .") is Śāntarakṣita's. Here Śāntarakṣita is clearly distinguishing himself from earlier thinkers in the Svātantrika tradition.

Set side by side, the three passages show two different approaches to the conventional existence of external objects. Bhāvaviveka and Jñānagarbha allow objects to be accepted conventionally while Śāntarakṣita denies them. This difference became the basis for the distinction in Tibetan literature between the Sautrāntika-Svātantrikas (Bhāvaviveka and Jñānagarbha) and the Yogācāra-Svātantrikas (Śāntarakṣita and Kamalaśīla). The distinction is helpful as a device for classifying different thinkers, but it can be misleading if it obscures the more complex historical relationships between them. Conceptual clarity is sometimes bought at the expense of historical accuracy. One problem with the Tibetan scheme of classification is that it overlooks the different purposes of the three passages. Bhāvaviveka and Jñānagarbha make their point in an attack on a Yogācāra position. Their primary purpose is not to state their own independent position. This is why the double negative in Bhāvaviveka's passage is so important and why there is nothing in Jñānagarbha's passage to correspond to the idea of investigating and finding a distinction between relative things. In Śāntarakṣita's passage the point is to make a positive assertion about conventional reality, not just to negate a negation. There is certainly a difference of approach, but the idea of using the conventional status of external objects as a distinguishing criterion only seems to have emerged after the time of Jñānagarbha.

An example of the complex relationships between different Svātantrika-Mādhyamikas in the period between the sixth and ninth centuries can be found in the argument against the real existence of things. The argument is the centerpiece of Madhyamaka thought. It would be hard to imagine Madhyamaka without it. But the argument can occur in a number of different forms, each showing a slightly different combination of interests. At the beginning of the *Madhyamakakārikās* Nāgārjuna frames the argument in terms of arising from self and other:

> Nothing ever arises anywhere from itself, from something else, from both, or from no cause at all.[21]

Bhāvaviveka and Candrakīrti generally follow Nāgārjuna's statement of the argument, not only in their commentaries on the *Madhyamakakārikās*, where commentarial style requires dependence on the master, but in their independent works as well.[22] But in the Madhyamaka literature of the eighth century other ways of framing the argument take center stage. The *Tattvāvatāra* of Jñānagarbha's teacher Śrīgupta begins with the following verse:

> In reality everything, both inside and out, is empty, because it is neither one nor many, like a reflection.[23]

This argument, based on the distinction between one and many, is repeated at the beginning of Śāntarakṣita's *Madhyamakālaṃkāra*:

> In reality the things that we and others talk about are empty, because they are neither one nor many, like a reflection.[24]

Śrīgupta and Śāntarakṣita rely on these verses to make the same point Nāgārjuna made in his verse on "arising from self and other." Each of the verses functions for its author as the fundamental argument against the ultimate existence of things. But the substance of the argument on the one and the many is closer to the Yogācāra thought of Vasubandhu's *Viṃśatikā* than to Nāgārjuna's *Madhyamakakārikās*.[25]

Jñānagarbha also uses the distinction between one and many to construct his argument, but the result is as different from Śāntarakṣita as it is from Nāgārjuna:

> Many do not produce one, many do not produce many, one does not produce many, and one does not produce one.[26]

The argument is almost a hybrid, borrowing Nāgārjuna's emphasis on the arising of things and combining it with the distinction between one and many found in Śrīgupta and Śāntarakṣita. The intellectual parentage of Jñānagarbha's verse has to include the Buddhist logicians, since Jñānagarbha has in mind particularly the arising of *cognitions* rather than the arising of objects.[27] But what is most striking from a historical perspective is that Jñānagarbha's argument occurs nowhere in Śrīgupta or in Śāntarakṣita's *Madhyamakālaṃkāra*, even though these two figures are closely associated with Jñānagarbha historically. It is picked up instead by Haribhadra in the *Abhisamayālaṃkārālokā*.[28] Haribhadra also shares key terminology with Jñānagarbha and quotes a number of his verses, but based on this argument alone, it would be plausible to argue that there was not one but two types of Svātantrika in the eighth century, one line leading from Śrīgupta to Śāntarakṣita, the other from Jñānagarbha to Haribhadra. It is more likely, however, that we face one tradition. The tradition is complex and flexible enough to incorporate and respond to sources as varied as the works of Nāgārjuna, Vasubandhu, and the Buddhist logicians.

CHAPTER 2

Jñānagarbha's Works

The Derge edition of the Tibetan canon contains seven works attributed to an author named Jñānagarbha. Of the seven, three are listed in the Tantric section of the canon and are not of direct concern to this study.[29] The four remaining works show enough similarities for us to suspect that they were written by the same author.

1. The Verses and Commentary on the Distinction between the Two Truths

The two most important works attributed to Jñānagarbha are *The Verses on the Distinction between the Two Truths (Satyadvayavibhaṅgakārikā*: Tohoku #3881) and *The Commentary on the Distinction between the Two Truths (Satyadvayavibhaṅgavṛtti*: Tohoku #3882).[30] Together *The Verses* and *Commentary on the Distinction between the Two Truths* form the work that is the focus of this study. In the Derge and Cone editions of the Tibetan canon, the verses and commentary are followed by a *Subcommentary* (*Satyadvayavibhaṅgapañjikā*: Tohoku #3883) attributed to Śāntarakṣita. The Peking and Narthang editions of the canon contain only the *Subcommentary* and omit the *Verses* and *Commentary*. With the exception of a few verses quoted in Haribhadra's *Abhisamayālaṃkārālokā*, the Tibetan translations found in these four canonical collections give us the only evidence we have to recover Jñānagarbha's text.

The title of the work is borrowed from a key phrase in the 24th chapter of Nāgārjuna's *Madhyamakakārikā*:

> Buddhas rely on two truths when they teach the Dharma: ordinary relative truth and ultimate truth.
>
> To ignore the distinction between these two truths is to ignore the profound meaning of the Buddha's teaching.
>
> Without relying on conventional usage, it is impossible to teach the ultimate, and without understanding the ultimate, it is impossible to attain nirvana.[31]

A well informed eighth-century reader would be aware that Nāgārjuna's verses themselves were part of a venerable discussion in Indian literature of what might be called simply the problem of appearance and reality. Even the terminology is not distinctively Madhyamaka. Terms such as ultimate (*paramārtha*), relative (*saṃvṛti*), and conventional usage (*vyavahāra*) were part of the general currency of Buddhist thought at an early stage. Many of Nāgārjuna's terms appear, for example, in the Theravāda text *The Questions of King Milinda*, as in the discussion of the meaning of the name "Nāgasena": "'Nāgasena' is a term, a word, a designation, a conventional expression, merely a name, but ultimately no person can be found here."[32] A reader would also know that around the two truths clustered some of the great questions of Buddhist thought. There is the obvious epistemological problem of distinguishing right forms of awareness from wrong, but the problem of right awareness leads instantly into every area of Buddhist thought. Nāgārjuna's own verses suggest an exegetical dimension: to know the distinction between the two truths makes it possible to distinguish the true meaning of the Buddhas' words. The two truths also have a moral or soteriological dimension: "without understanding the ultimate, it is impossible to attain nirvana." And behind the terminology of the verses, in such terms as *satya* (truth) and *tattva* (meaning), each of which could be translated "reality," lie questions of ontology. The two truths serve as a focal point on which the different dimensions of Buddhist thought converge.

The term "distinction" (*vibhaṅga*, or in its more common form, *vibhāga*) has complex associations of its own. In a non-dualistic system like the Madhyamaka, the idea of a distinction seems to tread dangerously close to the category of delusion. As Jñānagarbha says, from the ultimate perspective "[the Buddha] considers the relative and the ultimate to be identical in nature, because there is no difference between them."[33] To distinguish the two truths when they ultimately are identical would seem not only counterproductive, but misleading. But among the many ironies of a non-dualistic system is the fact that distinctions are necessary at least in the preliminary stages, if not throughout the system itself, if the system is to work. In non-dualistic (*advaita*) Vedānta the distinction (*viveka*) between eternal and non-eternal is a part of the preliminary discipline (*sādhana-catuṣṭaya*) that prepares for the understanding of non-duality itself.[34] Madhyamaka is like Vedānta in requiring a distinction between true and false cognition before going on to show that true cognition admits no duality. Jñānagarbha's *Distinction between the Two Truths* is thus one of a number of Buddhist texts, such as Maitreyanātha's *Distinction between the Middle and the Extremes* (*Madhyāntavibhāga*) and Dharmakīrti's *Discrimination of the Means of Knowledge* (*Pramāṇaviniścaya*), that discriminate correct from incorrect forms of awareness.[35]

The *Satyadvayavibhaṅgakārikā* and its commentary were originally written for a specialized audience who prized the virtues of elliptical expression. Because so much is left unstated, even the Sanskrit original would now present serious problems of interpretation. But without the Sanskrit original, the Tibetan translation virtually requires another level of commentary to make its meaning clear. Fortunately, we have such a commentary in the form of a *pañjikā* attributed to Śāntarakṣita. This *Subcommentary* is such an important source and so thoroughly determines our understanding of Jñānagarbha that it is difficult to determine whether the *Subcommentary* is faithful to Jñānagarbha's intent. It seems, however, that the *Subcommentary* follows Jñānagarbha quite closely. There are relatively few digressions or instances where the subcommentator clearly modifies the meaning of the text. Even then, the modifications are usually meant to overcome obvious and rather trivial flaws in the argument.[36]

A more difficult problem is the identity of the subcommentator himself. Tsong-kha-pa, along with much of the dGe-lugs-pa exegetical tradition, argues that the *Subcommentary* could not have been written by the Śāntarakṣita who wrote the *Madhyamakālaṃkāra*. Tsong-kha-pa bases his argument on two points, as he explains in his *Legs-bshad-snying-po*:

> As for the claim that Śāntarakṣita wrote the [sub-]commentary—it could have been someone with the same name or someone who borrowed the name, but it was not the author of such [works] as the *Madhyamakālaṃkāra*. There are two reasons: 1. [Kamalaśīla] refutes this [author's] explanation of the purpose (*prayojana*) of the text's composition in his commentary on the *Tattvasaṃgraha*. 2. [This author] approves the literal meaning of the statement made [by Jñāngarbha] in the commentary on the *Satyadvaya* [*vibhaṅga*], where [Jñānagarbha] says that the claim that subject and object do not exist as they appear (*yathādarśana*) contradicts perception and is denied by common sense.[37]

Tsong-kha-pa's first point is based on a comparison of the opening section of the *Subcommentary* on the *Satyadvayavibhaṅga* with the opening section of Kamalaśīla's *Tattvasaṃgrahapañjikā*. Tsong-kha-pa assumes that Kamalaśīla would not disagree outright with a point made in the *Subcommentary* on the *Satyadvaya* if the *Subcommentary* had been written by Kamalaśīla's teacher. But a close look at the two passages shows that the point is too complex to yield a simple solution. Even if we grant Tsong-kha-pa's assumption that Kamalaśīla would not have contradicted his teacher, it is not obvious from the texts of the two commentaries that the contradiction is as great as Tsong-kha-pa suggests. The two commentaries seem at first to give different accounts of the purpose (*prayojana*) of the texts. The author of the *Subcommentary* on the *Satyadvayavibhaṅga* says that the text is written simply to give a correct understanding of the two truths. In contrast Kamalaśīla says: "Mere comprehension of the True Doctrines is not the only purpose of composing the Treatise; as such an attempt would be useless."[38] But further reading of Kamalaśīla shows that he does not mean to characterize texts in general, but to distinguish his own text, which is a collection (*saṃgraha*) of various doctrines, from a text meant to discriminate (*viniścaya*) true from false doctrines. As the "distinction" (*vibhaṅga*) between the two truths, Jñānagarbha's text is meant to discriminate rather than to collect, so it need not be written with the same purpose as the *Tattvasaṃgraha*. On other points the two subcommentaries are remarkably consistent, even to the point of using identical terminology. Comparing the two introductory sections in their entirety, the single point of disagreement over the purpose of the text seems too slender to support Tsong-kha-pa's argument against Śānta-rakṣita's authorship.

Tsong-kha-pa's second point has more to do with the substance of the text. He focuses on the passage in the *Satyadvayavibhaṅga* where Jñānagarbha accepts the relative existence of the subject-object duality. If the subcommentator agrees to this, he would seem to accept the position that distinguishes Bhāvaviveka's Sautrāntika-Svātantrika from Śāntarakṣita's Yogācāra-Svātantrika. Here is the crucial passage with the subcommentator's explanation:

> [Yogācāra objection:] [Imagined nature] does not depend on anything because it does not exist.
>
> [Reply:] This contradicts perception (*pratyakṣa*). Subject and object are of imagined nature (*parikalpita-svabhāva*), but they are generally accepted (*prasiddha*) as perceptible.

Subcommentary:

> [Jñānagarbha first] summarizes the Yogācāra position: "[Imagined nature] does not depend on anything because it does not exist." That is, it never exists. This means that imagined [nature] alone does not exist, as is said [in *Triṃśikā* 24]: "The first is empty of identity." This [imagined nature] does not even exist as it appears (*yathādarśana*) and quite reasonably does not depend on any cause. Whatever exists as it appears, or in a relative sense (*saṃvṛtyā*), definitely depends on a cause.
>
> In reply [Jñānagarbha] says: "This contradicts perception." Why does this contradict perception or reject something that is both perceptible and generally accepted? He says: "Subject and object are of imagined nature . . . . They are generally accepted on the basis of means of knowledge (*pramāṇa*) acceptable to everyone, including such people as horse traders. So if you reject them, it is hard to claim that you are not contradicting perception. For [objects] such as blue and so forth, along with their subjects, are proven (*siddha*) in the perception of all living beings.[39]

The addition of the subcommentary on this passage simply sharpens the question of Jñānagarbha's relation to Śāntarakṣita, a question on which I have already commented. In one respect Tsong-kha-pa's position is beyond dispute. The subcommentator on the *Satyadvayavibhaṅga* allows a position to stand that the Śāntarakṣita of the *Madhyamakālaṃkāra* does not hold. Could the same person have written both texts? Not if we consider the dogmatic lines so clear that a philosopher of Śāntarakṣita's stature would not knowingly slip across them. But were they so clear? Could Śāntarakṣita's own opinions have evolved between the writing of the *Subcommentary* on the *Satyadvayavibhaṅga* and the *Madhyamakālaṃkāra*? Or was the position on the conventional existence of external objects even an issue of the same magnitude when Śāntarakṣita was at work on these texts?

Tsong-kha-pa developed his philosophical typologies in an era when clarity of classification was at a premium. Tibetan scholars were separated by at least two centuries from the source of the tradition in India and over five hundred years from the Indian authors themselves. Their challenge was to devise a system to rank what otherwise might have seemed a bewildering array of conflicting opinions. In that context Tsong-kha-pa's work was a singular success, at least if we are to judge from its impact on the scholarly literature of Tibet. But Tsong-kha-pa's clarity of vision was sometimes won by turning living philosophies into representatives of a type. In the Indian sources themselves there was all the experimentation and incipient contradiction of a tradition in the process of growth. Tsong-kha-pa points out a genuine contradiction—the *Subcommentary* on the *Satyadvayavibhaṅga* does, at one point, take a position different from the *Madhyamakālaṃkāra*—but how strongly should we weigh the difference in the Indian context? The answer to this question depends finally on the attitude we take toward the evolution of Śāntarakṣita's views and the views of those who worked in his circle. We now know so little about the complex texture of his work that it seems foolish to leap to a conclusion. I suspect that the tradition had good reason to attribute the *Subcommentary* to Śāntarakṣita, but in this work I will name Jñānagarbha's commentator simply as the "subcommentator" and leave the question of his identity to the reader's discretion.

A final word should be said about another commentary that is mentioned in Tibetan literature but that a determined search has not yet brought to light. In his compendium of philosophical views, the *Grub-pa'i-mtha'i-rnam-par-bzhag-pa*, written in the eighteenth century, lCang-skya refers to a commentary by rGyal-tshab on the *Satya-*

dvayavibhaṅga.[40] The commentary also is listed in the catalog of rGyal-tshab's works in Lokesh Chandra's *Materials for a History of Tibetan Literature.*[41] In spite of these references, the commentary does not appear in the collected works of rGyal-tshab presently available and does not seem to have survived to the present day.

2. A Commentary on the Maitreya Chapter of the Sandhinirmocana Sūtra

Among the other works attributed to Jñānagarbha in the Tibetan canon is a commentary on the eighth chapter of the *Sandhinirmocana Sūtra: 'Phags-pa-dgongs-pa-nges-par-'grel-pa'i-mdo-las-'phags-pa-byams-pa'i-le'u-nyi-tshe-bshad-pa* (Tohoku #4033). If this work was written by the same Jñānagarbha who wrote the *Satyadvayavibhaṅga*, it shows a very different side of his character. The Maitreya Chapter of the *Sandhinirmocana* is one of the best-known scriptural sources for the Yogācāra doctrine of "ideation-only" (*vijñapti-mātra*). In a commentary on the chapter, Jñānagarbha would be bound by the conventions of the Indian commentarial tradition to treat the text with reverence. But as a Mādhyamika, he would seem bound to reinterpret the text from a Madhyamaka perspective. The passages on "ideation-only" seem to give a perfect test of Jñānagarbha's authorship: either he accepts the doctrine at a face value, as a Yogācāra would, or he reinterprets it as a Mādhyamika. Either way he shows where his loyalty lies. Incredibly, the text itself defies such easy classification. An example of the commentary on one of the statements of "ideation-only" shows just how difficult it is to interpret.

Sandhinirmocana Sūtra 8.7:

> The Lord said: Is the image (*bimba*) that is the object (*gocara*) of concentrated insight different from the mind or not? O Maitreya, it is not. Why is it not different? Because the image is ideation-only (*vijñapti-mātra*). O Maitreya, the object (*ālambana*) of discursive cognition (*vikalpa*) is ideation-only.
>
> The Lord said: If the image (*bimba*) that is the object (*gocara*) of concentration (*samādhi*) is not different from mind (*citta*), how can the mind itself cognize the mind? O Maitreya, nothing cognizes

anything. As [discursive cognition] arises, the mind appears as [subject and object].

Commentary:

The Lord said: "Is the image (*bimba*) that is the object (*gocara*) of concentrated insight different from the mind (*citta*) or not?" Here he is asking whether the subject (*grāhaka*), which is the mind (*citta*), and the object (*grāhya*), which is the image that is the object of concentration (*samādhi*), are different from each other. He answers, "No." To explain why, he says: "Because the image (*bimba*) is ideation-only (*vijñapti-mātra*)." He means that the mind (*citta*) appears (*ābhāsate*) as an object, as if it were a [reflected] image (*bimba*), and [this image] is not different from the mind. To give further justification, he says: "The object (*ālambana*) of discursive cognition (*vikalpa*) is ideation-only." The object (*ālambana*) is the appearance of the mind in its object-aspect (*viṣayākāra*). That is not different from ideation (*vijñapti*), because it is cognized simultaneously.

"If the image that is the object of concentration is not different from mind, how . . ." is a question that would be asked by an objector. If whatever has the mark (*nimitta*) of the subject of cognition is the subject (*kartṛ*) and the image of the object of cognition is the object (*karma*), how can the two not be different? In ordinary usage (*loke*) the subject and the object appear to be different.

To demonstrate that they are not different in reality (*tattvena*) he says: "O Maitreya, nothing. . . ." The word "nothing" refers to the subject (*kartṛ*) and the word "anything" refers to the object (*karma*). They are not discrete entities. Thus the subject of cognition and the object of cognition, or the subject and object, in reality (*tattvena*) do not appear as discrete items among mind and mental phenomena. The terms (*prajñapti*) "subject" and "object" do not [have real reference]. They [refer] to combinations (*saṃghāta*), and are relative (*sāṃvṛta*), dependent, and powerless. Moreover, there is no independent entity. Thus one can only act on the basis of habitual misconception (*abhiniveśa*) about the subject (*kartṛ*). With no subject, there can be no [relationship between] subject, object, and action (*kriyā*).

[Objection:] Then why does mind (*citta*) appear to be differentiated into the aspects of subject and object?

> [Reply:] He says: "As [discursive cognition] arises, mind (*citta*) appears as [subject and object]." This means that, as discursive cognition (*vikalpa*) arises from the seeds of discursive cognition that have been nurtured (*paribhāvita*) from time immemorial by the traces (*vāsanā*) of talk about subject and object, the mind appears as subject and object.[42]

Formulas could be extracted from this passage to show that the author holds the Yogācāra doctrine of mind-only. The author says, for example: "The object (*ālambana*) is the appearance of the mind in its object-aspect (*viṣayākāra*)." But is the statement meant to apply to all objects of cognition? Perhaps not. The passage refers specifically only to objects perceived at a certain stage of concentration (*samādhi*). The commentator does not say whether the doctrine is meant to have universal application. To decide, we would have to know more about the practice of concentration than this passage tells us.

Then are there any signs that would mark this passage as a Madhyamaka interpretation of mind-only? The distinction between the real (*tattva*) and relative (*sāṃvṛta*) seems promising, but again may be misleading. The terminology is strongly reminiscent of Jñānagarbha the Mādhyamika, but it is used only to distinguish between parts and wholes. The wholes, or combinations (*saṃghāta*), are real only in a relative (*sāṃvṛta*) sense, so the terms (*prajñapti*) that name them do not have real reference. The distinction would be as much at home in a Theravāda work like *The Questions of King Milinda* as it would in Madhyamaka works. Here, in a Mahāyāna context, the distinction shows neither the influence of Madhyamaka ideas nor the opposite. It is simply a neutral rendering of a topic common to the Buddhist tradition as a whole. If we went to the text simply to learn about the meditative transformations of the mind, without any preconceived questions about its philosophical identity, the text itself would probably not even bring the questions to mind.

Given these considerations, can we decide anything about the text's authorship? Tibetan tradition indicates that there was at least one other Jñānagarbha, possibly two. A second Jñānagarbha was a teacher of the Tibetan translator Marpa in the eleventh century.[43] Another is listed as having translated the *Subcommentary* on the *Satyadvayavibhaṅga* into Tibetan at the beginning of the ninth century. This third Jñānagarbha could be identical to the Jñānagarbha who wrote the *Satyadvayavibhaṅga*, but it seems unlikely. There are thus three possible figures who might have written the commentary on the Maitreya Chapter of the *Sandhinirmocana* and no clear way to decide among them.

If we were only interested in fixing the authorship of this text. we would simply have to admit our frustration and move on. But we are interested at least as much in the intellectual environment in which Jñānagarbha (the author of the *Commentary* on the *Satyadvayavibhaṅga*) worked as in the narrow body of literature that can definitely be ascribed to him. About the larger environment this text tells us a great deal. It shows a type of literature that is loosely associated with the Madhyamaka tradition and yet avoids narrow sectarian identification. If it was written by a Mādhyamika, as the Tibetan traditions leads us to think, it was a Mādhyamika comfortable with a non-controversial presentation of a Yogācāra point of view. This is not the type of text that generates precise philosophical distinctions, but it shows the syncretic, conciliatory spirit of the eighth and ninth centuries just as well as the more formal philosophical discourse of the *Satyadvayavibhaṅga*.

3. The Path for the Practice of Yoga

The last non-tantric work attributed to Jñānagarbha is *The Path for the Practice of Yoga* (*Yoga-bhāvanā-mārga* or *-patha*). The work is listed twice in the Derge Tibetan Tripiṭaka (Tohoku #3909 and 4538). As David Seyfort Ruegg indicates in his history of Madhyamaka literature,[44] the work is similar to Kamalaśīla's *Bhāvanākrama*. It is likely to have come from a circle with which we know Jñānagarbha was associated, but it is too brief to give us much new information about the author of the *Satyadvayavibhaṅga*. The work does not show any evidence of the term *yathādarśana* ("corresponding to appearances"), which Jñānagarbha uses in a distinctive way in his definition of relative truth.[45] It does, however, follow his careful use of the term *vicāra* ("analysis") to distinguish between the ultimate and relative perspectives.[46] There seems to be no reason to deny that the Jñānagarbha who wrote the *Satyadvayavibhaṅga* wrote this work as well.

CHAPTER 3

The Structure of the Argument

To read Jñānagarbha's *Commentary* with no awareness of the patterns into which his thought naturally falls is to risk either complete bewilderment or, even worse, the suspicion that the text is no more than a pastiche of contradictions. Like other Madhyamaka writers, Jñānagarbha searches for a position of balance between extremes, matching assertions with denials and denials with assertions in a way that can be both frustratingly inconclusive and at the same time deeply revealing of the Madhyamaka view of reality. The key to interpreting this text is to sense the pattern of balance and read each element of the argument as part of a structured whole.

A. The Two Truths

The first structural feature to be aware of in the text is simply the distinction about which the text is written. The two truths are used throughout Madhyamaka literature as a device to express the balance of the Middle Path (*madhyamā pratipad*), the balance from which the Madhyamaka school acquires its name. Not all Mādhyamikas, however, interpret their "middleness" the same way. Bhāvaviveka set the pattern for the Svātantrika tradition when he argued that a Mādhyamika accepts (*siddha*) the existence of things in a relative sense, but denies them ultimately. With this distinction in hand, he was able to unravel the contradictions in some of Nāgārjuna's most paradoxical verses. Verse 18.8 of the *Madhyamakakārikās* is a good example. Here Nāgārjuna says:

> Everything is real or unreal, real and unreal, and neither real nor unreal—this is the teaching of the Buddhas.

This is truly a bewildering utterance—at least until the commentator begins his work. Bhāvaviveka explains the verse as follows:

> All *dharmas* are like nirvana; but we accept as real, in a mundane sense, certain things that are conducive to the acquisition of prerequisites (*saṃbhāra*) for the understanding of ultimate truth and are real according to ordinary conventional usage. We also accept that some are unreal. Therefore, *conventionally*
>
> Everything is real or unreal.
>
> As the Lord said, "Whatever ordinary people accept as real, I speak of as real. Whatever ordinary people do not accept, I speak of as unreal."
>
> On the other hand, [the Lord] also said that everything is real, in the sense that the sense media (*āyatana*), such as the eye, and objects, such as form, do not contradict *conventional truth*. He also said that everything is unreal, since *ultimately* nothing is established in its own right (*svabhāvena*), like magic. Hence nothing is what it seems. With regard to both truths, then,
>
> [Everything] is real and unreal.
>
> At the moment of insight (*abhisamaya*), a yogi is completely free from concepts of the reality of *dharmas*; therefore,
>
> [Everything] is neither real nor unreal—
> this is the teaching of the Buddhas.[47]

Bhāvaviveka dissolves the paradoxes by treating the verse as a mixture of the relative and ultimate perspectives—perspectives that yield first one result and then another.

The sense of balance in Madhyamaka thought, as in the Buddhist intellectual tradition as a whole, is related to issues that are more soteriological in flavor than the talk of "reality" and "unreality" in Nāgārjuna's verse would seem to indicate. The move from ontological to soteriological thinking is suggested at the end of the section on relative truth, where Jñānagarbha quotes a verse from the *Laṅkāvatāra Sūtra* about the balance between "reification" (*samāropa*) and "denial" (*apavāda*):

> There is no imagined entity, but there is a dependent [entity], because the extremes of reification and denial have to be avoided.

The terms "reification" and "denial" belong to both moral and ontological discourse. The first term refers to the mistake of attributing reality to something that is not real and the second to the mistake of denying the reality of something that is real, but both errors are also the intellectual counterparts of mistaken moral dispositions. "Reification" involves an attachment to the permanence of things and "denial" a sense of nihilism in which a person is unwilling to take seriously the pattern of responsibility and retribution that undergirds the moral life. As is true throughout Madhyamaka thought, ontology mirrors the problems of morality.

The moral dimension of Madhyamaka thought shows itself again in a variety of ways. It is never far away when one of the philosophers takes up the absence of a self (*nairātmya*), since "selfhood," in a pragmatic or conventional sense, is necessary to convince someone to be concerned for the results of his actions. But "selfhood"always is balanced with denials of self, as in *Madhyamakakārikā* 18.6:

> Buddhas use the word "self," they also teach no-self, and they teach neither self nor no-self.

Bhāvaviveka explains that the term "self" is used specifically to avoid the mistake of thinking that actions bring no results.

> There are sentient beings whose minds are stained by the false view of denying (*apavāda*) cause and effect. They mistakenly think that the present world and the world to come do not exist, good and bad actions do not bear fruit, and sentient beings are born spontaneously. They become obsessed with bad actions, and they hover on the brink of bad states of rebirth (*gati*). Buddhas have pity on them. Because of their vow to seek the welfare of others, they see that if these beings depend only on themselves, they would never escape rebirth, and [the Buddhas] use conventional designations to say, "There is a self."[48]

Bhāvaviveka's explanation shows how the problem of moral retribution is related to the problem of causation in general. Moral questions once again become questions of ontology. Do actions cause results?

Do things arise? According to Bhāvaviveka and his followers, they have to. Otherwise the controlled, disciplined pursuit of Buddhahood would be impossible.

The first step in understanding the two truths is simply to keep them apart. From the conventional perspective things arise and actions cause results. From the ultimate perspective all things are empty and nothing can arise in its own right. But the two perspectives also are related in such a way that each reinforces the other. Someone operating in the realm of relative truth, who wants to achieve the merit that comes from good actions, achieves it best by cultivating an awareness of emptiness. To know that things are empty reduces selfish attachment and makes it possible to act with a purity of motive that brings the best moral consequences. Conversely, to understand the emptiness of things, a person should put emptiness into practice, and practice involves a shrewd calculation of conventional gain and loss. The two truths represent contradictory perspectives, but they are opposites that complement each other. Each perspective helps to deepen and reinforce the other so that the two together make a balanced system.

B. From Affirmation to Negation

The sense of balance in the distinction between the two truths can also be felt at other levels in Jñānagarbha 's thought, even within the description of the truths themselves. In verses 4–7, for example, Jñānagarbha gives both an affirmative and a negative account of ultimate truth. In verse 4 he defines "the expressible ultimate" (*saparyāya-paramārtha*) as a rational cognition that can be distinguished from a merely relative cognition:

> 4abc. Since it cannot be contradicted (*avisaṃvāda*), reason (*nyāya*) is ultimate (*paramārtha*) and is not relative (*saṃvṛti*).

In the next three verses he explains what the ultimate *is not*. In the course of the explanation, he criticizes the Yogācāra conception of "self-cognition" (*svasaṃvedana*) and argues that the ultimate cannot even be regarded as an existing cognition. His full explanation has the paradoxical quality of Nāgārjuna's passages that mix the conventional with the ultimate. For him the ultimate is something about which much can be said and about which nothing can be said. It is something that can be distinguished from the relative and also something to which no distinctions apply. The affirmative element in the definition, in which Jñānagarbha accepts the validity of conceptual distinctions, gives way to a negative definition in which the distinctions are transcended.

The same is true in Jñānagarbha's account of relative truth. He starts with an affirmative definition in verse 8:

> A mere thing (*vastu-mātra*), which (A) is not confused with anything that is imagined and (B) arises dependently, is known as correct relative [truth]. Whatever is imagined is incorrect.

He goes on in the next seven verses to explain what he means by his two defining criteria: "not confused with anything imagined" and "arising dependently." But each section, in a curious way, shows how the distinctions do not apply if they are looked at from the perspective of the ultimate. At least it would seem curious if we were not already prepared to see a paradoxical relationship between the two truths. In his explanation of the first criterion, Jñānagarbha argues that the negation of imagined objects is ultimate. But when he looks at the negation from the ultimate point of view, it is only relative:

> 9. The negation of arising is consistent with Reality (*tattva*), so [we] also consider it [to be ultimate]. But if there is no object of negation, it is clear that in Reality there is not negation.

From one perspective the distinction applies, from another it does not.

The section on the "dependent arising" of relative truth follows a similar pattern. Jñānagarbha starts with a verse that uses Dharmakīrti's concept of effective action (*artha-kriyā*) to distinguish correct from incorrect relative truth:

> 12. Correct and incorrect relative [truth] are similar in appearance, but they are distinguished by their ability or inability to produce effective action.

But then, in one of the longest discussions of a single topic in the text, he argues that there can be no causal relationship at all. The discussion centers on a single verse:

14. Many do not produce one, many do not produce many, one does not produce many, and one does not produce one.

Again, the shift to an ultimate perspective turns the point upside down. He starts by telling us the way to distinguish and define relative truth, then shows how the distinctions ultimately do not apply.

The pattern of argument in which affirmation is followed by negation is familiar to anyone who has opened the pages of a Madhyamaka text. For that matter, it would be familiar to anyone who reads the literature of negative theology, whether it be the work of Pseudo-Dionysius or Śaṅkara. The system requires a preliminary recognition of distinctions, between the self and the goal or between the self and the Absolute, but the distinctions are established only to be overcome. Jñānagarbha begins by distinguishing the two truths, but finds again and again that the distinctions are relativized and left behind.

C. From Negation to Affirmation

If the argument stopped with the negation of distinctions it would be much less challenging than it is and, given Madhyamaka presuppositions, much less cogent. It would be equivalent to saying that there are two truths, but that from the perspective of one of them the other is groundless. To favor one perspective so completely over the other may seem necessary, but it offends the sense of balance that makes the Mādhyamikas search for the "middle" between extremes.

Once Jñānagarbha has shown how the relative and ultimate perspectives produce different conclusions, the next step in the argument is to apply the ultimate perspective to the ultimate itself:

16. From the standpoint of reason, the meaning of the words "ultimately [things] do not arise" also does not arise. Other [such statements] should be interpreted the same way.

17. [The Buddha] considers the relative and the ultimate to be identical in nature, because there is no difference between them. This is because reason also corresponds to appearances.

To say that reason (*nyāya*) corresponds to appearances (*yathādarśana*), in Jñānagarbha's terminology is to say that the ultimate (*paramārtha*) is relative (*saṃvṛti*). This is a striking conclusion, but one that is consistent with everything that has gone before. Up to this point, he has tied affirmative statements that distinguish the two truths to statements showing that the distinctions do not ultimately apply. The ultimate is a rational cognition, as he explains in verse 4, but not a *real* cognition, as he explains in his refutation of self-cognition in verse 6. The relative is something that arises dependently, but ultimately nothing arises dependently. Now even the distinction between ultimate and relative falls away. From one perspective he says that the two are different, from another he says that even the ultimate is no more than a reflection of the relative.

This argument is reminiscent of the contradictory, yet complementary relationship between the two truths in their moral aspect. From one perspective the two truths are distinct and have to be kept apart for the system to function, but from another perspective the two reinforce and complement each other. Someone who understands the system can hold the two perspectives together and not be confused by their apparent contradictions. To give up the attachments that stand in the way of action, it is important to understand that all distinctions are empty. But it is just as important to keep from being dazzled by the absence of distinctions and failing to put the awareness into practice. When Jñānagarbha turns the ultimate on the ultimate and finds it no different from the relative, he is giving the classic Madhyamaka argument for the return to the relative. The emptiness of emptiness itself compels a person to reappropriate and affirm, in a transformed way, the distinctions of the relative world.

In the third step in the argument, Jñānagarbha moves beyond the statement of non-distinction to a stage in which distinctions are reappropriated:

> 21. [The relative] corresponds to appearances, so it must not be analyzed. Something is contradicted if, when analyzed, it turns out to be something else.
>
> 22. [Objection:] Explain why one thing appears to be caused by another. [Reply:] It is just that one thing appears to be caused by another. What more is there to say?

Here the term no-analysis (*avicāra*) has a crucial function. In other Madhyamaka texts of the same period, as different as Śrīgupta's *Tattvāvatāra* and Atiśa's *Satyadvayāvatāra*, the term appears as one of a series of defining characteristics of relative truth.[49] Here Jñānagarbha extracts it from its normal place for emphasis and to make a point that is crucial to his argument: relative truth can only be reappropriated when one knows precisely what questions *cannot* be asked of it. To ask how it arises is to approach it from the ultimate perspective and to invite the answer, "It does *not* arise!" Relative truth is a category that "only satisfies when it is not analyzed" (*avicāraramaṇīya*). Then what can be said about the process of causation? "Just that one thing appears to be caused by another. What more is there to say?" There is much more that can be said about other things, as Jñānagarbha points out in the discussion of Vimalakīrti's silence in verse 11. But questions that come too close to the arising of a thing in itself cross the narrow line that separates ultimate from relative, and, under questioning, the relative dissolves into thin air.

After his section on the analysis of relative truth, Jñānagarbha digresses briefly to deal with opponents' objections. He then concludes the book with a section that brings the reappropriation of relative categories back to questions of morality and salvation. He takes up *karma*, transmigration, and Buddhahood as categories based only on relative truth. *Karma*, for example, exists only "as it appears."

> 31. [The Buddha] teaches action (*karma*) and its results just as they appear to him who sees them. This is why all [actions and results] are as they appear.

At the end of this section, he writes a luminous verse that captures as well as any in the text the complex ironies of self and non-self, distinction and non-distinction.

> 46. May the merit I have gained by distinguishing the two truths cause the whole world to develop the seed of understanding (*jñānagarbha*).

May the merit that I have gained by making these distinctions accrue to you, so that you can become identical to me! The patterns of distinction and non-distinction finally coalesce into a single image—the seed of understanding—which is the beginning of the path, contains the path in its totality, and at the same time is the name of the author himself.

D. Dialectic or Paradox?

To understand the elegance of Jñānagarbha's argument takes a certain instinctive affection for the topography of a circle: not the vicious circle of the logicians, but the empty circle of Zen or perhaps the spiraling movement of the bodhisattva's career, leading first into contemplative abstraction, then back into the world of suffering. Jñānagarbha revels in the irony of asserting a position, then showing that it can only be true if the opposite also is true. How else are we to understand the contrast of verse 2 with verse 17?

> 2. Those who know the distinction between the two truths do not misunderstand the Sage's teaching. They acquire all prerequisites and achieve perfection.
>
> 17. [The Buddha] considers the relative and the ultimate to be identical in nature, because there is no difference between them. This is because reason also corresponds to appearances.

Even the title of the work itself has an ironical dimension: to understand the Buddha's teaching correctly takes a correct understanding of the distinction (*vibhaṅga*) between the two truths, but ultimately there is no difference between them. A complete understanding of the two truths requires that they be understood both ways simultaneously.

The argument leads to the familiar but disorienting world of paradoxical discourse, where a thing is what it is precisely because it is not. Jñānagarbha often gives the impression that he is trying simply to "draw the cork out of an old conundrum and watch the paradoxes fizzle."[50] In another kind of work, where the author sets out deliberately to shroud the nature of ultimate reality in a veil of mystification, it would be enough to know why and how the paradoxes are generated without searching for a resolution. But

Jñānagarbha intends to give a precise specification of the ultimate, or, if not of the ultimate itself, of how the ultimate is to be understood. To be fair to Jñānagarbha's intention we should ask whether there is a stage in the argument, beyond distinction and non-distinction, in which the paradoxes are taken up and resolved. Is there a way to understand the two truths that transcends the contradiction of distinction and non-distinction, yet preserves what is valid in both of those two perspectives? A more precise way to pose the question is to ask whether Jñānagarbha's argument is meant to be a formal dialectic, in which thesis and antithesis give way to a synthesis, or whether Jñānagarbha intends only to generate a series of paradoxes, with no separate resolution outside the paradoxes themselves.

Some of the most influential modern studies of Madhyamaka characterize it in a general way as dialectical. This is done to emphasize the critical function of Madhyamaka thought: it attacks the reification of any *thing* in its own right and rejects the suggestion that any single position is able to express truth in its totality. The term "dialectical" is also used to emphasize Madhyamaka's dynamic character: Madhyamaka arguments move in a dialectical style not only to criticize other positions, but to criticize the criticism. In a sense, Madhyamaka never stands still. It is not content with any single formulation of the truth, however rarefied or intricately qualified, lest it slip into the intellectual "reification" that its philosophical method is meant to avoid. According to T.R.V. Murti, Madhyamaka thought is also dialectical in the sense that it transcends the contradictions of reason and moves to a further position in which the contradictions are resolved.

> The Mādhyamika dialectic tries to remove the conflict inherent in Reason by rejecting both the opposites taken singly or in combination. The Mādhyamika is convinced that the conjunctive or disjunctive synthesis of opposites is but another view; it labours under the same difficulties. Rejection of all views is the rejection of the competence of Reason to comprehend reality.[51]

Murti acknowledges the negative function of the dialectic in marking reason's limits, then goes on to say that the dialectic plays the positive role of clearing the ground for a "higher faculty" through which reality is accessible:

> The Mādhyamika denies metaphysics not because there is no real for him; but because it is inaccessible to Reason. He is convinced of a higher faculty, Intuition (prajñā) with which the real is identical.[52]

For Murti the contradictions between distinction and non-distinction or between being and non-being are resolved at the level of this higher intuition.

> The Mādhyamika Dialectic as negation of thought is intuition of the Absolute; as the rooting out of passions it is Freedom (Nirvāṇa); and it is perfection as union with the Perfect Being.[53]

This is not the place to discuss Murti's understanding of the reality (or lack of reality) to which the critique of the Madhyamaka is meant to point. I have argued elsewhere that the Madhyamaka criticism of Yogācāra shows how misleading it is to claim that Madhyamaka arguments point to an ultimate reality beyond words.[54] The issue here is simply the form of the arguments themselves. On the critical and dynamic aspects of Madhyamaka thought, Murti is surely correct. In these respects, Madhyamaka certainly has a dialectical character. But it is not as clear that Jñānagarbha's argument is dialectical in the more formal sense of yielding a resolution of opposites.

The difficulties can be seen by comparing the stages of Jñānagarbha's argument with the thesis, antithesis, and synthesis that make up a formal dialectic. The first stage of Jñānagarbha's argument, corresponding to the distinction between the two truths set out in verse 2, offers no problem. It can be understood as a simple affirmation or thesis. The second stage, corresponding to the denial of distinctions in verse 17, also is a straightforward antithesis. But the reappropriation of distinctions in verses 21 and 22, the third stage of Jñānagarbha's argument, is more of a return to an earlier position than a separate synthesis. To say otherwise would be to reify the synthesis as a third position different from the other two, when Jñānagarbha's intention is to argue that the two initial perspectives are exhaustive.

The point is a subtle one. It has to do with the extent to which the conclusion of the argument is reified. There is critical movement in the argument, and the movement does not rest in either the thesis or antithesis alone, but it is not resolved in a *separate* third position. It simply leads back to the other two. It is more of a return to the thesis and antithesis together than a "taking up" or "sublation" of thesis and antithesis in a new synthesis. The passage from the thesis to antithesis, then to the reappropriation of the thesis makes the argument more paradoxical than dialectical, if by dialectic is meant adherence to a pattern of argument in which a separate synthesis supersedes both the thesis and the antithesis. Jñānagarbha concludes his argument just where he began. But on the way to his conclusion he argues that the distinctions with which he began can only be affirmed if he can also affirm that there are no distinctions. Distinctions can apply only if they are relative, not ultimate.

In its fondness for such paradoxes, Jñānagarbha's argument is reminiscent of the treatment of opposites in the work of the modern Japanese philosopher, Keiji Nishitani. Nishitani uses a Japanese conjunction *soku* (Chinese *ji*), translated by Van Bragt with the Latin *sive*, to indicate the paradoxical identity of a thing and its opposite.

> When we say "being-*sive*-nothingness," or "form is emptiness; emptiness is form," we do not mean that what are initially conceived of as *being* on one side and *nothingness* on the other have later been joined together. In the context of Mahāyāna thought, the primary principle of which is to transcend all duality emerging from logical analysis, the phrase "being-sive-nothingness" requires that one take up the stance of the "*sive*" and from there view being as being and nothingness as nothingness.[55]

Nishitani uses *soku* to avoid suggesting that the conjunction of being and nothingness, or affirmation and negation, constitutes a third position different from both. That would be to reify the notion of emptiness as a separate position transcending both affirmation and negation. Emptiness does transcend them, of course, but not in a metaphysical sense and not as something separate. It transcends even itself and leaves the reader back at the start, with *mere* being as being and *mere* nothingness as nothingness.

The word "mere," with its analogs "only," "just," or "sheer," moves almost imperceptibly through the pages of both Nishitani and Jñānagarbha. It can go almost unnoticed, but it bears profound philosophical weight. It appears at points where Nishitani wants to suggest a resolution of the conflict of opposites without implying that there is anything else but the opposites themselves:

> But when we pursue the *essentiality* of this essential life to its very end, non-essential life appears where essential life reaches its outer limit, its point of consummation, where it is, as it were, on the point of being totally consumed. In other words, true nirvāna appears as samsāra-*sive*-nirvāna. Here life is sheer life and yet thoroughly paradoxical.[56]

Reading further in Nishitani shows that the phrase "sheer life" is related to the "just sitting" of Zen meditation:

> Dōgen tells us that when he was studying and practicing Zen under Juching, he attained the Great Enlightenment in a flash upon hearing Ju-ching say, "To practice Zen is to drop off body-and-mind. . . it is *just sitting*."[57]

In the translation of Jñānagarbha the term "mere" (*mātra*) appears in the definition of correct relative truth in verse 8 ("A mere thing, which is not confused with anything that is imagined . . . is known as correct relative [truth]"). It also is echoed in what may be the most important verse in the text, verse 22, where Jñānagarbha explains what it means to understand causation without analysis ("It is just that one thing appears to be caused by another. What more is there to say?").

The term "mere" has the same paradoxical flavor in English that its counterparts have in Sanskrit or Japanese. It is used to indicate that the reappropriation of the relative, or the understanding of the relative as relative-*sive*-ultimate, is both more and less than meets the eye. It is the ordinary, mistaken understanding of things *minus* what is imagined (*kalpita*), or the ordinary understanding of things minus what is negated by the understanding of emptiness.[58] Correct relative truth is the ordinary cognition of things *minus* the illusion that they are ultimately real. But, of course, less is more. To understand the "mereness" of a thing is to be free from illusion, know it as it really is, and appropriate it in the fullness of its being. The word initially sounds negative and suggests a subtraction. But the subtraction is a subtraction of illusion, with a result that is positive in the same way that the term "sheer" is positive in phrases like "sheer pleasure." It is meant to indicate reality plain and simple, but also reality in its fullness.

This term, whether it is the Sanskrit *mātra* or the English "mere," is another indication of the importance of paradox in Jñānagarbha's thought. It is crucial that Jñānagarbha *not* portray the resolution of his critique as "something more" than the elements of the critique itself. That would reify the outcome and lead to precisely the errors the critique is meant to avoid. The circular form of reasoning is essential; the argument must end "merely" where it began. But, of course, this is not the whole story. If the argument did nothing more than lead back to the beginning, it would be pointless. To be significant, the argument requires some statement of the positive point toward which the transformed understanding of what is "merely" relative is moving. To explain the goal of his argument, Jñānagarbha includes a discussion of Buddhahood as the last quarter of the text. The transformation of awareness mapped in the earlier parts of the text leads forward to the full awareness of things as they are, an awareness that is identified with the Buddhahood described at the end:

> 37. The Omniscient One sees everything that is empty of imagined nature and arises dependently, in a way that corresponds to appearances.
>
> 40. The place where he rests becomes the locus of every inconceivable virtue. It is incomparable, worthy of worship, a guide, and quite inconceivable.

To hold the awareness of the bare appearance of things together with an awareness of their emptiness is to possess the cognition of a Buddha.

Then is Jñānagarbha's argument finally dialectical or paradoxical? Certainly the element of paradox is essential. To suggest otherwise would imply that there is "something more" or "something beyond" the affirmations and negations that make up the argument itself. Such a suggestion would reify the outcome of the argument in precisely the way the argument is meant to avoid. But the argument does not stand still. In moving forward toward the goal of Buddhahood it shows the dynamism Murti had in mind when he spoke of the Madhyamaka dialectic. It is paradox, but paradox with the insatiably dynamic quality of a dialectic. It is never content to rest at any single point, lest it suggest that there is a real resting place short of Buddhahood, the place which is no place.

Perhaps the best category to describe Jñānagarbha's mode of argument is not dialectic or paradox but irony.[59] No one would make the mistake of claiming that Jñānagarbha is one of the world's great comic writers, but there is much in his argument that reminds a reader of the deep sense of playfulness that in Indian civilization characterizes the freedom of the enlightened mind. Nishitani alludes to this sense of play when he says:

> On the field of emptiness, then, all our work takes on the character of play. When our doing-being-becoming, when our existence, our behavior, and our life each emerges into its respective nature from its outermost extreme, that is, when they emerge from the point where non-ego is self into their own suchness, they have already cast off the character of having any why or wherefore. They are without aim or reason outside of themselves and become truly autotelic and without cause or reason, a veritable *Leben ohne Warum*.[60]

This is not some crude sense of comedy, but the exquisitely learned humor of a mind that perceives in each affirmation about the nature of things the presence of its opposite and senses in the irony and ambiguity of things a freedom from the bondage of ordinary conceptuality. In a civilization that elsewhere pictures the freedom of God in the mischief of a child, the philosophical investigation of ultimate reality takes on the character of play. In even the simplest and most cryptic philosophical utterances one senses the presence of complex levels of irony left unsaid, and behind the words the presence of a philosophical mind that, in E.B. White's words, laughs "the inaudible, the enduring laugh."[61]

CHAPTER 4

Jñānagarbha's Debt to Dharmakīrti

The structure of Jñānagarbha's argument makes the question of influence particularly complex. Even his own affirmations are shrouded in such a network of claims and counter-claims that piecemeal interpretation is impossible. It is difficult to know, when Jñānagarbha uses a term or style of argument derived from one of his opponents, whether the borrowing is genuine or whether he is adopting something simply to reject it. But to understand the spirit of Madhyamaka philosophy in the eighth century demands an effort to grasp the relationship between the Madhyamaka and the broad tradition that stems from Vasubandhu, particularly the tradition represented by the Buddhist logicians.[62] So much of the terminology and logical technique of Madhyamaka thought in this period reflects the terminology of Dignāga, Dharmakīrti, and their successors that the Madhyamaka cannot be understood in isolation. In the case of Śāntarakṣita and Kamalaśīla, whose writings in Buddhist logic far outweigh their writings in Madhyamaka, it is even unclear whether they should be called Mādhyamikas in an exclusive sense. They were practitioners of both traditions and drank equally from both streams of thought.

The close relationship between the Madhyamaka tradition and the tradition of Buddhist logic is marked on the Madhyamaka side by a tendency to reconceive traditional ontological questions in the epistemological form made popular by Dignāga and his successors. This epistemological shift is particularly pronounced in the works of the eighth century, but it is not confined to that period. Bhāvaviveka, in the sixth century, shows a heightened awareness of epistemological issues. His concern for formal logic is embodied in the name of the "independent inference" (*svatantra anumāna*), the name that is now used to designate the Svātantrika Madhyamaka of which he is the source. Less well-known is his tendency to define key terms in a way that emphasizes their epistemological dimension. He defines the term *paramārtha* (the ultimate), for example, as "that [cognition] whose object is ultimate."[63] Jñānagarbha follows Bhāvaviveka's lead when he defines *paramārtha* as the cognition that is "the ultimate (*parama*) meaning (*artha*)." Jñānagarbha takes the term as a *karmadhāraya* compound, while Bhāvaviveka takes it as a *bahuvrīhi*, but the result is the same. Both understand the term as referring primarily to a cognition. For both philosophers, discussion of the two truths is primarily a discussion of different epistemological perspectives.

In Jñānagarbha's work the shift toward epistemology is even more clear, particularly if we compare the way the two philosophers criticize the Yogācāra treatment of consciousness as ultimately real. In Bhāvaviveka's case, the argument is formulated as a critique of the ontological categories "dependent nature" (*paratantra-svabhāva*) and "absolute nature" (*parinispanna-svabhāva*).[64] In Jñānagarbha it is a critique of the cognitive category *svasaṃvedana* (self-cognition), the category used by the Buddhist logicians to refer to the aspect of every cognition that is aware of itself. The argument functions analogously for both, but for Jñānagarbha it takes an epistemological form missing in Bhāvaviveka.

A similar contrast can be found in their argument against the ultimate arising of things. In Bhāvaviveka's case, the argument does not differ substantially from the argument formulated by Nāgārjuna: both of them deny that anything can arise from itself, from something else, from both, or from neither. In Jñānagarbha the argument about self and other is replaced by the argument that many do not produce one, many do not produce many, one does not produce many, and one does not produce one. In his commentary Jñānagarbha explains that this argument is meant to accommodate all the possible combinations through which a *cognition* can arise. In Bhāvaviveka's argument, the examples are physical entities like the sense organs. Jñānagarbha, on the other hand, visualizes a situation that is strictly cognitive. As if to underline the importance of the shift, Jñānagarbha introduces verse 14, the verse in which this argument appears, with a series of interpolated verses (*antara-śloka*) to explain that no relationship of cause and effect can be *known*. He surrounds the whole argument with an epistemological framework.

What is most striking about this shift toward epistemology is how little the philosophers themselves seem to have been aware of "borrowing" either the techniques or the preoccupations of their opponents. Our own textbook categories, by which we tend to freeze "Buddhist Logic" and "Madhyamaka" into separate schools of thought, lead us to look for opposition and contradiction when the relationship between the philosophers who embodied these perspectives is much more fluid. Bhāvaviveka himself is a case in point. He divides his *Madhyamakahṛdayakārikās* into chapters that deal separately with schools such as that of the Śrāvakas, the Yogācāra, the Sāṃkhya, and so forth, and he takes a critical approach to their doctrinal assertions. But his criticism should not obscure the fundamentally inclusive character of his thought. When he criticizes the doctrine of mind-only, he does not reject the concept itself, only what he takes to be the Yogācāra interpretation of it.[65] He even goes so far as to admit that the Brahman of the Upaniṣads *is* the Dharma-Body of the Buddhas; he claims only that Vedāntins have misunderstood its true nature.[66] There is an element of irony in this, of course, since he explains, in the paradoxical style of which Bhāvaviveka also is fond, that the proper way to worship Brahman is "through the discipline of non-worship" (*anupāsana-yogena*). But the passage has a serious intent. He treats all the traditions as ways of approaching reality (*tattva*). His role is merely to discern (*viniścaya*) the reality in each.

The inclusive spirit of Bhāvaviveka's work is even more pronounced in the work of Jñānagarbha, where the traditions of Nāgārjuna and Dignāga are still more deeply interfused. Examples of such intermingling abound, as in Jñānagarbha's use of the term *artha-kriyā* (effective action) to define correct relative truth, and in the use of the term *avisaṃvāda* (not to be contradicted) to define the ultimate.[67] No one could hear these terms in Jñānagarbha's time and not be reminded of the discussion of the two truths in the works of Dharmakīrti. But alongside these points of convergence also are points of controversy, as in Jñānagarbha's criticism of Dharmakīrti's student Devendrabuddhi for his treatment of the etymology of *saṃvṛti* (the relative).[48] To what extent was Jñānagarbha influenced by Dharmakīrti and his followers? In the complex pattern of convergence and disagreement, the challenge is to find some consistency. What we need is a principle that can define the extent of Jñānagarbha's dependence on the Buddhist logicians, a principle that will make clear how far Jñānagarbha can go in adopting Dharmakīrti's point of view without compromising the integrity of his own Madhyamaka method.

The best way to formulate such a principle is to go back to the structure of Jñānagarbha's argument itself. There the pattern of affirmation, denial, and reaffirmation gives Jñānagarbha a way to absorb his opponents' ideas while still turning them to a Madhyamaka end. An example is Jñānagarbha's use of the term *artha-kriyā* (effective action). *Artha-kriyā* is a key element in Dharmakīrti's definition of the two truths, as in verse 2.3 of the *Pramāṇavārttika*:

> Here [the object] that is capable of effective action is called ultimately real and the other is relatively real.

Dharmakīrti's commentators explain that by *artha-kriyā* he means an action that is conducive to a useful purpose. A cognition of fire, for example, is valid if the "fire" is capable of burning and cooking; otherwise the cognition is not truly a cognition of fire.[75] According to Dharmakīrti, it is precisely what is capable of *artha-kriyā* that is ultimately real (*paramārtha-sat*). Jñānagarbha also uses the concept as a criterion of reality. He considers the ability to produce *artha-kriyā* to be the mark of a valid cognition, but only of a cognition that is valid in a relative sense (*saṃvṛtyā*):

> 12. Correct and incorrect relative [truth] are similar in appearance, but they are distinguished by their ability or inability to produce effective action (*artha-kriyā*).

The criterion of reality is the same, but Jñānagarbha does not consider it a criterion of *ultimate* reality.

To underline the importance of this distinction, Jñānagarbha moves on immediately after verse 12 to his critique of causation. He first indicates in verse 13 that he anticipates disagreement:

> 13. If you also think that [things] correspond to appearances [i.e. relative truth], rather than to Reality, we agree. But it is a completely different story if [you think that] they correspond to reason.

He then gives his arguments against the possibility of knowing a causal relationship and against the possibility of causation itself. All is meant to show that, while *artha-kriyā* may be an empirical reality, it cannot be ultimately real. Finally, the arguments are put together with the reappropriation of causality in the unanalyzed, relative sense described in verse 22 and the cycle is complete. Dharmakīrti's concept is drawn into Jñānagarbha's system, relativized from the point of view of the ultimate, then reappropriated to serve again as the basis of conventional distinctions.

In the cycle of affirmation, denial, and reappropriation we have the essential pattern through which the Madhyamaka logicians of the eighth century related to their Yogācāra critics. They accepted conventionally, while denying ultimately, many of the distinctive doctrines of the broad tradition of the Yogācāra. Different Mādhyamikas focused on different concepts, of course. We do not see in Jñānagarbha the same understanding of mind-only that is found in Śāntarakṣita. But the pattern of relationship is the same, and the pattern typifies the approach these Mādhyamikas took in absorbing the philosophical innovations of their critics. With this approach, they could appropriate others' categories and still defend the integrity of their own method. The verse that seems to express this relationship best comes from Jñānagarbha himself:

> What is ultimate for one is relative for another, just as one person's mother is considered another person's wife.[70]

Merely a shift in perspective adopts someone else's categories and turns them to a Madhyamaka end.

The solution seems terribly easy: merely a change in perspective gives an opponent's category a Madhyamaka meaning. The Mādhyamikas have one perspective, the Buddhist logicians another, and the acceptance of one seems to involve the denial of the other. But is the picture so simple? Were the perspectives so radically distinct in the minds of those who adopted them? A closer reading of Dharmakīrti casts doubt on some of the neat categories we now use to set these two traditions apart. In his discussion of the validity of a cognition in the first chapter of the *Pramāṇavārttika*, Dharmakīrti points out that the judgement of *artha-kriyā* can be made only in an empirical sense:

> From [the cognition] itself we understand the particular form (*svarūpa*). The validity [of a cognition is understood] through conventional usage (*vyavahāra*).[71]

The term *vyavahāra* (conventional usage) is a common synonym of *saṃvṛti* (relative). Dharmakīrti's commentator Manorathanandin explains that empirical application (*vyavahāra*) is the knowledge of *artha-kriyā*).[72] Dharmakīrti is not claiming, as Jñānagarbha would, that whatever possesses the ability to produce *artha-kriyā* is empirically real, but he moves a step closer by suggesting that *the knowledge* of *artha-kriyā* is an empirical reality.

The connection between Jñānagarbha and Dharmakīrti is even more clear in the interpolated verses (*antara-śloka*) that precede verse 14. I have already mentioned them as an example of Jñānagarbha's tendency to reconceive ontological questions in epistemological form. But the debt to Dharmakīrti is more than a vague shift in priorities. The second interpolated verse that precedes verse 14 ("For if a single [cognition] appears manifold, how can its forms [*ākāra*] truly exist, since it would lose its unity?") is almost a direct quotation of Dharmakīrti's *Pramāṇavārttika* 2.357 (repeated in *Pramāṇaviniścaya* 1.49). In the *Pramāṇavārttika* the verse is used as part of an argument to show that the distinction between subject and object cannot be established apart from consciousness itself. This can be interpreted as an assertion of mind-only. But Dharmakīrti's terminology leaves the nature of the appearance of duality deliberately vague: he speaks of it as "consistent with seeing" (*yathānudarśana*).[73] Dharmakīrti is a master of Sanskrit prose. When the occasion demands, he can use the language of philosophical Sanskrit as a finely honed instrument to express the most precise distinctions. But here vagueness seems to be more important than precision. *Yathānudarśana* treads a narrow line between the hypothetical term *yathāpratyakṣa* (consistent with perception) and *yathābhāsa* (consistent with appearance). "Perception" would suggest that the duality is real, "appearance" that it is unreal. "Seeing" leaves the question open.[74]

Jñānagarbha borrows Dharmakīrti's term (in the abbreviated form *yathādarśana*) in his account of relative truth: "Mere things are capable of effective action in a way that corresponds to appearances (*yathādarśana*)."[75] The term occurs again at other important points in the argument, particularly where Jñānagarbha wants to capture some of Dharmakīrti's scrupulous imprecision. Verse 17, for example, takes up the difference between relative and ultimate truth: "[The Buddha] considers the relative and the ultimate to be identical in nature, because there is no difference between them. This is because reason also corresponds to appearances." Does this mean that they are identical or not? Ask Dharmakīrti! The distinction between them is as real as the distinction between subject and object: it is *yathādarśana*—"the way we see." More could be said about the way Jñānagarbha uses the term *yathādarśana* to suggest the fusion of different perspectives in his argument, but beyond a certain point readers have to be left to find their own way to sense the nuances of Jñānagarbha's view of reality. In any case, the nuances owe as much to a borrowing of Dharmakīrti's method as they do to a rejection of it. Like so much in Madhyamaka thought, the borrowing and the rejection seem to be all of a piece.

This is not to say that the followers of Dharmakīrti, such as Devendrabuddhi, would agree in every detail. There still are basic differences that cannot be conjured away.[76] But Jñānagarbha's use of terms such as *yathādarśana* and *artha-kriyā* shows the dynamic nature of the relationship. Jñānagarbha's argument could just as well be understood, not as an attack on Dharmakīrti from *outside* his tradition, but as an attempt from *within* to interpret Dharmakīrti's actual intention. It is a reminder that, in the period in which both of these philosophers worked, the traditions of Buddhist Logic and Madhyamaka were less monolithic schools than fluid traditions of interpretation. Even at moments of conflict, their interests overlapped and even coincided.

The intricacies of the relationship between Jñānagarbha and Dharmakīrti indicate some of the intellectual atmosphere in the Indian Buddhist community at a time when Indian Buddhist thought was at the height of its powers. During these years, traditions of interpretation developed that in time produced the categories we now use to classify the different "schools" of Buddhist thought. But in the minds of the philosophers themselves the categories of philosophical affiliation do not seem to have been as sharp as they now seem to us, with nearly a thousand years of historical and philosophical study to color our understanding. In Jñānagarbha's time philosophical exploration crossed traditional lines, sometimes in conflict, sometimes in agreement, and sometimes in the complex combination of conflict and agreement that makes it hard to see clearly where one tradition starts and another ends. Through all this exploration, however, we hear the echo of a Madhyamaka motif: the balanced and paradoxical pattern of Madhyamaka thought, as old as Nāgārjuna and reverberating with the tones of Jñānagarbha's Svātantrika predecessors. In the balanced interplay of the perspectives of the two truths, new elements are brought together into an approach to Buddhist thought that is at once new and as old as the Madhyamaka tradition itself.

Notes To Part I

1. Ruegg points out that there is at least one and possibly two other authors named Jñānagarbha, one a teacher of Mar-pa in the eleventh century, the other a translator of several Madhyamaka works into Tibetan (Ruegg, *Literature*, p. 69).

2. Debiprasad Chattopadhyaya, ed., *Tāranātha's History of Buddhism in India* (Simla: Indian Institute of Advanced Study, 1970), pp. 252–3.

3. George N. Roerich, *The Blue Annals* (Calcutta, 1949; reprinted Delhi: Motilal Banarsidass, 1976), p. 34.

4. F. D. Lessing and A. Wayman, *Introduction to the Buddhist Tantric Systems* (The Hague: Mouton, 1968; 2nd ed. Delhi: Motilal Banarsidass, 1978), p. 90. Note that the division of the Madhyamaka tradition into Svātantrika and Prāsaṅgika, as well as subsequent subdivisions, is a product of Tibetan classification. Indian Mādhyamikas were aware of differences that separated them from other members of their tradition, but they did not honor them with these names.

5. On the date of Bhāvaviveka see Yuichi Kajiyama, "Bhāvaviveka, Sthiramati, and Dharmapāla," *WZKS* 12–13 (1968–9), pp. 193–203. Bhāvaviveka's works are discussed in Ruegg, *Literature*, pp. 61–6. Chr.

Lindtner differs from other scholars, notably Ruegg and Ejima, in assigning the *Madhyamakaratnapradīpa* to the 6th-century Bhāvaviveka ("À Propos Dharmakīrti—Two new works and a new date," *Acta Orientalia* 41 [1980], pp. 27–37; "Adversaria Buddhica," *WZKS* 26 [1982], pp. 167–94). I would prefer to withhold judgement on the point until Lindtner has published the *Ratnapradīpa* and had the chance to make his case in detail. For substantive studies of Bhāvaviveka's thought see Shotaro Iida, *Reason and Emptiness: A Study in Logic and Mysticism* (Tokyo: The Hokuseido Press, 1980); Yasunori Ejima, *Development of Mādhyamika Philosophy in India: Studies on Bhāvaviveka* (in Japanese) (Tokyo, 1981); Malcolm David Eckel, "A Question of Nihilism: Bhāvaviveka's Response to the Fundamental Problems of Mādhyamika Philosophy" (Ph.D. Diss.: Harvard University, 1980); and "Bhāvaviveka's Critique of Yogācāra Philosophy in Chapter XXV of the *Prajñāpradīpa*," in *Miscellanea Buddhica*, ed. Chr. Lindtner, Indiske Studier 5 (Copenhagen, 1985), pp. 25–75.

6. *Mūlamadhyamakakārikās de Nāgārjuna avec la Prasannapadā Commentaire de Candrakīrti*, ed. Louis de La Vallée Poussin, Bibliotheca Buddhica, vol. 4 (St. Petersburg, 1903–13), p. 25. See also Jan de Jong, "Text-critical Notes on the Prasannapadā," *IIJ* 20 (1978), pp. 25–59.

7. Edward Conze, *Buddhist Thought in India* (Ann Arbor: University of Michigan Press, 1967), pp. 238–9.

8. The study of the *Madhyamakahṛdayakārikās* was given great impetus by Rahula Samkrtyayana's discovery of a Sanskrit manuscript of the work in Zha-lu monastery in 1936. For a list of the portions that have appeared to date see the bibliographical entry in *'Sde Dge Tibetan Tripiṭaka Bstan Ḥgyur Preserved at The Faculty of Letters, University of Tokyo* (Dbu Ma) (Tokyo, 1977), vol. 3.

9. In addition to the work of V. V. Gokhale mentioned above see Hajime Nakamura, "The Vedānta Thought as Referred to in the Texts of Bhavya," *Professor M. Hiriyanna Birth Centenary Commemoration Volume*, ed. V. Raghavan and G. Marulasiddaiah (Mysore, 1972), pp. 174–6; and Hajime Nakamura, *A History of Early Vedānta Philosophy* (Delhi: Motilal Banarsidass, 1983), pp. 182–219. A portion of chapter five, containing a description of the eighteen *nikāyas*, has been used as a source for the study of early Buddhism. See André Bareau, "Trois traités sur les sectes bouddhiques attribués à Vasumitra, Bhavya, et Vinītadeva," *Journal Asiatique* 244 (1956), pp. 167–200.

10. Peking Tibetan Tripiṭaka (Tokyo Reprint Edition), vol. 96, *Dza* 160b/2–6.

11. *Madhyamakālaṃkāra* 92–3: *sems tsam la ni brten nas su / / phyi rol dngos med shes par bya / / tshul 'dir brten nas de la yang // shin tu bdag med shes par bya / / tshul gnyis shing rta zhon nas su / / rigs pa'i srab phyogs 'jug byed pa // de dag de phyir ji bzhin no // theg pa chen po nyid thob* (Derge Tibetan Tripiṭaka [Tohoku #3885] *Sa* 79b). The passage is mentioned in Kennard Lipman, "A Study of Śāntarakṣita's *Madhyamakālaṃkāra*," (Ph.D. Diss.: University of Saskatchewan, 1979), pp. 144–45; and Ruegg, *Literature*, p. 90.

12. *cittamātraṃ samārūhya bāhyam arthaṃ na kalpayet / tathatālambane sthitvā cittamātram atikramet / / cittamātram atikramya nirābhāsam atikramet / nirābhāsasthito yogī mahāyānaṃ sa paśyati (Saddharmalaṅkāvatārasūtram*, ed. P. L. Vaidya, Buddhist Sanskrit Texts Series, vol. 3 [Darbhanga: Mithila Institute, 1963], p. 124).

13. *tattvaprāsādaśikharārohaṇaṃ na hi yujyate / tathyasaṃvṛtisopānam antareṇa yatas tataḥ / / pūrvaṃ saṃvṛtisatyena praviviktamatir bhavet / tato dharmasvasāmānyalakṣaṇe suviniścitaḥ: Madhyamakahṛdayakārikā* 3.12–3, quoted from Iida, *Reason and Emptiness*, p. 67. The first verse appears almost verbatim in Haribhadra's *Abhisamayālaṃkārālokā Prajñāpāramitāvyākhyā* (Tokyo: The Toyo Bunko, 1932), vol. 1, p. 169. Compare also Kambala's *Ālokamālā*, quoted by Chr. Lindtner, "Adversaria Buddhica," *WZKS* 26 (1982), p. 192.

14. *Madhyamakahṛdayakārikā* 5.54: *tannirāsāya ced iṣṭo vidhyantaraparigrahaḥ / prakṣālanād dhi paṅkasya dūrād asparśanaṃ varam*. The Sanskrit is quoted by courtesy of Shotaro Iida. The Tibetan of the *Tarkajvālā* is found in the Peking Tibetan Tripiṭaka (Tokyo Reprint Edition), vol. 96, *Dza* 237b. The "maxim of washing away the mud" (*paṅkaprakṣālananyāya*) is a stock comparison in Indian literature (see V. S. Apte, *The Practical Sanskrit-English Dictionary* [Poona: Prasad Prakashan, 1957]: vol. 3, Appendix E, p. 66). Bhāvaviveka uses it to argue that if the doctrine of mind-only is false, one should avoid it from the start and not use it as a preliminary stage on the way to the correct understanding of Emptiness. See also my "Bhāvaviveka's Critique."

15. Derge Tibetan Tripiṭaka (Tohoku #3854), *Tsha* 280a/3–4. The verses correspond to *Laṅkāvatāra* 10.256–7 quoted in note 12 above.

16. E. Obermiller, trans., *History of Buddhism by Bu-ston* (Heidelberg: Otto Harrassowitz, 1932), part 2, p. 135.

17. See, for example, the classification used by lCang-skya in Donald Sewell Lopez, Jr., "The Svātantrika-Mādhyamika School of Mahāyāna Buddhism" (Ph.D. Diss.: University of Virginia, 1982).

18. Lessing and Wayman, p. 90.

19. Translation quoted from my "Bhāvaviveka's Critique," p. 50. For Tsong-kha-pa's use of the passage, see Thurman, p. 266.

20. Derge Tibetan Tripiṭaka (Tohoku #3884), *Sa* 78b.

21. *MMK* 1.1.

22. *Madhyamakahṛdayakārikās* 3.137–213; *Madhyamakāvatāra* 6.8–21.

23. Derge Tibetan Tripiṭaka (Tohoku #3892), *Ha* 39b.

24. *niḥsvabhāvā amī bhāvās tattvataḥ svaparoditāḥ / ekānekasvabhāvena viyogāt pratibimbavat.* The Sanskrit is found in *Bodhicaryāvatāra of Śāntideva with the Commentary Pañjikā of Prajñākaramati*, ed. P. L. Vaidya, Buddhist Sanskrit Texts Series, vol. 12 (Darbhanga: Mithila Institute, 1960), p. 173.

25. Compare *Viṃśatikā* 11 where a similar argument is applied to the existence of external objects (*Vijñaptimātratāsiddhi*, ed. Sylvain Lévi, vol. 1 [Paris, 1925], p. 1).

26. Verse 14.

27. Verse 14 immediately follows an argument drawn from Dharmakīrti about the single or multiple forms (*ākāra*) of a cognition.

28. *Abhisamayālaṃkārālokā*, pp. 970ff.

29. This study focuses on Jñānagarbha's Madhyamaka work and excludes the work attributed to Jñānagarbha in the Tantric section of the canon. The Derge Tibetan Tripiṭaka attributes four such works to an author named Jñānagarbha : 1. *Śmaśānavidhi* (Tohoku #1282), 2. *Caturdevatāparipṛcchāṭīkā* (Tohoku #1916), 3. *Ārya Anantamukhanirhāradhāraṇīvyākhyānakārikā* (Tohoku #2695), 4. *Ārya Anantamukhanirhāradhārṇaṇīṭīkā* (Tohoku #2696). Hisao Inagaki has shown that the fourth of these works is related to Haribhadra's *Abhisamayālaṃ kārālokā* ("Haribhadra's Quotations from Jñānagarbha's *Anantamukhanirhāradhāraṇīṭīka*," in *Buddhist Thought and Asian Civilization*, ed. Leslie S. Kawamura and Keith Scott [Emeryville, California: Dharma Press, 1977], pp. 132–44). The same is true of the verse portion of the text (work number three above). It quotes *Satyadvayavibhaṅgakārikā* 9cd, as does the *Abhisamayālaṃ kārālokā*. (See the note on verse 9cd below).

30. It is possible that the title of the text should read *vibhāga* rather than *vibhaṅga*. The colophons in the Derge and Cone editions of the Tibetan texts read *vibhaṅga*, but the Sanskrit of *Madhyamakakārikā* 24.9,

where the same phrase occurs, reads *vibhāga*. Nagao points out in the introduction to his edition of the *Madhyāntavibhāga-bhāṣya* (Tokyo: Suzuki Research Foundation, 1964) that the term *vibhaṅga* in the Tibetan version of his text should be changed to *vibhāga* on the basis of the reading of the Sanskrit manuscript. In Jñānagarbha's case we have no Sanskrit manuscript to support such a change. The Tibetan tradition may very well be in error, but *vibhaṅga* in the sense of "distinction" is acceptable Buddhist usage. In the absence of manuscript evidence to the contrary, it seems best provisionally to follow the testimony of the Tibetan sources.

The four editions of the Tibetan canon used in establishing Jñānagarbha's text are discussed in more detail in the introduction to the Tibetan text below.

31. *Madhyamakakārikā* 24.8–10.

32. V. Trenckner, ed., *The Milindapañho* (London: Williams and Norgate, 1880), p. 28.

33. Verse 17.

34. "Therefore, one should specify something subsequent to which the desire to know Brahman is taught. The answer is: the distinction (*viveka*) between eternal and non-eternal things. . . ." *Brahmasūtraśaṅkarabhāṣyam*, ed. J. L. Sastri (Delhi: Motilal Banarsidass, 1980), p. 37.

35. *Madhyāntavibhāga-bhāṣya*, ed. Gadjin M. Nagao (Tokyo: Suzuki Research Foundation, 1964); Tilmann Vetter, *Dharmakīrti's Pramāṇaviniścayaḥ: 1. Kapitel: Pratyakṣam* (Vienna: Österreichische Akademie der Wissenschaften, 1966); Ernst Steinkellner, *Dharmakīrti's Pramāṇaviniścayaḥ: Zweites Kapitel: Svārthānumānam*, 2 vols. (Vienna: Österreichische Akademie der Wissenschaften, 1973–9).

36. For example, the subcommentator revises the original argument against self-cognition (*svasaṃvedana*) in section II.B.

37. *'grel bshad de rtsom pa po zhi ba 'tsho yin zhes pa yang ming mthun pa'am kha g.yar ba yin gyi dbu ma rgyan la sogs pa rtsom mkhan ni min te / 'dis bstan bcos rtsom pa'i dgos pa bshad pa tshad ma'i de kho na nyid bsdus pa'i 'grel par bkag pa'i phyir dang / gzung 'dzin ji ltar snang ba bzhin du med par smra ba mngon sum dang 'gal zhing grags pas kyang gnod par bden gnyis rang 'grel las bshad pa smra sor bzhag gi don 'thad phyogs su 'grel ba'i phyir ro* (Tibetan quoted from *Drang-nges-legs-bshad-snying-po* of Tsong-kha-pa [Sarnath: Gelugpa Students Welfare Committee, 1973], pp. 141–2).

38. *Tattvasaṅgraha of Śāntarakṣita with the Commentary of Kamalaśīla*, vol. 1, pp. 8–9. Translation quoted from *The Tattvasaṅgraha of Śāntarakṣita with the Commentary of Kamalaśīla*, trans. Ganganatha Jha, Gaekwad's Oriental Series, vol. 80 (Baroda: Oriental Institute, 1937), p. 13.

39. Derge Tibetan Tripiṭaka (Tohoku #3883), *Sa* 40b/2–6.

40. Lopez, Dissertation, p. 509.

41. The commentary is listed under the title *Dbu-ma-rang-rgyud-pa'i-slob-dpon-ye-shes-snying-pos-mdzad-pa'i-dbu-ma-bden-gnyis-kyi-ṭīka* in Lokesh Chandra's *Materials for a History of Tibetan Literature* (New Delhi, 1963), part 3, p. 616.

42. Derge Tibetan Tripiṭaka (Tohoku #4033), *Bi* 321b/2–322a/4. The sutra itself is translated by Étienne Lamotte, *Saṃdhinirmocana Sūtra: L'Explication des Mystères* (Louvain: Université de Louvain, 1935), p. 211.

43. Ruegg, *Literature*, p. 69.

44. Ruegg, *Literature*, p. 69.

45. See the notes on verse 3 of the Translation.

46. See verses 21 and 22 of the Translation.

47. Translation taken from my "A Question of Nihilism," pp. 229–230.

48. "A Question of Nihilism," p. 218.

49. The *Tattvāvatāra* says: "It satisfies only when it is not analyzed, from such a thing something else seems to arise, and such things produce just this kind of effective action" (Derge Tibetan Tripiṭaka [Tohoku #3892] *Ha* 41b/1). Atiśa's verse reads: "A phenomenon (*dharma*) which arises and is destroyed; which only satisfies when it is not analysed (*avicāraramaṇīya*), and is capable of efficiency (*arthakriyāsāmarthyavat*) — is maintained to be the genuine relative truth" (Lindtner, "Atiśa's Introduction," p. 193). The importance of "no analysis" in the definition of relative truth is discussed further in the notes on verses 21 and 22 of the Translation.

50. The phrase belongs to Louis MacNiece, *Autumn Journal* (New York: Random House, 1939), p. 51.

51. T. R. V. Murti, *The Central Philosophy of Buddhism* (London: George Allen and Unwin, 1955), p. 128.

52. Murti, p. 126.

53. Murti, p. 143.

54. "Bhāvaviveka's Critique."

55. Keiji Nishitani, *Religion and Nothingness* (Berkeley: University of California Press, 1982), p. 97.

56. Nishitani, p. 180.

57. Nishitani, pp. 184–5.

58. Hence the importance of determining the negandum (*pratiṣedhya*) negated by the understanding of emptiness. In the commentary that introduces and follows verse 9, Jñānagarbha explains that the negandum is "what is imagined" (*kalpita*), namely that things are *ultimately* real.

59. By "irony" I mean the systematic use of two contradictory perspectives, each of which has to be brought to bear to interpret an author's words. This is similar to what Wayne Booth describes as irony in his *Rhetoric of Irony* (Chicago: University of Chicago Press, 1974). But it would have to be identified with what Booth calls unstable irony, in which each perspective simultaneously undermines the other, rather than stable irony, in which one perspective yields definitively to the other.

60. Nishitani, p. 252.

61. E. B. White and Katherine S. White, *A Subtreasury of American Humor* (New York: Coward-McCann, 1941), p. xvi.

62. Vasubandhu's influence was felt in two separate streams of thought: the tradition of figures such as Sthiramati and Dharmapāla, and the tradition of Dignāga and Dharmakīrti. The former are sometimes referred to as *āgamānusāriṇo vijñānavādinaḥ*, and the latter as *nyāyānusāriṇo vijñānavādinaḥ*, as in E. Obermiller, "The Sublime Science of the Great Vehicle to Salvation," *Acta Orientalia* 9 (1931), p. 99. Jñānagarbha clearly felt the presence of Sthiramati and Dharmapāla as oppponents, but it was the school of Dignāga and Dharmakīrti that had the greatest impact on his thought.

63. See the commentary and notes on verse 4ab of the Translation.

64. The full argument can be found in my "Bhāvaviveka's Critique," pp. 52–74.

65. "Bhāvaviveka's Critique," pp. 60–4.

66. V. V. Gokhale, "Masters of Buddhism Adore the Brahman through Non-adoration" *IIJ* 5 (1961–2), pp. 271–275.

67. See, respectively, verse 8 and verse 4 with accompanying commentary.

68. Devendrabuddhi's objection follows verse 15.

69. Masatoshi Nagatomi, "*Arthakriyā,*" *Adyar Library Bulletin* 31–2 (1967–8), pp. 52–72.

70. The verse appears in the commentary that precedes verse 20.

71. *Pramāṇavārttika* 1.6d–7a.

72. Manorathanandin on *Pramaṇavārttika* 1.6d–7a.

73. *Pramāṇavārttika* 2.357.

74. What is not vague, however, is Dharmakīrti's conviction that all discussion and analysis of the distinction between the two truths is carried out at the conventional (*sāṃvyavahārika*) level, as Christian Lindtner clearly shows in his "Marginalia to Dharmakīrti's Pramāṇaviniścaya I-II," *WZKS* 28 (1984), pp. 149–75.

75. Verse 8 and commentary.

76. As in the objections of Devendrabuddhi that follow verse 15.

Part Two

Jñānagarbha's Commentary on the Distinction Between the Two Truths

Outline of the Argument

I. Introduction
II. Ultimate Truth
  A. The Expressible Ultimate
  B. The Inexpressible Ultimate
III. Relative Truth
  A. Relative Truth is Not Confused with Anything that is Imagined
  B. Relative Truth Arises Dependently
    1. The Distinction between Correct and Incorrect Relative Truth
    2. It is Impossible to Know any Causal Relationship
    3. Nothing Ultimately Arises
      a. Many Do Not Produce One
      b. Many Do Not Produce Many
      c. One Does Not Produce Many
      d. One Does Not Produce One
      e. Concluding Verses
    4. The Etymology of *Saṃvṛti*
  C. The Relativity of the Ultimate
  D. Relative Truth Cannot Be Analyzed
  E. Reply to Particular Objections
    1. The Basis of Relative Truth
    2. Candrakīrti (?) on the Nature of Relative Truth
IV. Karma, Transmigration, and Buddhahood
  A. Action and its Result
  B. The Bodies of the Buddha
    1. The Dharma Body
    2. The Enjoyment Body
    3. The Manifestation Body
V. Conclusion

Homage to the crown prince Mañjuśrī!

Homage to the pure-minded, the Great Sage and his children, who understand the emptiness of things, yet in their compassion remain here has long as there is *saṃsāra* to accomplish what the whole world seeks.[1]

I. Introduction

I write this book to promote a correct understanding of the two truths.[2] For

1. The two truths have already been distinguished,[3] but because my great predecessors have misunderstood, to say nothing of others, I am distinguishing them again.

The Lord knew what would benefit others, and he distinguished the two truths in various ways to help those of lesser intelligence. Others, including Nāgārjuna, have explained them further. But great Buddhists[8] have misunderstood, to say nothing of the others who follow them.

2. Those who know the distinction between the two truths do not misunderstand the Sage's teaching. They acquire all prerequisites and achieve the goal.[5]

Those who understand the distinction between the two truths and are concerned about bringing benefit to living beings lead the world, which is illuminated by the Sugata's broad teaching, to acquire all the prerequisites of merit and knowledge (*puṇya-jñāna-sambhāra*). They also achieve the goal (*sampad*) for themselves and others indiscriminately. Others [such as Disciples] achieve the goal to which they aspire.[8]

3ab. [In various sūtras] the Sage taught two truths: the relative (*saṃvṛti*) and the ultimate (*paramārtha*).

"In various sūtras" should be supplied.

3cd. Only what corresponds to appearances (*yathādarśana*) is relative (*saṃvṛti*) [truth], and only something different [from appearances] is the opposite [i.e., ultimate truth].[7]

[The opposite] is ultimate truth. Whatever appears even to cowherds and women is true in a relative sense (*saṃvṛtyā*), but not in a real sense (*tattvataḥ*). [An appearance is true] if an object that corresponds to the appearance can definitely be cognized. Appearances are of two kinds: conceptual (*savikalpa*) and nonconceptual (*nirvikalpa*).[8] Only correct reason (*nyāya*) is ultimate truth. The word "only" has a restrictive meaning.

II. Ultimate Truth

A. The Expressible Ultimate

Truth in the ultimate sense is ultimate truth (*paramārtha-satya*),[9] and this is truth that is consistent with a rational (*nyāyānusārin*) [cognition].[10] Why?

4ab. Since it cannot be contradicted, reason is ultimate.[11]

[A cognition] that determines an object through reason cannot be contradicted.[12] Thus a cognition produced by a three-fold logical mark (*liṅga*) is ultimate (*paramārtha*), because it is the ultimate (*parama*) meaning (*artha*).[13] The ultimate also can be the object (*artha*) that is determined by that [cognition], just as a perception (*pratyakṣa*) [can be either a cognition or an object].[14]

4b. And [reason] is not relative.

[Reason] is ultimate, so it is not relative truth. The last word [in the phrase "relative truth"] is omitted [in the verse].

Why [is reason not relative]?

4c. Because [whatever is relative] can be contradicted.

The way in which [relative truth] is presented to cognition is impossible according to reason.

4d. But whatever corresponds to appearances is true [in a relative sense].

This means that whatever corresponds to appearances is relative truth. Although a double moon and so forth also correspond to appearances, ordinary people do not accept them as true. We will explain below that they are incorrect relative [truth] (*mithyā-saṃvṛti*).

B. The Inexpressible Ultimate

5. [The ultimate] cannot be classified as something that corresponds to appearances, [because] it does not appear at all as an object of cognition.

The ultimate does not correspond to appearances, because it does not even appear in the cognition of someone who is omniscient. This is why the sūtra says, "Not to see anything is to see Reality."[15]

[Objection:]

6ab. Someone may say that [to see Reality] is not to see any imagined nature (*kalpita-svabhāva*).[16]

That is, the statement "Not to see anything is to see Reality" is made with reference to imagined nature, and is [interpreted] correct[ly] this way. Otherwise, why would it say "anything"? It could be changed to say "Not to see any nature (*svabhāva*) [is to see reality]."[17]

[Madhyamaka reply:] This is wrong,

6c. Because self-cognition is impossible.[18]

[Self-cognition is] a cognition [that] cognizes [itself] as empty of duality and cognizes the absence [of duality]. It cannot [cognize the absence of duality], however, if it is not [empty of duality].[19] [In response to someone who says that a cognition cognizes itself as empty of duality, we say that] a cognition does not cognize itself, because it is empty of any image of itself (*svābhāsa*), like any other cognitions.[20] Not to admit that [it cognizes] the image of itself would imply that there is a difference [between the cognition itself and the image that it cognizes], as there is between blue and the cognition [of blue].[21]

[A cognition] cannot [cognize itself] merely because it is a cognition, because that would imply too much.[22] You may say that, if [a cognition cognizes itself] because it is a *self*-cognition, too much is not implied. But this also is wrong, because there is no special reason [why it should cognize itself rather than something else], and if there is no [special reason], too much is implied.[23] You may say that the nature of cognition is such that when [self-cognition] arises, it is its own cause, and for this reason [a cognition cognizes only itself]. But this is wrong again, either for the reason just given or because there is no reliable means by which this can be known. Someone who disagrees [with you] will have no respect if you simply assert your own position.[24]

When they respond to the objection raised by those who hold the doctrine that cognition has no form (*nirākāra-jñāna-vādin*), Dignāga and Dharmakīrti, among others, argue that [a cognition] must have the form of the object.[25]

6d. Because causal efficacy would be denied [if a cognition did not have the form of its object].

It also is wrong [to claim that self-cognition arises in the way that has just been described], because of the denial of causal efficacy [in verse 14] below.[26]

The statement "Not to see anything is to see Reality," therefore, does not support [the existence of self-cognition]. For

7. The Omniscient One knows what exists and what does not, and if he does not see something, one should analyze very carefully what kind of thing it is.[27]

This means that if [the Buddha], who is omniscient in the sense that [his] knowledge covers everything to be known, does not perceive something, it does not exist. This is why the sūtra says:

> What is relative truth? All ordinary designations, syllables, utterances, and words. Ultimate truth cannot even be known, let alone conveyed in syllables.[28]

An ordinary designation (*loka-prajñapti*) is an ordinary activity that is cognitive in nature (*jñāna-jñeya-lakṣaṇa*) rather than verbal in nature (*abhidhāna-lakṣaṇa*), since [syllables] are mentioned later [in the quotation].[29] The word "all" is meant to be inclusive. This[30] means that items cognized by perceptions (*pratyakṣa*) that are non-conceptual (*nirvikalpa*), such as perceptions of form (*rūpa*) or pleasure (*sukha*), are only relative truth. [The word "all"] is also to be taken with the subsequent [terms in the sentence]. Thus it applies to [the phrase "ordinary designations"], which has just been quoted from the sūtra, and to syllables, utterances, and words.

This is the way to understand [the sūtra's definition of relative truth],[31] because, in the definition of ultimate truth, [the sūtra] says [that ultimate truth] "cannot even be known." If relative truth consisted only of words, [the quotation] would say only that [ultimate truth] cannot be conveyed in syllables and would not mention knowledge. If both [knowledge and syllables] were not intended, as they are in this case, why would they be mentioned in the following order: "cannot even be known, let alone conveyed in syllables"? If [the word "knowledge"] referred only to conceptual (*savikalpa*) knowledge, [the quotation] would say that [ultimate truth] "cannot even be known conceptually" to avoid any confusion.[32] There is no definitive proof for the point [that the knowledge mentioned in the quotation is only conceptual knowledge]. It is wrong to narrow the scope of a general term without regard for meaning and context.

Furthermore, if the general term ["know"] referred only to conceptual knowledge, why would the one who used it mention both [knowledge and syllables]? In such a case [if "know" referred only to conceptual knowledge], "cannot even be known" would indicate that [the ultimate] cannot be conveyed in syllables. The word "even" would then be inappropriate. ["Syllables"] could not have been said with particulars (*svalakṣaṇa*) in mind, because [particulars] do not involve the designation of an object.[33] [If the word "syllables" did refer to particulars,] even though it is used as the second term, it would include the first, because "syllables" would be the more inclusive term. Thus the Lord held the view that, in a real sense (*tattvataḥ*), [the ultimate] cannot even be known by the cognition of a mere thing (*vastu-mātra*).[34] If [the quotation is interpreted] this way, everything fits.

Therefore,

(1) Consider whether it is reasonable for a cognition to be either pure or true, if [that cognition] cognizes itself and thus becomes an object of cognition.

The preceding [verse] is an additional verse (*antara-śloka*).[35]

III. Relative Truth

The relative (*saṃvṛti*) is of two kinds: correct (*tathya*) and incorrect (*mithyā*). Of these,

8abc. A mere thing (*vastu-mātra*), which is not confused with anything that is imagined and arises dependently, is known as correct relative [truth].

Imagined things (*kalpitārtha*) consist of real arising, the image of consciousness, primal matter (*pradhāna*), the transformation of elements (*bhūta*) and so forth.[36] [Mere things] are not to be confused with these. Mere things are capable of effective action (*artha-kriyā-samartha*) that corresponds to appearances (*yathādarśana*). [Mere things] also depend for their arising on causes and conditions, so they are known as correct relative truth.[37] If something appears consistently to be caused in the cognition of [everyone from a scholar] to a child, it is correct relative [truth], because something exists that is consistent with what appears in cognition.[38]

A. Relative Truth is Not Confused with Anything that is Imagined

Real arising has no appearance.[39] It is nothing more than a reification (*samāropa*) based on something else[40] or on a doctrinal position (*siddhānta*). If this were not the case [that is, if real arising did appear], there would be no disagreement [between different philosophical schools]. Neither party to an argument disagrees about something that appears to his cognition. If someone did disagree, he would be contradicted by perception and so forth.

> 8d. Whatever is imagined is incorrect (*mithyā*).[41]

Real arising is constructed by the imagination (*kalpanā*) and is incorrect relative truth (*mithyā-saṃvṛti-satya*).[42]

[Objection:] But the negation of real arising would also be incorrect relative truth, because when something appears, [the negation of its real arising] does not appear, just as [its] real arising [does not appear].[43]

[Reply:] This is not the case, because [the negation of the real arising of a thing] is not different from the thing itself (*bhāva-svabhāva*). [The negation of real arising] would be incorrect relative [truth] only if someone imagined it to be something other than what it is. Why?

> 9a. The negation of arising,

because it is the negation of the concept of real arising,

> 9b. is consistent with Reality (*tattva*), so [we] also consider it [to be ultimate].

That is, we consider it to be ultimate. Others [such as Yogācāras] consider it to be true, so the word "also" has an inclusive meaning.[44]

However, when [the negation of real arising] is analyzed from the standpoint of reason, it is only relative. Why?

> 9cd. If there is no object of negation (*pratiṣedhya*), it is clear that in Reality there can be no negation (*pratiṣedha*).[45]

If there is no object of negation, there can be no negation. That is, there can be no negation without any content (*viṣaya*).

[Objection:] If an opponent thinks that something like form (*rūpa*) arises, the object of negation is whatever [the opponent] imagines to be real.

[Reply:] In that case,

10ab. If [the object of a negation] is imagined, its negation also must be imagined.

If the object of negation is imagined, the negation also must be imagined, like the negation that the son of a barren woman has a dark complexion. However, even though there is no real negation [of arising], there still is no arising, because the absence of arising does not imply [the existence of] the negation [of arising], and because there is no reason for [arising] to exist.[46]

10c. So [the negation "in Reality there is no arising"] is relative.

"In Reality there is no arising" should be supplied.

10d. It is Reality-as-object (*tattvārtha*), but it is not [Reality] in a real sense.[47]

"Reality-as-object" is carried over [into the next verse].

Why [is Reality-as-object not Reality in a real sense]?

11a. In a real sense, [Reality-as-object] neither [arises nor does not arise].

The following [verse] is an additional verse (*antaraśloka*):

(1) This is why the Lord said: "It is not empty, it is not non-empty, and it is not both [empty and non-empty]," and "It does not arise and it does not not arise."

Why [does Reality-as-object neither arise nor not arise]?

11b. Because it is free from conceptual diversity (*niṣprapañca*).[48]

Only this [Reality viewed from the point of view of Reality] is free from the entire network of concepts.

11cd. This is why the *bodhisattva* said nothing when Mañjuśrī asked him about Reality.

It says in the [*Vimalakīrtinirdeśa*] *Sūtra*:[49]

> Then the crown prince Mañjuśrī said to the Licchavi Vimalakīrti: "O son of good family, now that each has given his own explanation, it is your turn to explain the non-dual entrance into the attributes (*dharmas*) [of Buddhahood]." The Licchavi Vimalakīrti remained silent. The crown prince Mañjuśrī then said to the Licchavi Vimalakīrti: "Well done, O son of good family. Syllables, words, and concepts do not apply to the *bodhisattvas*' non-dual entrance [into the attributes of Buddhahood]. Well done! Well done!"[50]

(1) [But] how could the Buddha's son remain silent if he were asked whether what is empty of duality were, in Reality, dependent (*paratantra*) nature?[51]

(2) Those who are knowledgeable somehow express their insight and do not remain silent.[52]

(3) If not, say clearly how logicians can say that particulars are beyond words.[53]

(4) But, in Reality, there still is nothing that can be expressed. So it is widely said that [Vimalakīrti] remained silent when he was questioned [by Mañjuśrī].

The preceding [verses] are additional verses.

Since the word *dharma* is used [in the description of Vimalakīrti's silence], it is not contradictory to say that a *bodhisattva* who sees *dharmas* after [rising from a state of concentration] does not see even the slightest *dharma* apart from those that arise dependently.[54]

B. Relative Truth Arises Dependently

1. The Distinction between Correct and Incorrect Relative Truth

Once again, relative truth is said to be two-fold:

> 12. Correct and incorrect relative [truth] are similar in appearance, but they are distinguished by their ability or inability to produce effective action.

Cognitions of such things as water or a mirage are similar in appearance or in the form they manifest, but ordinary people know that they are correct or incorrect [respectively] by determining whether they are true or false with regard to effective action (*artha-kriyā*). In fact (*vastutaḥ*), both are equally empty. But they are distinguished (*vyavasthita*) on the basis of appearances (*yathādarśana*). Whether they are true or false with regard to effective action is simply a matter of common consent (*yathāprasiddha*), because [effective action] also is empty.

[Objection:] Both of us agree that a mere thing arises dependently and produces effective action. How do we differ?

[Reply:] We do not.

> 13. If you also think that [things] correspond to appearances, rather than to reason, we agree. But it is a completely different story if [you think that] they correspond to reason.[55]

If you also think that [things] correspond to appearances, we agree, and I have no reason to boast. But if you think that [things] correspond to reason, we do not agree. It is a completely different story if [they are considered] from the standpoint of reason.

2. It is Impossible to Know any Causal Relationship

This is because there is no way to know for certain that there is any relationship of cause and effect.[56] For

> (1) A cognition that does not have the form (*ākāra*) [of an object] cannot cognize the object.[57] Neither can the opposite, because the form (*ākāra*) [of an object] is not a valid means of knowledge[58] and because [the form of an object] cannot be [the cognition of an object].[59]

(2) For if a single [cognition] appears to be manifold, how can its forms (*ākāra*) truly exist, because [if they did,] it would lose its unity?[60]

(3) If so [i.e., if no cognition can cognize an object, either with or without the form of the object], neither perception (*pratyakṣa*) nor non-perception (*anupalabdhi*) can prove cause and effect. Consider whether there is any other possibility![61]

(4) If you think that there is some other way of cognizing cause and effect, say what it is. Why be stingy to such a humble request?

(5) This is the reason [i.e., because there is no other way to establish cause and effect] that even those who are omniscient do not perceive the slightest causal relationship between dependent moments.[62]

(6) The object of a Buddha's knowledge is inconceivable. It is known only to someone who is omniscient. It is impossible even to say that [cause and effect] are consistent with reason.

The preceding [verses] are additional verses.

3. Nothing Ultimately Arises

There can be no causal relationship, because

14. Many do not produce one, many do not produce many, one does not produce many, and one does not produce one.[63]

a. Many Do Not Produce One[64]

Many do not produce one, for if a single effect arises from a multiple [cause], such as the eye and so forth, the multiplicity of the cause does not produce multiplicity [of the effect], since the cause is multiple but the effect is not. [Moreover] absence of multiplicity [in the cause] is not the cause of the absence of multiplicity [in the effect], because the effect lacks multiplicity, even when the cause does not lack multiplicity. Thus the multiplicity or lack of multiplicity [in the effect] would not have a cause. Since nothing is excluded from [the categories of multiplicity and non-multiplicity], nothing would have a cause. If this were the case, [everything] would either exist permanently or not exist at all.

b. Many Do Not Produce Many

[Objection:] It is not true [that there is no causation], because a multiple (*aneka*) cause produces a multiple [effect].[65] How? Particular aspects (*viśeṣa*) of [the cause] are associated by nature with particular aspects of [the effect], and because particular aspects of the effect are associated with [particular aspects of] the cause, there is no confusion. For it is from the antecedent condition (*samanantara-pratyaya*) that a visual cognition gets its cognitive nature (*upalambhātmatā*). From the eye comes a cognition's ability to perceive form (*rūpa-grahaṇa-yogyatā*). From the object (*viṣaya*) comes [a cognition's] conformity to a particular thing (*tat-tulya-rūpatā*). Actually (*vastutaḥ*) the effect is not multiple. It is multiple only with respect to the nature of its cause. Since the cause is multiple, the particular aspects of the effect also are multiple. Other cases should be interpreted in the same way.

[Reply:] This is wrong. If the cognitive nature and so forth [which are the cause] are mutually distinct, the cognition (*vijñāna*) [which is the effect] must also be multiple, because it is not different from them.[66] If it were different, they would not be its cause, because it would have to be associated with another efficient cause (*hetu-kāraṇa*).[67] [If the effect is not multiple,] the particular aspects of the cause cannot be mutually distinct, because the cognition (*vijñāna*) [which is the effect] cannot be multiple. There can be no possible benefit from imagining the cause to be multiple. This is why [the opponent's] position is wrong.

[Objection:] By nature the effect is not multiple, but it is a phenomenon (*dharma*) that we imagine (*kalpita*) to be multiple because of its association with the cause.[68] So the multiplicity of the effect, which is caused [by the cause], is imagined.

[Reply:] All right. If the efficient cause (*hetu-kāraṇa*) is conceptually constructed (*kalpanoparacita*), then in a real sense (*tattvā-*

rthena), it is only imagined (*kalpita*). In that case, the effect has no cause, because it is associated with an efficient cause that is imagined.

Furthermore, if you say that the particular aspects [of the effect] actually (*vastutaḥ*) are multiple, but the effect is not, then the subject (*dharmin*) is different from its properties (*dharma*), since [the properties] are multiple, and [the subject] is not. This leads to the problem mentioned before [namely that the effect must be associated with some other efficient cause].[69]

If the particular aspects are only imagined, it is wrong to say that multiple aspects arise from multiple causes. If the multiplicity [of the aspects] is conceptually constructed, it does not depend on an efficient cause.

(1) If you think that the effect is not multiple, but its particular aspects are multiple [and there is no difference between them], it must be an act of God![70]

(2) If [a cognition] is not different from its cognitive nature, it cannot arise from form (*rūpa*). If it is not different from the *ākāra* [of the object], it cannot arise from form (*rūpa*).

(3) If a single [effect] both arises and does not arise, and if [a single cause] both causes and does not cause [the effect] to arise, explain why there is no contradiction.[71]

(4) If you think that all [of the effect] arises from all [of the cause], then it is clear, from the standpoint of reason, that a multiple [cause] and a single [effect] cannot be causally related.[72]

(5) If you think that [an effect] arises from specific conditions (*pratyaya*), then the individual [conditions] separately cannot be the cause of its arising, and the effect cannot have a cause.[73]

(6) If you think that a [single] effect arises from [several] conditions, it follows, as before, that [the cause], which is multiple, and [the effect], which is not multiple, are not causally related.

(7) If [you think that] the two are not different, how reasonable is it to distinguish [aspects of the cause from aspects the effect]? You fall back into the same problems, like an elephant after a bath.[74]

The preceding [verses] are additional verses.

c. One Does Not Produce Many

Furthermore, if an additional factor (*atiśaya*), such as the eye, produces an effect, does it also produce a second [effect]?[75] If it does, this would be another case in which single and multiple [cause and effect] would have no causal relationship, since the effect would be multiple, but not the cause. If a second [factor produces the second effect], there would no longer be a single cause, since [the cause] would no longer be identical to the additional factor.

d. One Does Not Produce One

It is not right even to say that one cause produces one effect, because if the eye and so forth only produce the next moment (*kṣaṇa*) in their own continuum (*santāna*), everyone would be blind and deaf.[76] If they produce the cognition to which [they are related], their own continuum would be cut off. Neither [of these two options] is either possible or acceptable.

e. Concluding Verses

(1) [The preceding argument is] similar to [arguments against the existence of] God (*īśvara*). There is no God who creates the world, because objects of cognition [are not eternal]. If there were [a God who creates the world], he would have no objects of cognition.[77]

(2) The Master [Nāgārjuna] has refuted arising in many ways. But ignorant people still raise objections such as the following:[78]

(3) [Objection:] The terms (*prajñapti*) "from self" and "from something else" are imagined (*kalpita*), and to deny that

something arises [from itself or from something else] merely proves the obvious (*siddha-sādhana*). [Reply:] This is not the case.[79]

(4) If nothing has no cause and everything has some cause, you should have an answer when someone asks what it is.

(5) If there is a cause, such as a rice seed, is it different from or identical to [its effect]? These [two options] are mutually exclusive, and there is no other option.

(6) To say that you cannot specify [whether a cause is different from or identical to its effect] is as unreasonable as. . . a brahmin's mare (?). A reasonable person would answer another way.[80]

(7) It can be specified following conventional usage (*vyavahāra*), which would be acceptable in this case. Otherwise there would be nothing to say.[81]

(8) If you say that there is [a third option] other than these two, and we deny that there is, where is your skill in debate?[82]

(9) If the effect arises before [the cause] has ceased, how can it be an effect? If the effect arises after [the cause] has ceased, what is the cause of the effect?[83]

(10) If these distinctions seem pointless, set them aside. They would be like feeding a snake milk, only to increase its poison.[84]

(11) There is no single cause and there is no multiple cause. Apart from single and multiple [causes], tell us what other cause there can be.

(12) There is no single effect and there is no multiple effect. Apart from single and multiple, tell us what other effect there can be.

(13) You cannot claim "This arises when that is present" without a valid means of cognition (*pramāṇa*). But with

the forms (*ākāra*) discussed above, you have no valid means of cognition.[85]

(14) For us causation only corresponds to appearances. If you think [causation] is real, you have no place to stand.

(15) We would be delighted if you agreed. You would be better off if you were no longer haunted by the idea of real things (*vastu-grāha*).

(16) You claim again and again that there is causality, but you give no proof.

(17) Words alone do not prove it, for then anything could be proved. Yet you praise your own [position]—what subtle understanding![86]

The preceding [verses] are additional verses.

4. The Etymology of Saṃvṛti

What is called "relative" (*saṃvṛti*)?

15ab. The relative is considered either that by which or that in which Reality is concealed.[87]

The relative can be thought of as either the cognition by which or the cognition in which Reality is concealed, that is, [the cognition by which or in which things] are generally accepted (*prasiddha*). As is said in the [*Laṅkāvatāra*] *Sūtra*,

> Things arise in a relative sense (*saṃvṛtyā*), but ultimately they are empty. An erroneous cognition (*bhrānti*) of empty [things] is [rightly] considered a relative [cognition].[88]

15cd. Therefore everything is true [in a relative sense], and nothing is true in an ultimate sense.[89]

Everything is true in a relative sense (*saṃvṛtyā*). That is, [everything] is true according to common consent (*yathāprasiddha*). As is said in a sūtra,

O Subhūti, were it not for mistaken cognitions, foolish common people would not have even the slightest reason to conceive of real entities.

Mistaken cognition (*viparyāsa*) is generally accepted (*loka-prasiddha*). It is true as long as one cognizes the three marks of a [valid] inference.

Devendrabuddhi's Objection[90]

(1) If the relative is non-existent (*abhāva*) and also something that arises, then the same thing at the same time is both capable and incapable [of effective action].

(2) Furthermore, if the relative is something that arises, then, as far as scholars are concerned, the statement "things arise in a relative sense" has the astonishing meaning "what arises arises"![91]

(3) If "relative" is [a synonym of] arising and "ultimate" is [a synonym of] non-arising, you are saying that things do not arise because they do not arise.

(4) This simply proves the obvious (*siddha-sādhana*) and does not prove your point. Following reason, the same can be said of "remaining" and so forth.[92]

Jñānagarbha's Reply

(5) These [objections] do not apply. The word ["relative"] does not have the meaning you imagine. You should understand that these objections do not fit the definition of the relative.[93]

(6) When examined by reason [something] is not true (*satya*). Otherwise it is true. Why is it contradictory, then, for the same thing to be both true and untrue?[94]

(7) When examined by reason, [something] is not real (*bhāva*). Otherwise it is real. Why is it contradictory, then, for the same thing to be both real and unreal?[95]

The preceding [verses] are additional verses.

C. The Relativity of the Ultimate

Nevertheless,[96]

16. From the standpoint of reason, the meaning of the words "ultimately [things] do not arise" also does not arise. Other [such statements] should be interpreted the same way.

The words "ultimately do not exist," "ultimately are empty," and so forth should be interpreted the same way. From the standpoint of reason, they do not exist, are empty, and so forth.

(1) Others think that, from the standpoint of reason, arising is dependent. So what harm do their objections cause to [our conception of emptiness]?[97]

The preceding [verse] is an additional verse.

This is why

17ab. [The Buddha] considers the relative and the ultimate to be identical in nature.[98]

Why?

17c. Because there is no difference between [the relative and the ultimate].

The phrase "the relative and the ultimate" should be supplied.

17d. This is because reason also corresponds to appearances.

Reason also corresponds to appearances (*yathādarśana*), so it is only relative. Reason cannot function any other way.

18. The subject, property, and so forth [of an in-

ference] are constructed on the basis of an item that appears to the mind of both parties.

19. When this happens, there is an inference. Otherwise, there is not. If logicians use such [inferences], who can refute them?

The inference (*anumāna*) and the thing to be inferred (*anumeya*) are made up of a subject (*dharmin*), a property (*dharma*), and an example (*dṛṣṭānta*) that appear to the minds of both parties to the discussion. Otherwise there is no inference, because there can be no inference if the subject, property, and [example] are not established (*siddha*) for both parties. This is because there would be no agreement about any [items in the inference] between persons of different doctrinal positions. It is acceptable to start with this kind of subject to use this kind of reason (*hetu*), and so forth, to ask whether [the subject] is ultimate or not. If a logician uses such an inference, who can refute it? We have shown that this point is generally established, so we will not expand on it here.

It is because [reason corresponds to appearances] that the sūtra says:

> O Subhūti, the relative is not one thing and the ultimate another. The ordinary relative is identical in nature to the ultimate.[99]

Some [logicians] think that the negation of arising also is ultimate.[100] Others consider it to be real. But from [the ultimate] perspective, [our] interpretation of the quotation is correct. Why?

> What is ultimate for one is relative for another, just as one person's mother is considered another person's wife.[101]

20ab. [Objection:] From the standpoint of reason, there is no arising even in a relative sense.

If neither a cognition that bears the form [of its object] nor the opposite[102] can definitely cognize [an object], then, as explained earlier, there can be no definite cognition of cause and effect. [Cause and effect] are [also] impossible for the reasons explained in [verse 14], which began "Many do not produce one."

20cd. [Reply:] Yes, this is why [the Buddha's] teaching is based on appearances.

Why? It is precisely because [cause and effect are impossible when examined by reason] that the Lord's teaching about arising is based on appearances, as he said [in the *Sarva-buddha-viṣayāvatāra-jñānālokālaṃkāra Sūtra*]:

> *Dharmas* that do not arise are always [identical to] the Tathāgata, and all phenomena are like the Sugata. But in the world, foolish people apprehend signs and act upon phenomena that are unreal.[103]

D. Relative Truth Cannot Be Analyzed[104]

21ab. [The relative] corresponds to appearances, so it must not be analyzed.

The relative corresponds to appearances (*yathādarśana*), so it is inappropriate to subject it to the previous analysis [i.e., to ask whether there can be certain knowledge of a causal relationship or to ask whether many can produce one, and so forth].[105] Why?

21cd. Something is contradicted if, when analyzed, it turns out to be something else.[106]

We [Mādhyamikas] do not analyze [relative truth]. Instead, we deny such analysis. If something is impossible when it is analyzed, it is simply impossible. If you start with the relative, which corresponds to appearances, then analyze it, you only contradict it, since it turns out to be something else. However, if [the opponent's objection] refers to something other than what has just been described [i.e., to something that corresponds to reason rather than to appearances], the objection does not contradict us at all.[107]

[Objection:] If nothing arises ultimately,

22ab. Explain why one thing appears to be caused by another.

[Reply:] The answer is,

22cd. It is just that one thing appears to be caused by another. What more is there to say?

If the same thing appears to both of us, what more is there to ask about it? If you do ask, we will say no more than this. There is nothing to be said that has not been said before. The question ["Why does one thing appear to be caused by another?"] is based on nothing more than habitual misconceptions (*abhiniveśa*).

(1) Even though they see [such things as fire and smoke], some people do not understand [that these things are merely appearances]. They are known for creating false disputes by saying to others ["Why does one thing appear to be caused by another?"]. They are ignorant and of ill-repute.

The preceding [verse] is an additional verse.

E. Reply to Particular Objections

1. The Basis of Relative Truth

Do not say that, because [relative truth] would have no basis (*āśraya*), [the Madhyamaka conception of relative truth] is impossible.[108] For

23. The basis of [relative truth] is imagined, even though nothing appears anywhere [with a real basis]. Even something like a tree does not depend on a real basis.[109]

Branches and so forth make it possible to use the designation (*prajñapti*) "tree," and other things [make it possible to designate the branches and so forth].[110] Eventually [such an analysis] leads to the smallest atom (*paramāṇu*), and when one analyzes whether [the smallest atoms] have separate parts, [one finds that] they too do not exist.[111] So there can be no real cause for the designation of something like a tree. This is why we admit that [relative truth] is only consistent with appearances and does not depend on a real cause.

(1) If the relative were based on an [ultimate] basis, it would be [ultimately] real. But [since it is not ultimate,] why not [admit] that its basis is relative?[112]

The preceding [verse] is an additional verse.

Another reason why [the basis of relative truth is only imagined] is that, according to you [Yogācāras],

24ab. Imagined nature is not based on anything.

[Objection:] But [imagined nature] does not depend on anything because it does not exist.[113]

[Reply:] This contradicts perception (*pratyakṣa*). Subject and object are of imagined nature (*parikalpita-svabhāva*), but both are generally accepted (*prasiddha*) as perceptible.[114]

[Objection:] It is only a cognition (*vijñāna*) agitated by ignorance that cognizes [the duality of subject and object].

[Reply:] How can you deny that this contradicts perception? Ordinary people (*loka*) utterly reject anyone who is so ignorant of his own [experience].

[Objection:] But there is vision in dreams and so forth.[115]

[Reply:] Yes, there seems to be such vision, but it appears to you falsely because of wrong habitual notions (*abhiniveśa*).

[Furthermore,] is the appearance of subject and object dependent (*paratantra*)?[116] In Reality, [dependent nature] is empty of [the duality of subject and object], so how can it appear dualistically? You may say that it appears [dualistically] because it is agitated by ignorance, but [dependent nature] itself is not [dualistic], because, by nature, it is empty of duality. So when [dependent nature] appears, it cannot appear dualistically, because there is no connection [between dependent nature and duality].

[Objection:] But we have said that there is a connection.[117]

[Reply:]

24cd. If there is [such a connection], who can deny that it is dependent?

The other [i.e., the connection] must be dependent. Since it is the cause [of the appearance of dependent nature], in addition to being [the cause of duality], it must not be imagined.

If only the cognition arises from causes and conditions, how can duality [arise], when [cognition] arises?[118] If the cognition itself appears dualistically, then, as we have already said, the appearance [of duality] must be produced [by causes and conditions]. If you say that [cognition] is produced [so that it contains the appearance of duality], then the nature [of cognition] is not empty of duality, even though you claim that it is.

It is not enough to say that [a cognition] cognizes dualistically, even though it is not dualistic, because it is deluded by another cognition. The same analysis can be applied [to the other cognition].[119] Enough said!

2. Candrakīrti (?) on the Nature of Relative Truth

25. Some, who are notorious for their bad arguments,[120] argue that if things do not arise in a real sense, they also do not arise in a relative sense, like the son of a barren woman and so forth.

[The opponent claims that] if something does not arise in a real sense (*tattvataḥ*), it does not arise in a relative sense (*saṃvṛtyā*), like the son of a barren woman and so forth, and [that] this is true of such things as form (*rūpa*). But this is wrong.

(1ab) [This point] is not established, because it is refuted by common sense (*loka*) and so forth.[121]

(1c–2c) Perhaps you [the opponent] think that [the point] is not refuted because common sense itself does not arise, but then [your own] point (*sādhya*) cannot be proved,[122] because there is no reason (*hetu*) and so forth, and because your own statement is contradicted.[123]

(2d–3) If [your own point] is the only exception [to the claim that things do not arise], then you cannot avoid [the fault of] inconclusiveness (*anaikāntikatva*).[124] And if the inferring [property] (*sādhana-dharma*) does [not arise], it cannot be present in the example (*dṛṣṭānta*).[125]

(4) If you admit that the reason (*hetu*) implies the conclusion (*sādhya*), then [these problems apply]; but the same problems do not apply to us. Why did you start the argument?[126]

(5) If [the reason] is established by valid cognition (*pramāṇena siddha*) for us, it must also be for you. If you are such a scholar, why attribute your own faults to us?[127]

(6) Perhaps you will say that [the reason] is not established by valid cognition. But it is established repeatedly by denying the arising of things that already exist and do not yet exist. [In any case] you are the one who claims that [the reason] implies [the conclusion].[128]

(7) [Objection:] As far as we are concerned, neither no-real-arising nor no-relative-arising, which are [respectively] the subject (*vyāpya*) and the object (*vyāpaka*) of the implication, is established. So you are the one who is at fault.[129]

(8) [Reply:] We admit that they do not arise in a real sense, because we have denied that anything arises in a real sense. But we do not [admit] that they do not arise in a relative sense. So they are not [as you claim].[130]

(9) In a real sense, neither exists, because there is no conceptual diversity (*prapañca*). If [the opponent's objection] is considered from the standpoint of Reality, it lacks the reason (*hetu*) and so forth that are essential parts [of an inference].

(10) For if there is no duality, there can be no cause and effect.[131] From this it follows that the objection is refuted.

The preceding [verses] are additional verses.

Furthermore,

26a. If relative [truth] were impossible,

on the basis of a means of cognition (*pramāṇena*), then there could be no means of cognition, because there could be nothing to cognize (*grāhya*).

> 26b. What harm could this argument cause?

No one can be angry if . . . .[132]

If you accept (*abhyupagama*) [relative truth], you cannot claim that it is refuted by a means of cognition.

[Objection:] It is wrong to accept relative [truth] and then analyze whether it is reasonable or not. So you should not accept it in the first place.[133] For

> 26cd. Something should be accepted only when it has been analyzed by reason.[134]

You should not accept something and then investigate it, since you first have to examine the reliability and so forth of the means of cognition.

> 27a. [Reply:] This contradicts perception.

Relative [truth] is consistent with appearances, so it follows that, if you do not accept [relative truth], you contradict perception and so forth. If so, [the objection] contradicts perception and so forth.

> 27b. Why should [the problem of contradicting perception] not apply to [your] position?

There is no reason for you to be exempt or for [the problem of contradicting perception] not to apply to you. You may say that this does not frighten you. But we maintain the doctrine of emptiness (*niḥsvabhāva-vāda*) and are not frightened either.

> 27cd. If [a point] is contradicted on the basis of a means of cognition, it is impossible to be confident of its validity.

The relative corresponds to appearances, but if a means of cognition shows that it is impossible, it is simply impossible.[135] If perception is contradicted, we say that it is impossible to be confident of its validity. . . . Thus [the opponent's objection] has no effect, whether it [makes use of] a means of cognition or not.[136] [Without a means of cognition] it is impossible to deny relative [truth].[137]

> (1) If someone does not think that things [are real], who can tell him that [things are not] relative? If someone says that there would be no such thing as conventional usage (*vyavahāra*) [without the existence of real things], why not say the same thing in reply?[138]
>
> (2) Both of us have to use ordinary terminology. If so, what does all of your terminology finally come to?

The preceding [verses] are additional verses.

Therefore,

> 28. We do not deny the appearance of form: it is wrong to deny anything that is experienced,[139]

Because [to deny experience] is to contradict perception.

> 29. But we do deny such things as arising and so forth, which do not appear, but which others imagine to be real.

We only deny such things (*ākāra*) as ultimate arising, the appearance of consciousness, primal matter, the transformation [of elements], and so forth, which do not appear in cognitions of form (*rūpa*) and so forth, but are imagined on the basis of philosophical texts (*śāstra*) and so forth.[140] The denial of these things is not contradicted by perception and so forth. The phrase "and so forth" [in the verse] includes existence.

> 30ab. It is right to use [reason] to deny just what is imagined,

because problems [such as the problem of contradicting perception] mentioned earlier do not apply.

30cd. To deny something that is not imagined is only to contradict oneself.[141]

Not only is it impossible to deny the appearance (*ābhāsa*) of consciousness itself (*vijñāna-mātra*), which is unstained by the fault of conceiving of the aggregates as a body and is dependent in nature, but to [deny consciousness] is to be contradicted by perception and so forth.

(1) Even though concepts (*vikalpa*) appear (*ābhāsate*), we deny the primal matter and so forth that others imagine are, in a real sense, the cause of things.[142]

(2) When we negate [the things] that [others] imagine, [the qualification] "in a real sense" does not qualify the negation, so it does not mean that there is no relative [truth].[143]

The preceding [verses] are additional verses.

This is why it says in the [*Laṅkāvatāra*] *Sūtra*:[144]

> Imagined things do not exist, but dependent [things] do exist, because the extremes of reification (*samāropa*) and denial (*apavāda*) have to be avoided.[145]
>
> No *dharmas* arise with imagined nature. People develop concepts on the basis of dependent [nature].[146]

Similarly,

> O Subhūti, form has the nature of no-form.

And

> Venerable Śāriputra, form is empty of own-being. Whatever is empty of own-being neither arises nor ceases. Whatever neither arises nor ceases is not perceived as becoming anything else. Thus [the aggregates] from feeling to consciousness are the same.

This has been thoroughly explained and is now established.

IV. Karma, Transmigration, and Buddhahood

A. *Action and its Result*

Someone may wonder whether there can be any action (*karma*) or any result (*phala*) if things are only consistent with appearances.[147]

31. [The Buddha] teaches actions and results just as they appear to him as he sees them. This is why all [actions and results] correspond to appearances.

The Teacher has unimpeded vision and is the very essence of knowledge. He seeks the welfare of the world and his nature is compassion. He teaches specific actions and results as they appear to him.[148] Thus, while [actions and results] are not objects of the senses, they all exist just as they appear.

32. [The Buddha] whose very nature is compassion sees that concepts cause bondage, and he explains bondage and liberation through such [teachings] as mind-only.

The Lord understands actions and results, and the nature of his body (*kāya*) is compassion. He sees the world bound by conceptual chains in the prison of *saṃsāra*, and he teaches the world about bondage and liberation. That is, he dispels all ideas of real things (*bhāva-grāha*) by a gradual teaching of aggregates (*skandha*), realms (*dhātu*), sense media (*āyatana*), mind-only (*citta-mātra*), and the selflessness of *dharmas*, adjusted to the mental capacities [of his listeners].

[Objection:] What are concepts (*kalpanā*)?

[Reply:]

33ab. Concepts are a reification of mind and mental phenomena in the three realms.

Concepts are a reification (*samāropa*) of mind (*citta*) and mental phenomena (*caitta*) in the three realms (*traidhātuka*).

> 33cd. [The Buddha] sees that [concepts] cause bondage and teaches accordingly.

The Tathāgata sees that [concepts] cause bondage and teaches accordingly. He does not [teach that concepts cause bondage] from the standpoint of Reality. For

> 34ab. [We] consider even non-existent things to be effective in a way that corresponds to appearances.

It is not contradictory even for non-existent things to cause bondage and so forth in a way that is generally accepted (*yathāprasiddha*), but ultimately there is neither bondage nor anything that is bound.[149]

> 34cd. [Buddhas] do not see existent things as effective in any way.

Even Buddhas do not see existent things as capable of effective action, since there can be no definite cognition [of a causal relationship] either with or without the form (*ākāra*) [of an object] and there is no other way definitely to cognize [a causal relationship].

> (1) [Buddhas] see that one thing follows another—that is, that one thing definitely follows when another is present and one thing is absent when another is absent—so [our statement] does not imply too much (*atiprasaṅga*).[150]

The preceding [verse] is an additional verse.

> 35ab. Others [imagine] that conventional terms refer to things, but this is impossible.

Understand that all conventional terms (*prajñapti*) apply only in a way that corresponds to appearances. Realists hold the view that conventional terms refer to things, but from the standpoint of reason this is impossible, because this is not the way things appear. In the cognition itself, neither atoms nor non-dual [cognition] appear as things.[151] And what does appear is not a thing, because neither a combination [of atoms] nor dualistic [cognition] is a thing.[152] If conventional terms [refer] to either [a combination of atoms or a dualistic cognition], neither [a combination of atoms nor a dualistic cognition] is a thing.

[Objection:] If [conventional terms] only correspond to appearances, they do not specify [anything].

[Reply:] Why not refer to something [that is not precisely specified]? If you do not trust what we say about appearances, let us swear an oath! There cannot be any real thing, because there is no means of cognition [to prove that it exists] and there is a means of cognition to refute it. Why?

> 35cd. This statement is made from the standpoint of reason, because nothing can appear and nothing [can arise].[153]

Therefore, even if there were real things, there would be no reason to be attached to them simply because of conventional terms that conform only to appearances.[154]

> (1) Why be attached to your own views? How insightful are you if you are stubborn and fail to recognize your own faults?[155]
>
> (2) Stop being attached to your own views and resort to rationality. Accept as ultimate only what is confirmed by reason.

The preceding [verses] are additional verses.

[Our] view [i.e., the *darśana* of the Mādhyamikas] does not entail annihilation (*uccheda*).

> 36. If things arise from causes, in what sense are they annihilated? If [effects] cease when [their causes] cease, explain how they can be permanent.

If [a sentient being] appears to be reborn under the influence of defilements (*kleśa*) and actions (*karma*), in what sense is [that being] annihilated? That is, if a sentient being's continuum (*santāna*) continues to be reborn, it is not annihilated. If [a sentient being] burns all defilements and actions in the fire of insight and dwells in the city of nirvana, how can it be permanent? If things did not exist in the relative sense, they could very well be permanent or annihilated. But there is no opportunity [to hold] such a view if [they do not exist] in the ultimate sense. For

(1) How can something that does not arise in its own right be either permanent or annihilated? Conceptions of separate *dharmas* bring about conceptions of own-being.[156]

(2) If [things] do not arise, it is as difficult to conceive of them as separate *dharmas* as it is to write letters in the sky.[157]

The preceding [verses] are additional verses.

37. The Omniscient One sees everything that is empty of imagined nature and arises dependently, in a way that corresponds to appearances.[158]

Things are empty, but [exist] as they appear. Someone who is omniscient is someone who completely and in a single moment perceives that all things are empty of ultimate arising and arise dependently.

38. This is not contradicted in the least by those [Yogācāras who think that] because it is impossible to cognize an object in someone else's continuum, omniscience is [only] imagined.

According to [the Yogācāras], who claim that objects of knowledge are only internal, omniscience is only imagined, because it is impossible to determine an object in someone else's continuum (*santāna*) as if it were in one's own continuum. The reason is that neither a cognition that bears the form (*ākāra*) [of the object] nor the opposite can definitely grasp [an object].[159] This problem does not apply to those who hold the doctrine of emptiness, since [we hold that an object] is determined only with regard to what is generally accepted (*yathāprasiddha*).[160]

B. *The Bodies of the Buddha*

1. The Dharma Body

To be [omniscient] is [first] to understand that even such [ideas] as "*dharmas* do not arise" are imagined, because they are the negations of concepts such as "ultimate arising," and [second] to analyze the nature of things and see nothing at all. For,

> 39. When [the Buddha] takes no notice of subject, object, or self, signs (*nimitta*) do not arise, and when his concentration is firm, he does not get up.

When the Lord has uprooted the seeds of all concepts, along with their traces (*vāsanā*), and no signs (*nimitta*) arise [in his mind], he has no reason to get up [from concentration]. For he has worshipped for many countless eons and his concentration (*samādhi*) is firm from uninterrupted practice.[161]

> 40. The place where he rests becomes the basis of every inconceivable virtue. It is incomparable, worthy of worship, a guide, and quite inconceivable.[162]

> 41. It is the Dharma Body of the Buddhas in the sense that it is the body of all *dharmas*, the basis of every inconceivable virtue, and rational in nature.

The Dharma Body is explained three ways: (1) It is the body of all *dharmas* in the sense that no beings surpass the nature of the Tathāgata.[163] (2) It is the body, or basis (*āśraya*), of all ordinary and extraordinary virtues, either in the sense that [it is the basis on which] they are amassed or that it is [the place where] *dharmas* are proclaimed.[164] It is conceived to be the basis [of virtues] because one who attains it obtains [virtues].[165] (3) The Dharma Body also is that whose nature is discerned by reason, because it is consistent with reason.[166]

2. The Enjoyment Body

(1) Then [when the Dharma Body is attained] concepts are absent, but by the power of a previous [vow], it serves the needs of sentient beings always, everywhere, and in every way.[167]

(2) In a moment of insight it encompasses every object of knowledge. It is the basis of a mass of precious virtues and of inconceivable concentrations (*samādhi*) and trances (*dhyāna*).[168]

(3) It has eliminated all concepts and defilements, along with their traces, and has left behind all ignorance concerning the objects of knowledge.[169]

(4) It contains no faults, but it does contain an ocean of virtues. It always accomplishes what everyone desires.[170]

(5) Like a wishing jewel, it has no equal, and it continues as long as there is *saṃsāra*. Great compassion brings it about, and it is the supreme product of inconceivable merit and knowledge.[171]

(6) It is inconceivable, so it is accessible [only] to the eyes of *bodhisattvas* who attain true excellence and acquire greatly meritorious *karma*.[172]

(7) Since it provides *bodhisattvas* at will with the enjoyment of the Dharma, it is thought of as the Enjoyment Body.

3. The Manifestation Body

(8) From it springs a stream of manifestations (*nirmāṇa*) that, at the proper time, accomplish what every being desires.

(9–10) From the Sage's pores and so forth come specific manifestations, in just the right shape and at just the right time to bring fortunate beings to maturity.

(11) The Conqueror (*jina*) uses it to accomplish all that the world must accomplish. It is his Manifestation Body, which instills the world with confidence.[173]

(12) The manifestation is manifested by the power of the Lord.
It acts at will, as if it were undertaking every action.[174]

The preceding [verses] are additional verses.

This is a brief explanation of the three forms of the Lord's body. Even a sage who possesses all knowledge could not describe it completely in all its forms, much less someone such as I. If one were to go in that direction [and attempt to explain it completely], one would also have to understand the distinction between the bodies of the Disciples (*śrāvakas*) and so forth.[175]

V. Conclusion

42. So do not be one-sided. Consider whether there are any faults in this distinction between the two truths.

43. It is hard to be born as a human being; a pure mind is very weak, the wilderness of rebirth is hard to cross; even life itself is very fleeting.[176]

44. A good teacher is hard to find. So do not be resentful, even if, for lack of merit, you have no conviction (*adhimukti*).[177]

45. [Conviction] will come after gradual practice. But if you practice. But if you are angry, the opportunity will be quite remote.

46. May the merit I have gained by distinguishing the two truths cause the whole world to develop the seed of understanding.[178]

Here ends the distinction between the two truths written by Jñānagarbha, a seeker of perfect insight.

Part Three

Selections from the Subcommentary with Explanatory Notes

1. *Subcommentary:*

> I compose this brief commentary (*pañjikā*) on the distinction between the two truths so that those of lesser intelligence may increase in the various kinds of wisdom.

"At the beginning of the text [Jñānagarbha] says: 'Homage to the pure-minded . . . accomplish what the whole world seeks.' This is an auspicious statement of homage to a chosen divinity (*iṣṭa-devatā*). In one sense, this is an expression of respect. In another, it is the homage to a teacher at the beginning of a text that either generates respect for the text or shows that it has a salutary goal (*artha*) that its teaching aims to bring about. That is, there is [a goal] that has already been accomplished and one that has not yet been accomplished. The expression of homage reflects the goal of the text and expresses the kind of goal the author is seeking.

"This verse expresses three goals (*artha*): (1) *Correct understanding* of the nature (*tattva*) of things is expressed by the phrase 'who understand the emptiness of things.' Emptiness transcends being (*bhāva*) and non-being (*abhāva*) since it has the nature of neither being nor non-being. The word 'thing' (*bhāva*) refers to own-being (*svabhāva*). (2) The *remaining* [of the Buddha and his children] is described as great in five ways: (a) It is great with respect to its cause (*hetu*), in the sense that its cause is compassion (*karuṇā*). Compassion is of three kinds depending on the sentient beings (*sattva*) and so forth to whom it is directed. (b) It is great with respect to duration in that [the Buddhas and *bodhisattvas*] remain as long as there is *saṃsāra*. (c) It is great with respect to the ones who do it, since it is done by the Buddha and *bodhisattvas*. Disciples (*śrāvaka*) and Solitary Buddhas (*pratyeka-buddha*) are silent (*mauna*) in body, speech, and mind, but the Lord (*bhagavān*) is the greatest of these, because he is uniquely silent in body, speech, and mind. This [silence] is explained by the description of the secret of the body (*kāya-guhya*) and so forth in the *Tathāgataguhyaka Sūtra*. 'And his children' indicates that the Lord has an entourage that is always large and pure. (d) It is great with respect to its purpose, as is indicated by the words 'world' and so forth . . . . (e) It is great in the sense that it is not stained by any fault, as is indicated by the word 'pure-minded.' A pure mind is one in which moral and cognitive hindrances (*kleśa-jñeyāvaraṇa*) have been abandoned. That is, it is one in which moral and cognitive hindrances have been abandoned, in which they have been abandoned along with their traces (*vāsanā*), and in which all hindrances to concentration (*samādhi*) and attainment (*samāpatti*) have also been abandoned. A pure mind is one that is unstained by worldly things (*laukika-dharma*) or the samsaric faults of those who reside in *saṃsāra*. The word 'yet' indicates a *viṣamālaṃkāra* [*Sāhityadarpana* 10.7 ab]. It shows that while they correctly understand the nature of things from the perspective of ultimate truth, from the perspective of relative truth they remain [*in saṃsā*ra]. This is not a contradiction, since the Enjoyment Body (*saṃbhoga-kāya*) arises from the prerequisites of merit and knowledge (*puṇya-jñāna-saṃbhāra*) in accordance with the aspiration of the *bodhisattvas* and with the appearances of [external objects?] such as blue. In short, the expression of respect [in the opening verse] expresses goals (*artha*) consisting of three actions" (*Sa* 15b/2–16a/6).

Explanation: According to the subcommentator, the opening verse serves a double purpose: it induces respect for the teaching that is being transmitted in the text, and it indicates the goal that the text is meant to promote. The double purpose reflects a number of important features in Jñānagarbha's intellectual method. Philosophical texts were understood in Jñānagarbha's day as a transmission of the words of an authoritative teacher. References to the Buddha and bodhisattvas, including Nāgārjuna, at the beginning of a Madhyamaka text are not just perfunctory gestures of respect, but indications of the authoritative source of the teaching the text is meant to expound. Candrakīrti explains the importance of Nāgārjuna at the beginning of Chapter 6 of the *Madhyamakāvatāra*: "It is hard to be certain of the intention (*abhiprāya*) of scripture, so people like us are incapable of explaining reality even on the basis of scripture. This applies to someone who acts independently. But a treatise (*śāstra*) is written by someone authoritative (*pramāṇa-bhūta*). He is certain of the meaning of scripture because he perceives the correct explanation of scripture. Nāgārjuna's method, which follows scripture (*āgama*) and reason (*yukti*), is like [a bodhisattva's] understanding of the profound nature of *dharmas*. My explanation follows his method" (*Madhyamakavatāra*, p. 75). Dignāga also acknowledges the authority of the Buddha in the opening words of his *Pramāṇa-samuccaya*: "To him who is the embodiment of valid knowledge (*pramāṇa-bhūta*) . . . I do homage": Sanskrit found in Hattori, *Dignāga*. p. 23. On the relationship of scripture and reason in Madhyamaka thought see Shotaro Iida, "*Āgama* (Scripture) and *Yukti* (Reason) in Bhāvaviveka," *Kanakura Festschrift* (Kyoto, 1966), p. 76–96. On the role of Dignāga's verse in the formation of Dharmakīrti's *Pramāṇavārttika* see Masatoshi Nagatomi, "The Framework of the Pramāṇavārttika, Book One," *JAOS* 79 (1959), pp. 263–6.

The subcommentary also draws attention to the relationship between the text and the larger goals of human life. In spite of their rarefied content, philosophical texts in Jñānagarbha's day had a pragmatic flavor. They were expected to have relevance to some specific goal (*artha*). In Jñānagarbha's case the goal is Buddhahood, characterized by the acts of understanding (the emptiness of things), remaining (in *saṃsāra*), and accomplishing (what the whole world seeks). In other texts the purpose might be more mundane. But for a text to be considered meaningful it had to give a clear statement of its connection to a goal someone might wish to seek. The purpose (*prayojana*) of a text (to use terminology the subcommentator introduces in the next section) is to impart the right knowledge that will help bring about this goal. For a clear expression of the relationship between right knowledge and the goals of human life see the beginning of Dharmakīrti's *Nyāyabindu*: "The achievement of all human goals is preceded by right knowledge; thus this [knowledge] is to be investigated" (*samyagjñānapūrvikā sarvapuruṣārtha-siddhir iti tad vyutpadyate*: Pandita Dalsukhbhai Malvania, ed., *Dharmottarapradīpa*, 2nd ed., Tibetan Sanskrit Works Series, vol. 2, [Patna: Jayaswal Research Institute, 1971], p. 61).

Although the term *artha* (goal) is not used by Jñānagarbha until later in the text, its use here by the subcommentator deserves comment, since the term can be used to unlock the layers of meaning in the text. According to *A Critical Pāli Dictionary,* the Pāli term *attha* (Skt. *artha*) can mean, among other things, "aim" or "purpose," "thing," and "meaning." To these three meanings might be added a fourth: "cognitive datum" or "content" of a cognition. In the case of a cognition of a tree, for example, the tree itself is an *artha* in the sense of "thing," but the image "tree" in the cognition of the tree also can be referred to by the term *artha*. The four separate meanings of the term reflect the different dimensions of Jñānagarbha's thought. The first meaning ("purpose") is related to its teleological or soteriological dimension. The third meaning ("meaning") is related to its exegetical dimension. The second and the fourth ("thing" and "cognitive content") are related to its ontological and epistemological dimensions.

Later sections of the text take up epistemological and ontological questions in greater detail, but here, in the verse of homage to Buddhas and *bodhisattvas* and in the verse that states the subject matter of the text, Jñānagarbha shows that the text has *artha* in the sense of purpose and in the sense that it is a legitimate explanation of the words of his teachers.

2. *Subcommentary:* "This book would not be written if it had no purpose (*prayojana*). To show that there is no reason to accuse him of counting crows' teeth, [Jñānagarbha] says: 'to promote a correct understanding of the two truths.' The word 'correct' indicates that, while others have already distinguished the two truths, they have not done so correctly. The relevance (*saṃbandha*) [of the text] is not stated separately, because it is implied by the purpose. The relevance of any text or action to its purpose should be

stated, but it is not necessary to state separately relevance that is causally related [to the purpose], since it is not a necessary part of the text. For example, medical treatises and so forth should be written if they have a purpose. This book also is one that has a purpose. If medical treatises and so forth have relevance, those who already know their relevance will take them up. This book also is one that has relevance. The phrase 'to promote a correct understanding of the two truths' should be supplemented by the addition of the phrase 'by people who have prior knowledge'" (*Sa* 16 a/7–16b/4).

Explanation: This passage bears a close relationship to a similar passage in Kamalaśīla's *Tattvasaṃgrahapañjikā*. "Relevance that is causally related [to the purpose]," for example, is similar to "the relationship of cause and effect" (*sādhya-sādhana-bhāva-lakṣaṇa*) mentioned by Kamalaśīla as a reason for omitting explicit reference to the relevance (*sambandha*) of a text (vol. 1, p. 12). Tsong-kha-pa based his argument against Śāntarakṣita's authorship of the *Subcommentary* in part on a comparison between the *Subcommentary* and Kamalaśila's *Tattvasaṃgrahapañjikā*. This question is taken up in the section on Jñānagarbha's works in Part One.

3. The title "distinction between the two truths" is discussed in the section on Jñānagarbha's works in Part One.

4. "Dharmapāla and so forth": *Subcommentary* (*Sa* 16b/7).

5. The prerequisites of merit and knowledge are said to result in two benefits (*sat*), the Form Body (*rūpa-kāya*) and the Dharma Body (*dharma-kāya*). These two benefits are discussed by Candrakīrti in the *Yuktiṣaṣṭi-kāvṛtti* (Peking Tibetan Tripiṭaka, vol. 98, *Sa* 33a) and *Madhyamakāva-tāra*, p. 62.

6. The subcommentator identifies the others as Disciples (*śrāvaka*) and so forth (*Sa* 17b/1–2).

7. The translation equivalents *rigs pa* = *nyāya* and *ji ltar snang ba* = *yathādarśana* are based on verse 17, which is quoted in the *Abhisamayā-laṃkārālokā*, p. 407. The Tibetan translator had as much difficulty capturing the nuances of the phrase *yathādarśana* in Tibetan as we do in English. In the verse the phrase is translated *ji ltar snang ba* ("corresponding to appearances"), as it is throughout most of the text. In the commentary, however, the translator changes to *ji ltar . . . mthong ba* ("corresponding to what is seen"). Both phrases can be used to represent the same Sanskrit original, but in English, as in Tibetan, a translator has to choose between a term like "appear," which emphasizes the passive and illusory quality of the cognition, and "see," which emphasizes the agent's own engagement in the cognition. Here I have chosen to show the relationship in Sanskrit between

snang and *mthong* by translating both as "appear." The nuances of the Tibetan translation would be better rendered, however, by leaving "appear" in the verse and changing the commentary to "see." The translation would then read: "Whatever even cowherds and women see is true in a relative sense but not in a real sense. [Their seeing is true] if an object can definitely be cognized that corresponds to that seeing. Seeing is of two kinds: conceptual and non-conceptual."

Jñānagarbha's use of the formula *yathādarśana* indicates the depth of his relation to Dharmakīrti. At first his definition of the two truths seems to turn Dharmakīrti upside down. In the verse Jñānagarbha associates the relative with seeing (*darśana*), and in the commentary he associates the ultimate with reason (*nyāya*). This definition reflects Dharmakīrti's distinction between perception (*pratyakṣa*) and inference (*anumāna*) but with the values reversed. For Dharmakīrti, perception grasps what is ultimately real and inference what is real only in a relative sense: "Here the [object] that is capable of effective action is ultimately real and the other relatively real: these are respectively the particular and the universal" (*Pramāṇavārttika* 2.3). But Jñānagarbha's reversal of Dharmakīrti's distinction between perception and inference also reflects Dharmakīrti's own argument about the nature of the distinction between subject and object in *Pramāṇavārttika* 2.354–67 (parallel to *Pramāṇaviniścaya* 1.45–59). It is from this argument that Jñānagarbha seems to draw the term *yathādarśana*. For more on the significance of this term see the section on Jñānagarbha's debt to Dharmakīrti in Part One.

The phrase "even to cowherds and women" (*ba lang rdzi mo*) is a stock phrase in Madhyamaka literature. It occurs twice in the *Prasannapadā* (pp. 260 and 418) and at least once in the *Madhyamakāvatāra* (p. 105). In Sanskrit it is unclear whether the compound *gopālāṅganā* means "female cowherds" or "cowherds and women." Candrakīrti's Tibetan translators agree, however, in reading the compound as a *dvandva: ba lang rdzi dang bud med* "cowherds and women."

8. A similar distinction is found in the discussion of incorrect relative [truth] in the *Madhyamakārthasaṃgraha*: [The incorrect relative (*mithyā-saṃvṛti*)] "again has two forms: one with discursive thinking (*savikalpa*) and one without discursive thinking (*nirvikalpa*). *Savikalpa* is [e.g.] to take a rope for a snake, *nirvikalpa* is [e.g.] to 'perceive' two moons" (quoted from Chr. Lindtner, "Atiśa's Introduction to the Two Truths, and its Sources," *JIP* 9 [1981], p. 201). This explanation of *mithyā-saṃvṛti* may explain the otherwise puzzling comment on this sentence by the subcommentator: "'Appearances are of two kinds . . . ' shows that relative truth (*saṃvṛti-satya*) consists of correct (*tathya-*), and so forth." Jñānagarbha could not be

making a simple, one-to-one correspondence between *tathya-saṃvṛti* and *savikalpa* cognition and between *mithyā-saṃvṛti* and *nirvikalpa* cognition. The subcommentator may be taking the entire sentence as a reference to *mithyā-saṃvṛti*.

9. According to the subcommentator, verse 4 is an account of the first of two kinds of ultimate (*paramārtha*) (*Sa* 18b/3–4). The subcommentator calls the first kind of ultimate "the ultimate that is consistent with the ultimate" (*don dam pa dang mthun pa'i don dam pa*). The meaning of this formula is not immediately obvious, but it becomes clear by contrast with the second kind of ultimate, which the subcommentator calls "the inexpressible ultimate" (*rnam grangs ma yin pa'i don dam pa / aparyāya-paramārtha*). He has in mind the distinction between the expressible (*paryāya*) and inexpressible (*aparyāya*) ultimates found in texts such as the *Madhyamakārthasaṃgraha*: "The absolute is devoid of the principle of language (*prapañca*), and it is of two kinds, viz. the absolute which can be rendered into words (*paryāya-paramārtha*) and the absolute which cannot be rendered into words (*aparyāya-paramārtha*)" (Lindtner, "Atiśa's Introduction," p. 200).

lCang-skya gives a helpful breakdown of the different meanings of the term "ultimate" in his *Presentation of Tenets (grub pa'i mtha' rnam par bzhag pa)*. He explains that the term can refer either to an object of cognition or to the cognition itself, and in each case can be either conceptual or non-conceptual: "The object (*viṣaya*), which is the nature of things (*dharmatā*), can be referred to as ultimate (*paramārtha*), and the subject (*viṣayin*), which is a rational cognition, can also be referred to as ultimate. Each of these in turn can occur in two forms. The object, which is emptiness, is the *actual* ultimate in a pure state of concentrated awareness, free from discursive ideas (*prapañca*) of the duality [of subject and object] and discursive ideas of real existence. In a conceptual, rational cognition, [this object] is free from discursive ideas about real existence but not from dualistic discursive ideas, thus [in a rational cognition] it is only partially free from discursive ideas. In general, then, emptiness-the-object is the actual ultimate. But [the emptiness that is known] in a conceptual, rational cognition is not an ultimate that is free from both kinds of discursive ideas. These are the two ways of talking about the ultimate as object. When the non-conceptual awareness of a saint in a state of concentration (*samādhi*) is focused on Reality (*tattva*), it is capable of eliminating both kinds of discursive ideas. Thus this [non-conceptual awareness] also is the actual ultimate. Through logical marks (*liṅga*), a conceptual, rational cognition of Reality is capable of eliminating discursive ideas of the real existence of its object, but it cannot eliminate dualistic discursive ideas. Because it is merely consistent in form with the former [non-conceptual awareness], it is [called] the ultimate that is consistent with the ultimate. These are the two ways of talking about the ultimate-as-subject." (Translation of lCang-skya adapted from Donald Lopez's translation of *The Presentation of Tenets* in "The Svātantrika-Mādhyamika School of Mahāyāna Buddhism" [Ph.D. Diss.: University of Virginia, 1982], p. 506–7.)

The *locus classicus* of the distinction between conceptual and non-conceptual ultimates is the third chapter of Bhāvaviveka's *Tarkajvālā*: "The ultimate is of two kinds: The first is effortless, transcendent (*lokottara*), free from impurity, and free from discursive ideas (*niṣprapañca*). The second is accessible to effort, consistent with the prerequisites of merit and knowledge, pure, and accessible to discursive ideas (*saprapañca*) in the sense that it can be referred to as worldly knowledge (*laukika-jñāna*)." The Tibetan text of this passage is found in Shotaro Iida, *Reason and Emptiness: A Study in Logic and Mysticism* (Tokyo: Hokuseido Press, 1980), p. 86. The translation is mine.

10. On the addition of the term "cognition" see notes 13 and 14 below.

11. The term "not to be contradicted" (*avisaṃvāda*) recalls verse 1.3 of the *Pramāṇavārttika: pramāṇam avisaṃvādi jñānam*: "A means of knowledge is a cognition that cannot be contradicted." But it is also found in traditional Madhyamaka works such as Nāgārjuna's *Ratnāvalī* (Lindtner, "Atiśa's Introduction," p. 203).

12. In this passage Jñānagarbha gives only the briefest indication of what he means by reason (*rigs pa / nyāya*). He leaves unanswered several key questions. He defines reason as a cognition produced by a three-fold logical mark (*liṅga*). But there are different kinds of cognitions produced by logical marks. Does he mean that every valid inference (*anumāna*) is an ultimate cognition? If so, he would be elevating ordinary inferences such as "There is fire on the mountain because there is smoke on the mountain" to the level of ultimacy. Given the Madhyamaka understanding of Buddhahood, this would be an absurd position for even the most devoted rationalist. The subcommentator addresses this problem in his subcommentary.

Subcommentary: "Why is reason called ultimate? [Jñānagarbha] says: 'Reason is ultimate because it cannot be contradicted.' In what sense is it not contradicted? He says: '[A cognition] that determines an object through the use of reason cannot be contradicted. Thus a cognition produced by a three-fold logical mark (*liṅga*) is ultimate (*paramārtha*) because it is the ultimate (*parama*) meaning (*artha*).' 'Through the use of reason' means through a relationship of either identity or causality. 'Not to be contradicted' means to be unmistaken about a cause on the basis of an effect, because [if the cause were absent] it would follow that there would be no effect; or to be unmistaken about the identity of a thing, because [if a *śiṃśapa*, for example, were not a tree] it would follow that it would not have the same identity [as a *śiṃśapa*]. . . .

"[Objection:] If the cognition produced by a three-fold logical mark is ultimate, then the cognition that there is fire when there is smoke must be ultimate, and the object specified by that cognition must be ultimate as well.

"[Reply:] This is not the way to understand [Jñānagarbha's point]. Such things as smoke do not exist, since they do not arise in the first place. How then can either the cognition that they produce or the object that they specify exist? If [you are claiming that] a logical mark, such as smoke, that corresponds to appearances (*yathādarśana*) establishes the existence of an object such as fire, we agree and there is no problem. We accept as ultimate the argument that proves the non-existence of such things as fire, since it is consistent with the ultimate. This is because the ultimate is defined as the elimination of the entire network of concepts" (*Sa* 18a/1–7).

13. Svātantrika tradition recognizes a number of different explanations of the compound *paramārtha*. The *Madhyamakaratnapradīpa*, for example, says: "[In the word '*paramārtha*'] 'meaning' (*artha*) denotes the object of inquiry (*vikalpanīya*) and the object of comprehension (*avagantavya*). 'Ultimate' (*parama*) indicates that it is supreme (*uttama*). It is meaning and ultimate, i.e., the ultimate meaning [or, in one word, absolute]. Or, again, the absolute is *paramārtha* as it is the object (*artha*) of the supreme cognition (*paramajñāna*)" (Lindtner, "Atiśa's Introduction," p. 72). The *locus classicus*, however, is again Bhāvaviveka's *Tarkajvālā*: "In the word *paramārtha*, the word *artha* means an object of knowledge (*jñeya*). It refers to the object that is to be investigated and understood. The word *parama* means 'supreme'. The compound *paramārtha* [as a *karmadhāraya* compound] can mean ultimate object, in the sense that it is both ultimate and an object. Or [as a *tatpuruṣa* compound] it can mean the object of the ultimate, in the sense that it is the object of non-conceptual knowledge, which is the ultimate. Or [as a *bahuvrīhi* compound] it can mean [the cognition] that is consistent with the ultimate object. [Such a cognition] is consistent with the ultimate object because it is the wisdom (*prajñā*) that is consistent with the ultimate object and possesses the ultimate object. When we say 'ultimately' (*paramārthena*), it is just this *paramārtha* [i.e., *paramārtha* in the third sense] that we mean." The Tibetan of this passage is found in Iida's *Reason and Emptiness*, pp. 82–3. The translation is mine.

Jñānagarbha's explanation does not strictly follow Bhāvaviveka's. Jñānagarbha understands the term *paramārtha* as a *karmadhāraya* compound meaning "the cognition that is the ultimate meaning." Bhāvaviveka prefers to take it as a *bahuvrīhi* compound meaning "the cognition whose object is ultimate." But both take it as referring primarily to a cognition. When they use the term in constructing their own arguments, the term refers to the cognition of emptiness.

14. In this sentence Jñānagarbha recognizes that the term *paramārtha* can also refer to the *object* that is ultimate. His example is somewhat cryptic, but it shows how he gives priority to the cognition rather than to the object. The subcommentator explains that the term "perception" (*pratyakṣa*), like the term "measure," can refer both to the cognition that perceives an object and to the object itself. When someone is measuring a certain "measure" of grain, the word "measure" can refer either to the cognition of the grain or to the grain itself, but what makes the grain a "measure" is the cognition of the grain rather than the grain itself (*Sa* 18a/4–5).

15. This scriptural quotation is often used as part of the Madhyamaka criticism of Yogācāra conceptions of the ultimate. See, for example, my "Bhāvaviveka's Critique," p. 72. Compare also *Madhyamakahṛdayakārikā* 3.246 and verse 7 of Atiśa's *Satyadvayāvatāra* (Lindtner, "Atiśa's Introduction", p. 194). The quotation is similar to a passage in the *Dharmasaṃgīti Sūtra: adarśanaṃ bhagavan sarvadharmāṇām darśanaṃ samyagdarśanam* ("O Lord, not to see is to see all *dharmas*: this is true seeing"). The passage is quoted in the *Śikṣāsamuccaya of Śāntideva*, ed. P. L. Vaidya, Buddhist Sanskrit Texts Series, vol. 11 (Darbhanga: Mithila Institute, 1961), p. 140.

16. With this objection, Jñānagarbha begins an important digression on the Yogācāra doctrine of the three natures (*svabhāva*). His argument corresponds to Bhāvaviveka's argument against "absolute nature" (*pariniṣpanna-svabhāva*) in my "Bhāvaviveka's Critique,"pp. 70–4. The form of the argument is quite similar. It even uses the same scriptural quotations to support its point. But, unlike Bhāvaviveka, Jñānagarbha focuses on the concept of self-cognition (*svasaṃvedana*).

17. Compare Dignāga's *Prajñāpāramitāpiṇḍārtha* 28ab: *nāstītyādi-padaiḥ sarvaṃ kalpitaṃ vinivāryate* ("Words such as 'there is not' rule out everything that is imagined"), Giuseppe Tucci, "Minor Sanskrit Texts on the Prajñā-pāramitā," *JRAS* (1947), p. 57.

The objector argues that the term *kiṃcit* / *'ga' yang* (which can be translated as "something," "anything," or "a certain thing") should be understood as referring only to imagined nature (*kalpita-svabhāva*), the first of the three natures (*svabhāva*). This allows the objector to interpret the phrase "not to see anything" so that it does not deny *all* cognition, only the cognition of imagined nature. The objector's position is consistent with the relationship between the three natures described in the first verse of the *Madhyāntavibhāga: abhūtaparikalpo 'sti dvayan tatra na vidyate / śūnyatā vidyate tv atra tasyām api sa vidyate* ("The imagination of what is unreal exists, and in it there is no duality. In it is emptiness, and it is in [emptiness]"). The Sanskrit is found in Gadjin M. Nagao, ed., *Madhyāntavibhāga-bhāṣya* (Tokyo: Suzuki Research Foundation, 1964), p. 17. In this verse, "the imagination of what is unreal" corresponds to dependent nature (*paratantra-svabhāva*), the second of the three natures, and duality corresponds to imagined nature. According to the *Madhyāntavibhāga*, imagination exists, but what is imagined does not exist. Here the opponent argues that the seeing of Reality is a real seeing (like the real imagination of the *Madhyāntavibhāga*), from which the unreal dualities of imagined nature have been removed.

In his response, Jñānagarbha, like Bhāvaviveka, criticizes the idea that there is a real cognition. Bhāvaviveka did this by arguing against dependent nature (*paratantra-svabhāva*). Jñānagarbha argues against the concept of self-cognition (*svasaṃvedana*). But the point is the same: nothing ultimately real is left behind after dualities have been stripped away. These arguments strike at the heart of what has been known in Madhyamaka scholarship as "the problem of the Absolute." See, for example, Jan de Jong, "The Problem of the Absolute in the Madhyamaka School," *JIP* 2 [1972], pp. 1–6. Jñānagarbha's argument shows how unwilling he is to attribute any ultimate reality to *paramārtha* or to the cognition of emptiness. For more on this question see my "Bhāvaviveka's Critique."

18. According to Dignāga, "self-cognition (*svasaṃvedana*) is the aspect of a cognition that is aware of itself. This aspect is distinguished from the aspects that serve as the subject and object. See Dignāga's *Pramāṇa-samuccaya-vṛtti*: "Every condition is produced with a two-fold appearance, namely, that of itself [as subject] (*svābhāsa*) and that of the object (*viṣayābhāsa*). The cognizing of itself as [possessing] these two appearances or the self-cognition (*svasaṃvitti*) is the result [of the cognitive act]" (Maasaaki Hattori, *Dignāga on Perception* [Cambridge, Mass:. Harvard University Press, 1968], p. 28).

The subcommentator gives a helpful introduction to the argument: "[The Yogācāras] claim: There exists a self-referential cognition that arises dependently and is free from the duality of subject and object, and the phrase 'not to see anything' refers to imagined nature (*kalpita-svabhāva*). [To express this objection Jñānagarbha] says: 'Someone may say that [to see Reality] is not to see any imagined nature.' [This means that imagined nature] is utterly non-existent, and thus makes no appearance. 'This is correct' means that the statement is made with reference to imagined nature. 'Otherwise,' if [the statement] referred to all the natures, why would it say 'anything'? The word 'why' indicates that [the word 'anything'] could have been omitted. If [the statement] were inclusive, it would say 'Not to see any nature.' To say that would have been sufficient. Anything else would be inappropriate" (*Sa* 18b/7–19a/3).

19. *Subcommentary:* "'The absence' means the absence of duality. 'If it is not' means if it is not empty [of duality]. To 'it cannot' should be supplied 'cognize the absence of duality.' This indicates that [self-cognition] is similar to a case [of non-cognition (*anupalabdhi*)] in which one does not cognize the absence of a pot in a [particular place] without cognizing the place (*āśraya*) that is empty of the pot" (*Sa* 19a/3–4).

Explanation: The subcommentator uses the technical category of non-cognition (*anupalabdhi*) to clarify Jñānagarbha's opening definition. To cognize the absence (*abhāva*) of an object in a particular place (*āśraya*), such as the absence of a pot on a particular spot on the ground, Buddhist logicians require the cognition of the place itself, empty of the object that is absent. Cognition of the absence of the pot is equivalent to the cognition of the ground on which the pot is absent. The absence of the pot and the ground on which it is absent correspond to the two elements in Jñānagarbha's definition of self-cognition: "Cognition cognizes [itself] as empty of duality" corresponds to the cognition of the ground on which the pot is absent, and "cognition of the absence [of duality]" corresponds to the cognition of the absence of the pot. The second of these elements is impossible without the first. Jñānagarbha's strategy as the argument unfolds is to attack the possibility of a cognition cognizing itself as empty of duality. He says that the cognition cannot cognize itself unless it has an image of itself (*svābhāsa*), but because it is empty of duality it also must be empty of any image of itself. For a more complete explanation of the theory of non-cognition (*anupalabdhi*) see Th. Stcherbatsky, *Buddhist Logic* (New York: Dover Publications, 1962), vol. 1, pp. 363–6 and vol. 2, p. 60.

20. *Subcommentary:* "To someone who says that [cognition] cognizes itself as empty of duality, [Jñānagarbha] responds by saying: 'A cognition does not cognize itself, because it is empty of any image of itself (*svābhāsa*).' This is the first statement of the argument, but it is not a conclusive statement. If it were, the example 'like any other cognition' would lack the inferred (*sādhya*) [property]. As far as the opponent is concerned, cognitions do cognize themselves. The argument here should read as follows: [A cognition] does not cognize an image of which it is empty, just as one cognition does not cognize another cognition, and the cognition in question is empty of any image of itself" (*Sa* 19a/4–7).

Explanation: The subcommentary on this passage is one of the few places in the text where the subcommentator clearly changes Jñānagarbha's argument. He makes the change to avoid an obvious flaw. As it is first formulated, Jñānagarbha's argument reads as follows:

> A cognition (the *dharmin* or subject of the inference)
> does not cognize itself (the *sādhya-dharma* or inferred property)
> because it is empty of any image of itself (the
> *sādhana-dharma* or inferring property)
> like other cognitions (the *dṛṣṭānta* or example).

For the inference to be valid, the example has to give an instance in which the opponent agrees that both the *sādhya-dharma* and the *sādhana-dharma* are present. Here, because the opponent thinks that all cognitions cognize themselves, the *sādhya-dharma* ("not cognizing itself") is not established. The subcommentator rewrites the inference in a more roundabout way to avoid this difficulty.

21. The focus of the argument then shifts to the reason (*hetu*) of the inference ("because it is empty of any image of itself"). One way for the opponent to reject Jñānagarbha's argument would be to claim that the reason is not valid. This would mean denying that a cognition is empty of any image of itself, or asserting that a cognition cognizes an image (*ābhāsa*) of itself that is different from the cognition itself. Jñānagarbha rejects this possibility by suggesting that such a distinction would result in an infinite regress. Self-cognition is identical to the cognition itself; it is merely a cognition being aware of itself while it is aware of whatever is its object. But if the self-cognition of cognition A is a cognition of the *image* of cognition A, then it is no longer identical to cognition A itself, since cognition A is a cognition of the image of the object, not of the image of cognition A. If the self-cognition of cognition A is different from cognition A, then it must require *another* cognition to be aware of itself, and so on *ad infinitum*. The subcommentator gives the following explanation:

"To show that the reason (*hetu*) is not unestablished (*asiddha*) he says: 'Not to admit that [it cognizes] an image of itself would imply that there is a difference [between the cognition and the image it cognizes], as there is between blue and the cognition [of blue].' This means that the cognition and the self-image (*svābhāsa*) of the cognition would be different, just as blue and the cognition of blue, or of the image [of blue], are different, since blue and [a cognition of] the image of blue are not identical. This would not be acceptable, since there would be an infinite regress in which one cognition would be understood to cognize another. This is how [Jñānagarbha] shows that the reason is not unestablished" (*Sa* 19a/7–19b/2).

22. The argument then shifts in another direction. Assuming that self-cognition cognizes only itself, rather than a separate image of itself, what *causes* it to cognize itself? Normally the image of an object would provide the occasion for such a cognition, but in this case there is no object different from the cognition itself. The first possible explanation is that a cognition A cognizes cognition A "because it is a cognition." Taken literally, this means that *any* cognition would also cognize cognition A, because it too is a cognition. This is a result in which "too much is implied" (*atiprasaṅga*): it leads to an absurd conclusion.

Subcommentary: "[Objection:] [A cognition] both cognizes itself and is empty of its own form (*svākāra*) because it is a cognition. Furthermore, there is no contradiction between these two [assertions]. There is doubt, therefore, as to whether the reason (*hetu*) is excluded (*vyāvṛtta*) in the contrary instance (*vipakṣa*).

"[Reply:] [Jñānagarbha] says: '[A cognition] does not [cognize itself] merely because it is a cognition.' 'Cognize itself' is carried down [from the previous paragraph]. Why? 'Because too much would be implied (*atiprasaṅgāt*).' That is, every cognition would cognize every other cognition and no cognition would fail to cognize any [other cognition]. You may say that a cognition of blue is not a cognition of yellow. But the fact that it is a cognition is not sufficient justification, because there is no distinguishing factor, as there would be in the cognition of an object (*viṣaya*), to indicate that it is a cognition of blue rather than a cognition of yellow" (*Sa* 19b/2–4).

The opponent's reason ("because it is a cognition") may represent an argument found in Dharmakīrti's *Pramāṇaviniścaya:* "What is called 'cognition' is conscious, because it has the nature of [cognition]. [The cognition of the object] is not different from [cognition], like self-cognition. This also is why [the cognition] does not cognize another object. If blue and so forth are not objects different from perception, blue and so forth are cognized, because something is conscious in that way that has the nature of [cognition]. But when something appears that way, it brings about consciousness of itself and of something else, because it has the nature of [cognition]. This is why we think that the subjective aspect (*grāhakākāra*) proves self-cognition." (Translation adapted from Tilmann Vetter, *Dharmakīrti's Pramāṇaviniścayaḥ: 1 Kapitel: Pratyakṣam* [Vienna: Österreichische Akademie der Wissenschaften, 1966], pp. 98–9.)

23. The discussion then shifts to another point. What if the opponent attempts to explain self-cognition by saying not simply that it is a cognition but that it is a cognition of *itself*? The subcommentator explains Jñānagarbha's response:

"'You may say that, if [a cognition cognizes itself] because it is a *self*-cognition, too much is not implied.' Here 'cognizes itself' is carried down. 'But this also is wrong.' That is, it is unreasonable. Why? 'Because there is no special reason.' This means that there is no special reason for this [cognition] to cognize itself rather than to cognize something else. It also indicates that [the opponent] has no reason for saying this [rather than something else]. 'If there is no' means if there is no special reason. Too much is then implied, as before" (*Sa* 19b/4–6).

Explanation: The over-implication (*atiprasaṅga*) seems similar to the one in the preceding argument: If there is no special reason to require that a particular cognition cognize itself rather than something else, then self-cognition A could just as well cognize cognition B as cognition A. The reason "because it is a self-cognition" would allow no distinction. But the subcommentary indicates cryptically that the point may actually be different. The subcommentator says:

"This is a reference to an earlier problem (*doṣa*). That is, if there is a cause and that cause is different from its form (*ākāra*), then to admit that [a cognition] cognizes itself implies that there is a difference [between the cognition and the form it cognizes]" (*Sa* 19b/6–7).

Explanation: Here the subcommentator is not referring to the immediately preceding argument but to the earlier argument that begins "Not to admit that [it cognizes] the image of itself would imply that there is a difference . . . ." The over-implication would then be an infinite regress: if the self-cognition were different from the image it cognizes, it would require another cognition to cognize itself and so on. To make the text of Jñānagarbha fit this new explanation requires only a slightly different interpretation of the phrase here translated as "if there is no" (*de lta ma yin na*). If it means "otherwise," i.e., if it were not the case that there is no special reason, then the special reason would lead to the same infinite regress brought about by the separate image in the earlier argument. But the subcommentator's point still seems unusually obscure.

24. The next argument follows naturally from the arguments that precede. If the opponent attempts to argue that the nature of cognition is such that self-cognition is its own cause, Jñānagarbha's reply is two-fold. He points out first that the opponent is still taking "the nature of cognition" as his reason. Jñānagarbha has already shown that this reason alone fails to prove why cognition A should cognize only cognition A and not every other cognition that has the nature of a cognition. Jñānagarbha's second response is to say simply that the opponent is begging the question. The opponent is just asserting that it is the nature of cognition to do what the opponent thinks it does. As Jñānagarbha points out, this is not a position likely to win much respect from opponents in a debate.

25. Here Jñānagarbha uses an unusual reference to Dignāga and Dhar makīrti (the *lakṣaṇa-* and *vārttika-kāras*) to support his own point that there can be no cognition without an image of what is cognized. In *Pramāṇa-*

vārttika 2.13–18, Dharmakīrti criticizes the doctrine of *nirākāra-jñāna-vāda* (the doctrine that a cognition does not possess the form of its object) by making a claim very similar to the one made by Jñānagarbha here. He argues that the opponent's position does not explain how someone can take "initiative" (*pravṛtti*) toward an object.

26. Jñānagarbha is referring to the "one and many" argument in verse 14 where he denies that any cognition can ultimately arise.

27. The terminology of this verse echoes *Ratnāvalī* 2.5–6: "This world ultimately is neither true or false. This is why, in reality, [the Sage] does not think that it either exists or does not exist. If it does not in any way [exist or not exist], how can one who is omniscient say that it is finite or infinite, dual or non-dual?" Sanskrit and Tibetan is found in Michael Hahn, ed., *Nāgārjuna's Ratnāvalī* (Bonn, 1982), pp. 40–43.

The term *shin tu zhib pa'i lta ba / sūkṣmekṣikā* (here translated as "very carefully") occurs in the *Ālokamālā* (ed. Chr. Lindtner) and in the *Prasannapadā* (p. 418). In both cases it has an ironical meaning. The authors use it to suggest that even "subtle vision" fails to turn up what someone is looking for. In the *Prasannapadā* it is contrasted with what "cowherds and women" see, as in Jñānagarbha's commentary on verse 3. For Jñānagarbha, careful analysis is precisely what distinguishes the relative point of view from the ultimate. See verses 21–22 below.

28. *Akṣayamatinirdeśa Sūtra*, partially quoted in the *Prasannapadā: yatra jñānasyāpy apracāraḥ kaḥ punar vādo 'kṣarāṇām* (p. 374). Also quoted by Bhāvaviveka in his commentary on *Madhyamakakārikā* 18.6.

29. Jñānagarbha is using the sūtra quotation to support his claim that cognition is not ultimately real. At first glance, the definition of relative truth seems hostile to Jñānagarbha's interpretation. "Designations, syllables, utterances, and words" seem to refer only to words, rather than to acts of cognition. But Jñānagarbha interprets the word *prajñapti* (designation) as an act of cognition rather than as a word. This allows him to include cognition in the category of relative truth. On the cognitive meaning of the term *prajñapti* (Pāli *paññatti*), see A. K. Warder, "The Concept of a Concept," *JIP* (1971), pp. 181–96 and Paul M. Williams, "Some Aspects of Language and Construction in the Madhyamaka," *JIP* 8 (1980), pp. 1–45.

30. The subcommentator explains that "this" can refer either to the word "all" or to the statement "an ordinary designation is an ordinary activity that is cognitive in nature" (*Sa* 21a/2).

31. *Subcommentary*: "This is the way to understand [the first part of the quotation]. That is, both what is cognitive in nature and what is verbal in nature are relative truth" (*Sa* 21a/4).

32. The subcommentator explains that this sentence is aimed at a hypothetical objection: "He says this in case someone says: Speech (*abhidhāna*) is relative truth and conceptual cognition (*vikalpa-jñāna*) also is [relative truth], because it arises from [speech]. How then can pleasure and so forth, which are cognized by non-conceptual cognition, be relative truth? Here 'cannot even be known' refers only to conceptual cognition" (*Sa* 21b/4–6).

33. The subcommentator again provides a hypothetical objection: "[Jñānagarbha] says 'particulars . . . ' in response to the following objection: Syllables (*akṣara*), which are particulars (*svalakṣaṇa*), are not entailed by conceptual cognition, and it is with these [particulars] in mind that [the sūtra] says 'let alone conveyed in syllables" (*Sa* 22a/6–7).

34. The subcommentator explains that a cognition of a mere thing (*vastu-mātra*) is a cognition whose object (*viṣaya*) is a particular (*svalakṣaṇa*) (*Sa* 22b/3). In verse 8 the term *vastu-mātra* (mere thing) is used as the definition of correct relative truth. This brief comment by the subcommentator indicates that for Jñānagarbha a "mere thing" is an object of perception, as the particular (*svalakṣaṇa*) is for Dharmakīrti.

35. "Additional" or "interpolated" verses (*antara-śloka*) are added by the commentator (in this case Jñānagarbha himself) either to summarize an argument or to expand a point that has not been mentioned in the *kārikās*. To distinguish "additional verses" from other verses in the text I have numbered each series of such verses with numbers enclosed in parentheses. For a more extensive explanation of the use of *antara-ślokas* in this type of text, see K. Mimaki, "Sur le rôle de l'*Antaraśloka* ou du *Saṃgrahaśloka*," in *Indianisme et Bouddhisme: Mélanges offerts à Mgr Étienne Lamotte* (Louvain-la-Neuve: Institut Orientaliste, 1980), pp. 233–44.

36. The subcommentator makes only two brief remarks about this sentence. He explains that "such things as real arising" means arising, continuation, and so forth, and he points out that the term "real" (*tattva*) should be taken with each item in the sentence. He does not indicate, however, which schools hold the doctrines mentioned. "Real arising" is not a view held by any particular school, but is taken by Mādhyamikas as typical of any school that considers things to be ultimately real. "The image of consciousness" refers to a Yogācāra conception of ultimate reality. "Primal matter" is the *pradhāna* of the Sāṃkhya system. "The transformation of elements" refers to a Cārvāka conception of ultimate reality.

Verse 8 is the starting point for the comparison of Jñānagarbha and Dharmakīrti. Contrast this verse and its commentary with *Pramāṇavārttika* 2.3: "Here [the object] that is capable of effective action is said to be ultimately real and the other relatively real. These two are respectively the particular and the universal" (*arthakriyāsamarthaṃ yat tad atra paramārtha-sat / anyat saṃvṛtisat proktaṃ te svasāmānyalakṣaṇe*). Jñānagarbha's "mere thing" (*vastu-mātra*), like Dharmakīrti's "particular" (*svalakṣaṇa*), is capable of effective action (*artha-kriyā-samartha*). But unlike Dharmakīrti, Jñānagarbha begins by defining the "mere thing" as relatively real (*saṃvṛti-sat*). Jñānagarbha's first step in appropriating Dharmakīrti's terminology is to accept it from the relative point of view, then deny it from the ultimate point of view. For more on the relationship between Jñānagarbha and Dharmakīrti, see the section on Jñānagarbha's debt to Dharmakīrti in Part One. On the meaning of the term *artha-kriyā* and its significance in the works of Dharmakīrti, see Masatoshi Nagatomi, "*Arthakriyā*," *Adyar Library Bulletin* 31–2 (1967–8), pp. 52–72.

37. The subcommentator does not distinguish between "the correct relative" (*yang dag pa'i kun rdzob / tathya-saṃvṛti*) and "correct relative truth" (*yang dag pa'i kun rdzob kyi bden pa / tathya-saṃvṛti-satya*). See, for example, *Sa* 23b/4, where the longer formula is substituted for the former without any change in meaning.

38. *Subcommentary*: "Something like a pot, which appears to those whose knowledge has been deepened by [the study of] the *śāstras* just as it appears to children, is correct relative truth. This means that something that does not appear, but is a reification (*samāropa*) made on the basis of *śāstras* and so forth, is incorrect relative truth" (*Sa* 23b/6–7).

39. The phrase "real arising and so forth" has been abbreviated simply as "real arising." The reader should bear in mind that "real arising" also implies real continuation and cessation.

40. The subcommentator glosses "something else" (*ji lta bur yang rung ba*) as "primordial (*anādikālika*) error (*mithyā-parikalpa*)" (*Sa* 24a/3).

41. Jñānagarbha's account of incorrect relative truth (*mithyā-saṃvṛti-satya*) is quite brief compared to that of other Mādhyamikas. In *Madhyama-kāvatāra* 6.26, for example, Candrakīrti distinguishes between false doctrinal conceptions, such as the three *guṇas* of the Sāṃkhya, and illusory forms of perception, such as magic or a mirage. (See the summary of Candrakīrti's position in C. W. Huntington, Jr., "The System of the Two Truths in the Prasannapadā and the Madhyamakāvatāra: A Study in Mādhyamika Soteriology," *JIP* 11 [1983], pp. 77–106.) Atiśa uses a formula very similar to Candrakīrti's: "The relative [truth] is maintained to be twofold: there is a false (*mithyā*) and a genuine (*tathya*) [relative truth]. The former is twofold: the moon in the water (*udakacandra*), and misconceptions (*kukalpanā*) in the settled doctrine (*siddhānta*)" (Lindtner, "Atiśa's Introduction," p. 193).

Jñānagarbha makes room for two kinds of *mithyā-saṃvṛti* by referring to reifications that are "based on something else or on a doctrinal position," but his attention is clearly focused on the latter.

42. Jñānagarbha adds a grammatical comment: "[The particle] *ni* either has an emphatic meaning or reverses the order [of the sentence]." Apparently he is referring to a Sanskrit particle in verse 8d, which in Tibetan reads *yang dag min ni kun brtags yin*. (The Derge and Cone texts of the *Kārikās* seem clearly to be in error when they read *ma yin* for *min ni*.) The Tibetan of the verse means literally "What is incorrect is imagined." The commentary then reverses the order to make "what is imagined" the subject and "incorrect relative truth" the predicate. Evidently it is this reversal of order that Jñānagarbha intends to indicate by the Sanskrit that lies behind the Tibetan *ni*.

The subcommentator raises another grammatical problem. If the word order is changed to make "what is imagined" the subject, it could be understood as meaning that *only* what is imagined (*kun brtags pa kho na*) is incorrect. The verse would then rule out other types of incorrect relative truth, such as the moon reflected in the water. The subcommentator explains that the particle *ni* is not meant to rule out these other types of incorrect relative truth (*Sa* 24a/7).

43. Jñānagarbha's point here is quite simple in the nominal style of philosophical Sanskrit, but it seems to defy easy translation into English. The opponent begins with Jñānagarbha's claim that real arising is incorrect relative truth because it does not appear. By this Jñānagarbha means only that when we observe things coming into existence, we do not observe that they come into existence in a real or ultimate sense. The conception of their real or ultimate arising is based only on doctrinal misconceptions. The opponent then argues that the *negation* (*pratiṣedha*) of real arising must also be incorrect relative truth because it is equally lacking in appearance. This would be an innocuous argument if "the negation of real arising" were not another word for emptiness. If the opponent's claim were correct, emptiness would be reduced to the status of an incorrect relative truth! Jñānagarbha's reply is typically paradoxical. He argues that the negation of the real arising of a thing (i.e., its emptiness) is no different from the nature of the thing itself (*bhāva-svabhāva*). This is equivalent to saying that the nature (*svabhāva*) of things is that they have no nature (*niḥsvabhāva*). This form of paradoxical discourse is quite common in Madhyamaka literature. For examples in the writing of Candrakīrti, see C. W. Huntington Jr., "The System of the Two Truths," pp. 91–4.

44. *Subcommentary*: "Others, namely Yogācāras, consider the negation of arising to be true or ultimate, so 'also' has an inclusive meaning" (*Sa* 24b/6–7).

45. *niṣedhyābhāvataḥ spaṣṭam na niṣedho 'sti tattvataḥ*: quoted by Haribhadra in the *Abhisamayālaṃkārālokā Prajñāpāramitāvyākhyā*, ed. Unrai Wogihara (Tokyo: Toyo Bunko, 1932–5), p. 45; and in Jñānagarbha's *Anantamukhanirhāradhāraṇīvyākhyānakārikā* (Tohoku #2695), *Nu* 5a/7.

A similar point is made in the discussion of *paramārtha-śūnyatā* in Jñānagarbha's commentary on the Maitreya chapter of the *Sandhinirmocana Sūtra*: "The distinguishing mark of the ultimate (*paramārtha-nimitta*) is empty by virtue of the emptiness of the ultimate (*paramārtha-śūnyatā*). Neither the object of negation (*pratiṣedhya*) nor the negation itself (*pratiṣedha*) is ultimate, and there is nothing to negate, hence there is nothing to indicate that there is any negation. There is thus no ultimate other than the cognition of emptiness" (Derge Tibetan Tripiṭaka *Bi* 336a/7–336b/1).

46. In this sentence Jñānagarbha is responding to a hypothetical objection: If (A) the negation of arising does not exist, then (B) arising does exist. But instead of attacking the objection directly, he attacks it by rejecting its contrapositive:

If (—B) arising does not exist, then (—A) the negation of arising does exist. Since the objection is formally equivalent to its contrapositive, a rejection of the latter is equivalent to a rejection of the former.

The subcommentator's explanation simply sets out this formal equivalence: "There is a chance that someone might say: 'If the negation of arising does not exist in reality, then arising does exist.' In response [Jñānagarbha] says: 'Even though there is no real negation, there still is no real arising.' Why? 'Because (—B) the absence of arising does not imply (—A) [the existence of] the negation [of arising].' This means that the absence of arising does not imply [the existence of] the negation—that is, the negation of arising. This is because (A) the absence of the negation [of arising] is the opposite of (—A) the negation of arising, and (B) the existence of arising is the opposite of (—B) the absence of arising. [Jñānagarbha claims that] it is not the case that, when (—B) there is an absence of arising, (—A) there exists the negation of arising. There continues, however, to be no arising. [Jñānagarbha's claim] is a contradiction of the argument that (—B) the absence of arising implies (—A) the existence of the negation of arising, and (A) the absence [of the negation of arising] implies (B) the existence of arising. [He makes this claim] because [the opponent's argument] would imply the existence of something like the son of a barren woman" (*Sa* 25a/5–25b/1).

Behind the question of formal equivalence is the more basic question of the nature of negation itself. Jñānagarbha is assuming the distinction, so important for Bhāvaviveka, between *prasajya-pratiṣedha* (verbally bound negation) and *paryudāsa-pratiṣedha* (nominally bound negation). He is arguing that the negation "no negation of arising" means that "there does not exist a negation of arising" (verbally bound negation), rather than "there exists a negation of the negation of arising" (nominally bound negation). The distinction is fundamental, since Jñānagarbha does not want to imply that, when he negates an entity, he is affirming the existence of its opposite. For more on the distinction between verbally bound and nominally bound negation, see B. K. Matilal, *Epistemology, Logic, and Grammar in Indian Philosophical Analysis* (The Hague: Mouton, 1971), pp. 162–5; and Yuichi Kajiyama, *An Introduction to Buddhist Philosophy: An Annotated Translation of the Text of the Tarkabhāṣā of Mokṣākaragupta* (Kyoto, 1966), pp. 38–9. For Bhāvaviveka's use of the distinction see Iida, *Reason and Emptiness*, p. 84.

47. Jñānagarbha's term *tattvārtha* (Reality-as-object) is similar to the term *śūnyatārtha* (Emptiness-as-object) in *Madhyamakakārikā* 24.7: "We reply: You do not understand Emptiness-as-goal, Emptiness[-as-cognition], or Emptiness-as-object. This is why you fail." In his commentary on the verse, Bhāvaviveka explains that "Emptiness-as-goal" is the quieting of all conceptual diversity (*prapañcopaśama*), "Emptiness" is the cognition of Emptiness, and "Emptiness-as-object" is Thusness ("A Question of Nihilism," p. 270). Bhāvaviveka's commentator Avalokitavrata explains that Thusness is the ultimate non-arising of things. Candrakīrti takes a different tack and explains that Emptiness is dependent arising (*pratītya-samutpāda*) (*Prasannapadā*, p. 591). The terms are all closely related, but in this case Jñānagarbha comes closest to the terminology of Avalokitavrata.

The best way to understand verses 10 and 11 is to refer to the discussion of the expressible (*saparyāya*) and inexpressible (*aparyāya*) ultimates (*paramārtha*) in verses 4 and 5. The term *tattvārtha* refers to the expressible ultimate, or the ultimate that can be known as an object (*artha*) of cognition. Essentially it is the ultimate understood from the relative point of view (*saṃvṛtyā*). When the ultimate is considered from the ultimate point of view, or when "Reality-as-object" (*tattvārtha*) is viewed from the point of view of Reality, it is inexpressible or "free from conceptual diversity" (*niṣprapañca*). The verses are meant to show what happens when "the negation of arising" (another term for Reality or Emptiness) is considered from the ultimate point of view (or from the point of view of Reality).

48. Conceptual diversity (*prapañca*) is associated particularly with the differentiation of a thing from its opposite. "We may say that the verbal activities necessary to make a simple statement, such as 'The chalk is white,' are pursued in terms of dichotomies of A and non-A . . . .By '*prapañca*' Nāgārjuna understands that those dichotomies are necessarily part of our verbal activities" (Musashi Tachikawa, "A Logical Analysis of the *Mūlamadhyamakakārikā*." in M. Nagatomi et al., eds., *Sanskrit and Indian Studies* [Boston: D. Reidel, 1980], p. 160).

49. The account of Vimalakīrti's silence in the *Vimalakīrtinirdeśa Sūtra* is one of the best known scriptural passages in the Mahāyāna tradition. The Sanskrit version of the sūtra is no longer extant, but translations of the Tibetan and Chinese versions have been made by Robert A. F. Thurman (*The Holy Teaching of Vimalakīrti* [University Park: Pennsylvania State University Press, 1976]) and Ētienne Lamotte (*The Teaching of Vimalakīrti* [London: The Pali Text Society, 1976]).

50. The phrase "non-dual entrance into the attributes (*dharmas*) [of Buddhahood]" (*advaya-dharma-mukha*) is translated on the basis of the subcommentary: "The entrance into the attributes (*dharmas*), in which dualities such as that of arising and non-arising are absent, is non-dual. It is non-dual and is the entrance into attributes (*dharmas*) that begin with the ten powers (*bala*) and [four] bases of confidence (*vaiśāradya*)" (*Sa* 25b/7–26a/1). Both Thurman and Lamotte take *dharma* as teaching rather than as attribute, an interpretation that would seem quite natural were it not for this passage of the subcommentary. The sūtra itself agrees with the subcommentator's interpretation of the term in chapter 10, where it uses the phrase *sarvabuddhadharmamukhapraveśa*, a phrase that appears in some Chinese versions as the title of the text itself (Lamotte, pp. xxvii and lv). Here *sarvabuddhadharma* almost certainly means "all Buddha attributes," although Lamotte avoids the choice by translating *dharma* as both doctrine and attribute (pp. xxvii, lvi, and 226).

51. The Tibetan of this verse is obscure. Apparently it anticipates Jñānagarbha's attempt in the following verses to limit the range of questions to which Vimalakīrti's silence applies. Here Jñānagarbha is saying that Vimalakīrti may remain silent when asked to describe non-duality, but silence would not be an appropriate answer if he were asked whether a relative (or dependent) entity were ultimately empty.

Behind this verse lie issues of considerable significance to philosophers in Jñānagarbha's tradition. Mādhyamikas insist that while the ultimate may in one sense be beyond words, in another it must be capable of precise specification. Otherwise the rational analysis of the philosopher would be incapable of specifying the nature of ultimate reality. *How* it should be specified is a question about which there was much discussion, but all agreed that some mode of specification must be possible. Bhāvaviveka makes a brief reference to this point at the end of his critique of Yogācāra in the *Prajñāpradīpa*: "The ultimate (*paramārtha*) . . . is not the object (*viṣaya*) of inference, but [inference] has priority, because there is no other way of investigating what is true and false." See my "Bhāvaviveka's Critique."

52. The subcommentator glosses the word "somehow" as "relatively" (*saṃvṛtyā*).

53. The subcommentator identifies the logicians as Dignāga and so forth (*Sa* 26a/7).

54. According to the subcommentator, Jñānagarbha is presupposing the following objection: "But is it not true that the ultimate (*paramārtha*) is included in dependent arising (*pratītya-samutpāda*)? If so, the statement in the sūtra is contradicted" (*Sa* 26b/5–6). Jñānagarbha replies that the sūtra quotation does not refer to dependently arising *dharmas* (about which it is possible to speak) but to *dharmas* viewed from the ultimate perspective.

55. The subcommentator explains the last half of the verse by saying that from the standpoint of reason all would be impossible (*Sa* 27b/2).

56. This sentence marks the beginning of Jñānagarbha's argument against causality. The first part of the argument, however, is not against causality per se, but against the possibility of knowing a causal relationship. He takes up causality directly in verse 14. On the importance of this argument as a mark of the "epistemological shift" in Jñānagarbha's thought see the section on Jñānagarbha's debt to Dharmakīrti in Part One.

57. *Subcommentary*: "In case someone wonders why there is no way [of knowing cause and effect] he says: 'Why? A cognition that does not have the form (*ākāra*) [of the object] cannot cognize the object.' It has not been established that a formless (*nirākāra*) cognition can be determined as being a cognition of one thing rather than another (lit. 'of blue rather than of yellow'), because there is no immediate cause. How then can it cognize an object?" (*Sa* 27b/3–4). On the argument against formless cognition, see Hattori, *Dignāga on Perception*, p. 98.

58. *Subcommentary*: "'The opposite' is a cognition that possesses form (*sākāra-jñāna*). 'Cognize an object' is carried down. Why [can it not cognize an object]? Because an *ākāra* is not a means of valid cognition (*pramāṇa*). The *ākāra* [of an object] does not imply that [the object] is present, just as being an object of knowledge (*prameyatva*) does not imply being imperma-

nent (*anityatva*). For in a dream and so forth, blue and so forth appear to the mind even though the blue and so forth are not present. How can the *ākāra* [of an object] bring about cognition of the presence [of an object]? If it did bring about the cognition [of the presence of an object], being an object of knowledge (*prameyatva*) could bring about cognition of impermanence (*anityatva*)" (*Sa* 27b/4–6).

59. The last clause in the verse gives a second reason for Jñānagarbha's claim that a cognition that bears the form of the object (*sākāra-jñāna*) cannot cognize an object. The second reason is then explained further in verse 2. *Subcommentary*: "'Cannot be' refers to the form (*ākāra*). That is, [the *ākāra*] cannot be the cognition of an object. Why not? For the following reason: 'If a single [cognition] appears to be manifold—that is, if it [appears] to be a [manifold] cognition—how can its forms truly exist?' Why would its forms not truly exist? 'Because it would lose its unity'" (*Sa* 27b/6–7).

60. This verse is virtually identical to *Pramāṇavārttika* 2.358 and *Pramāṇaviniścaya* 1.49.

61. For reasons that are not entirely clear the subcommentator adds a clause to the verse and changes the clause "neither perception nor non-perception can prove cause and effect" from the conclusion of the sentence into its reason. The subcommentator then interprets the verse as follows: If it is the case that no cognition can cognize an object, either with or without the form of the object, then it cannot cognize cause and effect. Why? Because neither perception nor non-perception can establish cause and effect (*Sa* 28a/2). "Any other possibility" means other than perception and non-perception.

62. If it is impossible ultimately to know that two moments are causally related, even a Buddha does not ultimately know the effects of action. *Subcommentary*: "If this is the case, there can be no knowledge that the *karma* in someone's continuum (*santāna*) has a certain effect. Thus even those who are omniscient do not engage in the understanding [of cause and effect], since the object of knowledge is merely itself (*rang gi ngo bo tsam yin pa'i phyir*). This is because there is no other way of knowing that [one thing causes another]" (*Sa* 28b/2–3).

63. Verse 14 introduces Jñānagarbha's version of the "one and many" argument against real causation that replaced the Nāgārjuna's "self and other" argument as the central argument against real causation in the Svātantrika works of the eighth century. The argument itself occurs in two forms. The first, used by Śrīgupta and Śāntarakṣita, has to do with whether a thing can *be* one or many. The second, used by Jñānagarbha and

Haribhadra, has to do with whether a thing, whether it is one or many, can *arise* from a cause that is one or many. The significance of the two varieties is discussed at some length in the section on Jñānagarbha and his Madhyamaka background in Part One. The notes that follow will be concerned with the interpretation of the argument itself, particularly as it is illuminated by the more detailed version of the argument found in Haribhadra's *Abhisamayālamkārālokā*, here abbreviated as *AAA*.

The "one and many" argument has recently received attention from Tom Tillemans in "The «neither one nor many» argument for *Śūnyatā*, and its Tibetan interpretations: background information and source materials," *Études de Lettres* 3 (1982), pp. 103–28.

Similar arguments are found in several of Nāgārjuna's verses, such as *Madhyamakakārikā* 2.20–1 and 21.6, and in Āryadeva's *Catuḥśataka* 9.12–9. But the argument moves to center stage in the works of the eighth century.

64. *Subcommentary*: "With regard to the first of these [options] he says: 'many do not produce one.' Why do many not produce one? He says: 'For if a single effect arises from a multiple [cause], such as the eye and so forth. . . .' 'And so forth' includes form (*rūpa*), light (*āloka*), mental activity (*manaskāra*), and so forth. 'A single effect' refers to a visual cognition (*cakṣur-vijñāna*). If you accept that [a single effect] arises [from a multiple cause], then the multiplicity of the cause would not produce multiplicity [in the effect]. Why? Because the cause would be multiple, but the effect would not be multiple. In that case, absence of multiplicity in the cause would not be the cause of absence of multiplicity in the effect, because the effect would lack multiplicity, even in the absence of a lack of multiplicity in the cause. If the multiplicity or lack of multiplicity in the effect were related by invariable cocomitance (*anvaya-vyatireka*) to multiplicity or lack of multiplicity in the cause, [the effect] would have a cause. But this is not the case. Therefore, the multiplicity or lack of multiplicity in the effect does not have a cause. If you say that multiple and non-multiple effects have no cause, he says, 'Since nothing is excluded'—that is, nothing is excluded from [the categories of] multiplicity and non-multiplicity—'nothing has a cause.' And if nothing has a cause, everything must either exist permanently or not exist at all. The word 'everything' is to be supplied. Why [must everything either exist permanently or not exist at all]? Because it does not depend on anything else as a cause. If it did [not?] depend [on other causes], things could appear at random (*kadācit*).

"[Objection:] (parallel to *AAA*: 970.6) But the cause of the effect is a combination (*sāmagrī*). The multiplicity or lack of multiplicity in the effect is related to the multiplicity or lack of multiplicity of that [combination] and is related by invariable concomitance (*anvaya-vyatireka*). So how can [the effect] have no cause?

"[Reply:] This is wrong, because there is nothing that can be called 'combination' apart from the elements [such as the eye and so forth] that make up the combination. Furthermore, these [elements] are multiple (*bhinna*), since they are mutually exclusive. How can they produce a single, non-multiple effect?

"Furthermore, why would elements [such as earth and so forth] that are included in another combination not produce the [same] effect [i.e., visual cognition]?

"[Objection:] [Earth and so forth] do not produce [visual cognition] because they are different [from the eye and so forth].

"[Reply:] Our answer is the same. [Haribhadra's version of the argument repeats the earlier question: 'How can the eye and so forth, which are mutually distinct, produce (a single effect)?']

"[Objection:] (parallel to *AAA*: 971.5) Those [elements] which, as causes of experience, possess an additional factor (*svabhāvātiśaya*) that causes [visual cognition], are the causes of [visual cognition]. The others [such as earth and so forth] are not.

"[Reply:] This also is mistaken. To claim that [these elements] possess a single additional factor that causes [visual cognition], when the eye and so forth are mutually distinct, is to contradict perception and so forth. Furthermore, the [additional factor] that causes [visual cognition] would have to be multiple if the eye and so forth are multiple. So the argument that the eye and so forth are diverse shows that this position is not very satisfactory.

"[Objection:] The additional factor that causes [visual cognition] is different from [the eye and so forth].

"[Reply:] This would also involve a problem, since the cause of experience would be something that possesses the additional factor that is capable of bringing about the effect. Something that possesses the factor that brings about the effect would be acceptable, but not the eye and so forth, which are different [from the factor that brings about the effect] . . . . Therefore, you contradict perception and so forth" (*Sa* 28b/7–29b/5).

65. Parallel to *AAA*: 974.20–7.

66. Different from the cognitive nature and so forth, which are the particular aspects of the cause (*Sa* 30a/4–5).

67. By "efficient cause" Jñānagarbha seems to mean some additional, intervening factor to mediate between the cause, which is multiple, and the effect, which is not. See the further use of the term "efficient cause" below.

68. Parallel to *AAA*: 973.12ff.

69. *Subcommentary Sa* 31a/5.

70. "And there is no difference between the effect and its particular aspects" is supplied from the subcommentary (*Sa* 31b/2).

71. The subcommentator fills in the terms "effect" and "cause" in the appropriate places without indicating how this verse is connected to the rest of the argument. Apparently it refers to the opponent's equivocation about whether the effect is actually single or multiple.

72. The lack of specific commentary on this verse makes the construction unclear.

73. Here the argument shifts to a consideration of conditions (*pratyaya*) rather than of the different aspects (*viśeṣa*) of a multiple cause. The argument remains essentially the same, however, since it is still a case of a multiple cause bringing about a single effect.

74. The point is that the opponent will suffer the same problems whenever there is an attempt to relate multiple causes to single effects. He may wash away the mud of one mistaken position, but, like an elephant that bathes in a river and then covers itself with dust, he simply covers himself with it again. The verse is expanded on the basis of the subcommentary (*Sa* 32a/4–5).

75. Here Jñānagarbha turns to the possibility of a single cause producing a multiple effect. The "additional factor" (*atiśaya*) indicates a causal process in which there is an underlying cause that is always present, but that needs to be triggered by some additional factor before it can produce its effect. The additional factor can enter the causal process at a number of different points, as is shown in Mādhava's reconstruction of Buddhist arguments on causation in the *Sarvadarśanasaṃgraha*, but all configurations eventually involve a multiplicity of causes, since the effect requires the presence of at least two separate causal elements (the underlying cause and the additional factor) before it can arise. For a more detailed analysis of the role of "additional factors" in the causal process, see *Sarva-darśana-saṃgraha of Sāyaṇa Mādhava*, ed. V. S. Abhyankar, 3rd edition (Poona: Bhandarkar Oriental Research Institute, 1978), Chapter 2.

76. Here Jñānagarbha takes up the fourth and final option mentioned in verse 14. He assumes that the eye and so forth are momentary entities and that each moment (*kṣaṇa*) in the continuum of moments has the function not only of producing the cognition that is its effect, but of producing the next moment in its own continuum. That is, the eye at moment 1 must be the cause not only of visual cognition 1, but of the eye at moment 2. If an opponent claims that single causes produce single effects, he has to choose whether the eye at moment 1 produces the eye at moment 2 or visual cogni-

tion 1. If he chooses the former, there is no cognition ("everyone would blind and deaf"). If he chooses the latter, the eye itself would cease to exist ("its own continuum would be broken"). The passage is parallel to *AAA* 976.14–7.

77. The subcommentator gives us relatively little to go on in interpreting this enigmatic verse. The verse may give a version of the argument in *Pramāṇavārttika* 1.10–11: "There is no such thing as an eternal means of knowledge (*pramāṇa*), (1) because a means of knowledge is always a cognition of a thing, (2) because the things-to-be-known (*jñeya*) are not eternal and the cognitions of them cannot be lasting, and (3) because it is inadmissible that things should arise consecutively from something that is eternal, for the eternal [viz. God] cannot be dependent on [auxiliary causes]" (translation by Masatoshi Nagatomi). In Dharmakīrti's verse "because things-to-be-known are not eternal" is not one of the reasons God could not have created the world. It indicates only that there cannot be a God who is an eternal source of knowledge. But the absence of a creator is at least connected in Dharmakīrti's mind with the presence of impermanent objects of knowledge.

78. *Subcommentary:* "'In many ways' means by such statements as 'not from itself and not from something else'" (*Sa* 33a/2). This is a reference to the critique of causation in the first chapter of Nāgārjuna's *Madhyamaka-kārikās*.

79. *Subcommentary:* "It is impossible to say whether [a thing] arises from itself or from something else. This is because particulars transcend words. Terms (*prajñapti*) such as 'something else' are constructed by the imagination (*kalpanā*). So it is clear that to say '[a thing] does not arise from [something else]' is to prove the obvious (*siddha-sādhana*)" (*Sa* 33a/3–4).

80. *Subcommentary:* "Because particulars transcend words, it is said that one cannot specify [whether a cause is identical to or different from its effect]. 'Another way' means a relative [way] which is capable of being expressed" (*Sa* 33a/6). The meaning of the comparison (*bram ze'i rgod ma bzhin*) is unclear.

81. *Subcommentary:* "It is possible to use such terms as 'pot' and 'cloth' following conventional usage (*vyavahāra*). Similarly, it is acceptable to use terminology such as 'the seed is different from or identical to the sprout.' Otherwise, if nothing could be expressed, there would be nothing to say" (*Sa* 33a/7–33b/1).

82. *Subcommentary:* "If you say that there is a third option apart from these two, namely, that the seed is either different from or identical to the sprout . . . " (*Sa* 33b/1).

83. The verse contains a simple dilemma. If both cause and effect are momentary, the effect must arise either before or after the cause has ceased. If it arises *before* the cause has ceased, it cannot actually be the effect of that cause. If it arises *after* the cause has ceased, the cause is no longer present to bring it into being. *Subcommentary:* "If the effect arises before [the cause] has ceased, then at that moment, how can there be an effect? If there were [an effect], the cause and the effect would both be present at the same time. And if that were the case, they would no longer be [cause and effect]. If the effect arises after [the cause] has ceased, then from what cause does the effect arise? The effect cannot arise from a cause that has already ceased" (*Sa* 33b/4–5).

84. The subcommentator considers verses 10–12 sufficiently clear to require no explanation.

85. The subcommentator explains that the verse is a response to the following objection: "The statement 'This [arises] when that is present' occurs both in scripture (*āgama*) and among ordinary people (*loka*). This is the condition for the existence of a causal relationship between such things as a seed and [a sprout]. Thus [the causal relationship] ultimately exists" (*Sa* 34b/2–3).

"The forms discussed above" is a reference to the argument found in the commentary preceding verse 14.

86. With no explanation in the subcommentary, the meaning of the last half of the verse is unclear.

87. *Subcommentary*: "'By which [Reality] is concealed' refers to the instrument [of the action]. 'In which' refers to the locus (*āśraya*). 'Considered' means considered by the Lord (*bhagavān*)" (*Sa* 35a/2–3). The explanation of *saṃvṛti* as a "concealment" is common in Madhyamaka literature. See, for example, Candrakīrti's commentary on *Madhyamakakārikā* 24.8: "*Saṃvṛti* is a complete concealment (*samantād vāraṇam*). Ignorance (*ajñāna*) is called *saṃvṛti* because it completely conceals the Reality of things" (*Prasannapadā*, p. 492).

88. *Bhāvā vidyanti saṃvṛtyā paramārthe na bhāvakāḥ / niḥsvabhāveṣu yā bhrāntis tat satyaṃ saṃvṛtir bhavet // Saddharmalaṅkāvatāra Sūtram*, ed. P. L. Vaidya (Darbhanga: Mithila Institute, 1963): 135. The Tibetan translation gives a slightly different version: for *vidyanti* (exists) it reads *skye ba* (= *jāyante* / arises) and for *bhavet* (is) it reads *'dod* (= *matam* / is considered).

89. Compare *Madhyamakakārikā* 18.6: "[Everything] is true (*tathya*) and untrue (*atathya*)." Bhāvaviveka's explanation is similar to Jñānagarbha's:

"[The Lord] says that everything is true, since the sense media (*āyatana*), such as the eye and so forth, and objects, such as form (*rūpa*) and so forth, do not contradict conventional truth. He also says that everything is untrue, since ultimately [everything] is like magic, in that it has no own-being and is not as it seems." See "A Question of Nihilism," p. 230.

90. The next four verses summarize an argument found in Devendrabuddhi's commentary on *Pramāṇavārttika* 2.4, one of the few verses in that work to make specific reference to a Madhyamaka argument. Verse 3 contains Dharmakīrti's statement of the two truths: "Here the [object] that is capable of effective action is said to be ultimately real and the other relatively real. These two are respectively the particular and the universal." Verse 4 then responds to a Madhyamaka objection: "[A Madhyamaka] might say that everything is incapable [of effective action]. But we can see that a seed and so forth have the capability [of producing] a sprout and so forth. If you consider this [capability] to be relative, so be it." In his commentary on this verse, Devendrabuddhi argues that the Madhyamaka position is either inconsistent or trivial. If to be real in a relative sense (*saṃvṛti-sat*) means to arise in a relative sense but not in an ultimate sense, then contradictory properties are attributed to the same thing. But if *samvṛti-sat* means that things arise, without any further reference to a perspective from which arising is denied, then the Mādhyamikas are not saying anything new at all. To say that things arise in a relative sense (*saṃvṛtyā*) would mean only that what arises arises.

Devendrabuddhi on *Pramāṇavārttika* 2.4: "Then what do you consider to be *saṃvṛti-sat*? Do you consider it to be what arises in a relative sense, but does not [arise] the other way [i.e., ultimately]? If something that does not exist in its own right is relative (*saṃvṛti*), then to say that something is relative means that it is incapable (*aśakta*) [of effective action], and to say that it arises means that it is capable. But capability and incapability are mutually exclusive. . . . Futhermore, if you think that the term *saṃvṛti* means 'arising' and so forth, yet [things] do not arise, because they are characterized ultimately as non-arising, then you accept something that others do not accept, namely the arising of something that does not arise and so forth. On the other hand, to say 'what arises [in a relative sense] arises' is inelegant, since what arises has no other choice" (Derge Tibetan Tripiṭaka, *Che* 124b/7–125a/3).

Devendrabuddhi is not the first to argue that the Madhyamaka understanding of two truths attributes contradictory properties to the same thing. The argument is also found in Dharmapāla's commentary on Āryadeva's *Catuḥśataka*. See Yuichi Kajiyama, "Bhāvaviveka, Sthiramati, and Dharmapāla, *WZKSO* 12–13 (1968–9), p. 201.

91. A similar etymology is found in Candrakīrti's commentary on *Madhyamakakārikā* 24.8. Candrakīrti first defines *saṃvṛti* as ignorance, which is consistent with verse 15 above. Then, as an alternative, he defines *saṃvṛti* as mutual dependence (*parasparasambhavana*). Mutual dependence or mutual coming into being is close to the meaning of arising. Candrakīrti then adds a third definition, in which he equates *saṃvṛti* with *saṃketa* (verbal conventions). Sources in Pāli and Hybrid Sanskrit indicate that this third definition is actually prior to the other two. See Franklin Edgerton, *Buddhist Hybrid Sanskrit Dictionary* (New Haven: Yale University Press, 1953) on *saṃvṛti*. By Jñānagarbha's time the definition of *saṃvṛti* as ignorance or concealment of Reality had taken priority.

92. "This" is the statement "Things do not arise because they do not arise." "To say the same of 'remaining' and so forth" refers not just to the argument in verses 3 and 4, but to the whole objection in verses 1–4. As the subcommentator explains, "This means that if *saṃvṛti* is [a synonym of] remaining (*sthiti*) and so forth, then in the same thing at the same time there is both capability and the lack of capability" (*Sa* 35b/4–5).

93. The subcommentator indicates that verse 5 is a response to both Dharmapāla and Devendrabuddhi: "'Such as these' refers to Dharmapāla's question 'Is *saṃvṛti* a synonym of unreality?' as well as to statements others have made that start from relative truth" (*Sa* 35b/5–6).

94. The subcommentator identifies this verse as a response to Dharmapāla. Lindtner has pointed out that similar objections occur in Kumārila's *Ślokavārttika* ("Atiśa's Introduction," p. 163).

95. This verse is directed against Devendrabuddhi.

96. Jñānagarbha was able to respond to the last set of objections only by making a sharp distinction between the relative and ultimate points of view. Now he examines the difference between the two from the ultimate standpoint (or from the standpoint of reason) and finds that expressions of the ultimate are themselves relative.

97. The subcommentator explains that Dharmapāla as well as certain unnamed logicians question the meaning of the term ultimate (*paramārtha*) and suggest that it too is only imagined (*parikalpita*). Jñānagarbha points out that from the standpoint of reason these objections only confirm his position (*Sa* 36b/1–4).

98. Verse 17 is quoted by Haribhadra: *saṃvṛtes tathatā yaiva paramārthasya sā matā / abhedāt so 'pi hi nyāyo yathādarśanam āsthitaḥ* (*AAA*, p. 407). Read *gyi* for *gyis* in the Tibetan text of the verse to follow the San-

skrit. The first half of the verse is a reference to the sūtra quotation that begins "O Subhūti . . ." in the commentary on verse 19 below.

99. Compare the *Āryadharmadhātuprakṛtyasaṃbhedanirdeśa Sūtra* quoted in the *Madhyamakaratnapradīpa* (Lindtner, "Atiśa's Introduction," p. 169).

100. *Subcommentary*: "There is another explanation [of the sūtra]. In the phrase 'the negation of arising also,' the word 'also' means in addition to reason. 'Some' means that, because it is consistent with the ultimate absence of conceptual diversity, logicians consider [the negation of arising] to be ultimate (*paramārtha*). Others consider the negation that consists of non-arising to be Reality (*tattva*) or ultimate (*paramārtha*), because, according to the Yogācāras, Emptiness (*śūnyatā*) is Reality (*tattva*). But from this perspective—that is, from the ultimate perspective—the words of the sūtra—namely, 'the relative is not one thing and the ultimate another'—have been interpreted correctly—that is, correctly understood. For in this context, the negation of arising is relative in nature. This has already been established when we said [in verse 9], 'If there is nothing to negate, it is clear that in Reality there is no negation'" (*Sa* 37b/1–4).

101. The subcommentator attributes this verse to Nāgārjuna and explains that "one" refers to the Yogācāra and "another" to the Mādhyamika (*Sa* 37b/4–5).

102. The subcommentary glosses *snang ba dang ldan pa* (*sābhāsa*) as *rnam pa dang bcas pa* (*sākāra*). "Its opposite" is a *nirākāra* (formless) cognition (*Sa* 38a/3). In this paragraph, Jñānagarbha is referring to the two arguments against causation found in verse 14 and the preceding commentary.

103. Derge Tibetan Tripiṭaka (Tohoku #100), *Ga* 284b/3–4, quoted by Candrakīrti in the *Prasannapadā: anutpādadharmāḥ satataṃ tathāgataḥ sarve ca dharmāḥ sugatena sādṛśāḥ / nimittagrāheṇa tu bālabuddhayo 'satsu dharmeṣu caranti loke* (p. 449; see also J. W. de Jong, "Textcritical Notes on the Prasannapadā," *IIJ* 20 [1978], p. 237). The verse also appears in the *Madhyamakaratnapradīpa* and related works (see Lindtner, "Atiśa's Introduction", pp. 176 and 204).

104. Madhyamaka works of this period often define correct relative truth with a three-part formula: the correct relative "arises dependently," is "capable of effective action," and is "not subject to analysis." See for example, the *Madhyamakaratnapradīpa*: "The [genuine] relative truth of the confined outlook / Is, however, like the pith of plantain (*kadalīskandha*): / When you do not examine it, it affords pleasure, / And it is causally pro-

duced and efficient" (Lindtner, "Atiśa's Introduction," p. 170). The same three-part formula occurs in verses from Śrīgupta and Atiśa quoted in note 49 of Part One and again in Śāntarakṣita's *Madhyamakālaṃkāra*: "Whatever satisfies only when it is not analyzed, has the property of arising and ceasing, and is capable of effective action is considered relative" (Derge Tibetan Tripiṭaka, *Sa* 70b/6–7). The phrase "satisfying when not analyzed" occurs alone in Śāntarakṣita's commentary on Dharmakīrti's *Vādanyāya* (ed. Rāhula Sāṃkṛtyāyana, *Journal of the Bihar and Orissa Research Society* 21–22 [1935], p. 26) and in the *Abhisamayālaṃkārāloka* (pp. 698 and 723).

The three elements of the formula could not have been brought together before the time of Dharmakīrti, since he introduced the term *artha-kriyā* into the vocabulary of Buddhist logic. But elements of the formula occur separately in earlier works. See, for example, Bhāvaviveka's use of the term "analysis" (*vicāra*) to mark the shift to an ultimate perspective in the *Madhyamakahṛdayakārikās: vicāryamāṇās tu dhiyā kim ayaṃ paramārthataḥ* (Iida, *Reason and Emptiness*, p. 77). The element of "no analysis" is also important in Candrakīrti's understanding of relative truth, as in the *Prasannapadā*: "An ordinary person does not enter into analysis (*vicāra*) about whether [something arises] from itself or from something else; he understands only (*etāvanmātram*) that an effect arises from a cause" (p. 27). Compare also *Madhyamakāvatāra* 6.35: "If things are analyzed, one finds that they have no real identity as things. So ordinary relative truth should not be analyzed" (p. 121).

What is unusual about Jñānagarbha among Mādhyamikas of the eighth century is not that he uses the three-part formula, but that he splits it apart. He takes up "dependent arising" and "effective action" in verse 8 and saves the idea of "no analysis" until verses 21 and 22. His departure from the norm is a measure of the importance of "no analysis" in the structure of his argument. His introduction of the concept here marks the point at which relative truth is reappropriated. For a more extensive discussion of this aspect of Jñānagarbha's argument see "The Structure of the Argument" in Part One.

105. The subcommentator explains that "the previous analysis" is the analysis of causation in verse 14 and the preceding commentary: "It is inappropriate to subject it to the previous analysis, by asking 'Is relative causality cognized by a cognition that has the form [of its object]?' and 'Is one produced by many or many produced [by many and so forth]?'" (*Sa* 38b/6–7).

This way of specifying the "analysis" that should not be applied to relative truth is again consistent with other Madhyamaka texts. See, for example, the *Bodhicaryāvatārapañjikā*: "Real things do not arise from themselves, from something else, or from both [themselves and something else], as is said [in the *Madhyamakakārikās*]: 'Never, anywhere, is there anything that arises from itself, from something else, from both, or from no cause at all.' Nothing is real, for analysis as to whether it is one or many shows that it has no own-being. This is why mere causality (*idaṃpratyayatāmātraṃ*) satisfies only when it is not analyzed (*avicāramanohara*), like a dream, magic, or a reflection" (p. 173).

106. The word translated as "contradicted" (*gnod par 'gyur* / *bādhita*) might be better rendered as "sublated," as it often is in translations of Vedānta literature. The word does not indicate that an item is completely denied, but rather that it is transcended by the adoption of a new perspective. The experiences of a dream are sublated by the experience of waking, but they are still real from the perspective of the dream. Here Jñānagarbha is arguing that "analysis" is a perspective that sublates the truths of the relative perspective.

107. It would be a serious objection to show that something someone claims to be consistent with reason is not actually reasonable. But Jñānagarbha only claims that relative truth corresponds to appearances (*yathādarśana*), so the objection causes him no harm.

108. Lindtner points out that this argument appears in Sthiramati's *Triṃśikābhāṣya* ("Atiśa's Introduction," p. 199).

109. The subcommentator's explanation has been incorporated into the verse.

110. "The cause of its designation" (*gdags pa'i rgyu* / *prajñapti-hetu*) consists of the parts into which a composite object can be analyzed. The causes of the designation "chariot," for example, are the pole, wheels, and so forth that make up the chariot. In Madhyamaka thought the parts into which a composite entity is analyzed are ultimately considered no more real than the composite entity itself. When Nāgārjuna says in *MMK* 24.18: "We call dependent arising emptiness; it is a dependent designation (*prajñaptir upādāya*) and it is the middle path," he means that "dependent arising" is dependent on parts that are themselves dependent. It is a metaphor based on an endless array of other metaphors. Yogācāra commentators, such as Sthiramati, preserve some of the character of the earlier tradition by arguing that everyday experience consists of a real substratum overlaid by the falsehood of imagined dualities.

111. "When one analyzes whether these have separate parts" is a reference to the argument against the existence of atoms (*paramāṇu*) found in *Triṃśikā* 11–14.

112. *Subcommentary:* "If relative [truth] depended on an ultimate basis, it would be an [ultimate] entity. In other words, it would cease to be relative, since effects conform to their causes, and it would become an ultimate entity. If it did not cease to be what it is [i.e., relative], why would your basis not be relative" (*Sa* 40a/7–40b/1)? See also *Ālokamālā* (trans. Lindtner), vs. 31.

113. *Subcommentary*: "'It does not depend on anything because it does not exist' means that imagined [nature] is simply non-existent, as is said [in verse 24 of the *Triṃśikā*]: 'The first is empty of identity.' This is why [imagined nature] does not even exist in a way that is consistent with appearances and cannot depend on any cause. For something to exist consistent with appearances, or in a relative sense, it must depend on a cause" (*Sa* 40b/3–4).

According to the Yogācāra theory of the three natures, for something to exist it must have dependent nature (*paratantra-svabhāva*). Imagined nature (*kalpita-svabhāva*), or the duality of subject and object, does not depend on a cause, so it does not exist at all. Or so, at least, is the ontology of texts such as the *Triṃśikā* and the *Madhyāntavibhāga* as interpreted by the Mādhyamikas Bhāvaviveka and Jñānagarbha. Jñānagarbha responds to the Yogācāra position as Bhāvaviveka did. He argues that imagined entities are not utterly non-existent, since they are widely accepted as the basis of ordinary discourse. For more on this argument, see my "Bhāvaviveka's Critique" and the section in Part One on Jñānagarbha and his Madhyamaka background.

114. "The duality of subject and object" is another name for imagined nature.

115. *Subcommentary:* "'And so forth' includes magic, a city of ghosts, and so forth" (*Sa* 41a/5).

116. As the subcommentator explains, this paragraph is meant to lend greater emphasis to Jñānagarbha's critique of the idea of imagined nature. Jñānagarbha has just argued that for imagined nature not to exist involves a denial of categories that ordinary people accept. Here Jñānagarbha offers the Yogācāra another option: perhaps imagined nature (or the duality of subject and object) does not exist, but the appearance (*ābhāsa*) of duality does exist. This claim would be consistent with the Yogācāra conception of dependent nature (*paratantra-svabhāva*), since "appearance" is imagination itself (*parikalpa*), rather than the duality that is imagined (*parikalpita*). But Jñānagarbha points out that even this device fails to solve the problem. Dependent nature and duality are still as different as night and day. One is real and the other is not. In fact, dependent nature is real precisely to the ex-

tent that it is empty of duality. Jñānagarbha argues that there is no way to explain how dependent nature by itself can appear as something that it is not.

The subcommentator summarizes the argument in the form of an inference: "The syllogism (*prayoga*) is as follows: If one thing is empty of another, or if one thing is unconnected to another, then when one does not appear, the other does not appear, just as form (*rūpa*) [does not appear] in an olfactory cognition" (*Sa* 41b/6).

117. Jñānagarbha next raises the possibility of a connection (*saṃbandha*) between dependent nature and duality that would permit the Yogācāra to explain why dependent nature appears dualistically, even though dependent nature itself is empty of duality. The key to the argument is the nature of the connection, which the subcommentator identifies as ignorance (*avidyā*). If the connection is dependent in nature and causes duality to appear, then duality must also be dependent, since it is caused by something that is dependent.

118. To say that ignorance is real is not in itself troubling to the Yogācāra, since the Yogācāra can argue that an ignorant cognition is real insofar as it is a cognition and unreal insofar as it is dualistic. But Jñānagarbha argues that such an ambivalent position still cannot account for the appearance of duality. Either cognition can appear dualistically, in which case it is not empty of duality, or it cannot.

The subcommentator introduces this step in the argument with a statement of the Yogācāra position: "[Objection:] We hold that the cognition in which duality appears is dependent (*paratantra*), since it arises from causes and conditions, but duality is not" (*Sa* 42a/3).

119. *Subcommentary:* "The same analysis can be applied to the other cognition. That is, the other cognition is also empty of duality. If so, it is open to the whole argument that begins 'When [dependent nature] appears, it cannot appear as duality, because there is no connection [between dependent nature and duality]'" (*Sa* 42b/2–3).

120. Neither Jñānagarbha nor the subcommentator identifies the objector against whom this argument is directed. Ruegg points out (*Literature*, pp. 70–71), however, that the objection is similar to Candrakīrti's conception of relative truth. If so, it is one of the few places in Svātantrika literature where the views of Candrakīrti are addressed. The relevant passage in Candrakīrti is *Madhyamakāvatāra* 6:36–38: "The same reason that shows arising from self or other is unreasonable from the point of view of reality also shows that it is unreasonable conventionally. How can you have any arising at all? Such things as reflections, which are empty and depend on a combination of

causes, are not unaccepted (*aprasiddha*). Likewise, from empty things such as reflections, arise cognitions with the form of those [things]. Thus, while all things are empty, they arise from empty [things]. There is no own-being from the point of view of either truth, so things are neither permanent nor destroyed."

121. *Subcommentary:* "'And so forth' includes refutation by perception and so forth" (*Sa* 42b/6).

122. *Subcommentary:* "The reason (*hetu*) and so forth are included in common sense (*loka*)" (*Sa* 42b/7).

123. *Subcommentary*: "For if someone wishes to make an assertion (*pratijñā*), he presupposes (*abhyupagama*) the arising of his own words. To presuppose [a point] and then reject it is clearly to contradict one's own words" (*Sa* 43a/1).

124. The subcommentator does not explain why the argument would be subject to inconclusiveness (*anaikāntikatva*), but the point is easy to imagine. The original argument would be stated in the following form: (1) Form and so forth do not arise in a relative sense, (2) because they do not arise in Reality, (3) like the son of a barren woman. If the opponent's own words are an exception to the assertion in clause 1, then the reason in clause 2 becomes inconclusive (*anaikāntika*). In some cases "not arising in Reality" might imply "not arising in a relative sense," but in the case of the opponent's own words the implication does not hold.

125. The subcommentator helps supply the terms necessary to complete the verse. He explains that if the *hetu* does not arise, it cannot occur in the example and cannot establish a valid inference.

126. The subcommentator explains that "the same problems do not apply to us [i.e., Jñānagarbha]" because Jñānagarbha accepts the *hetu* ("form and so forth do not arise in Reality") but does not agree that this implies the *pratijñā* ("form and so forth do not arise in a relative sense"). The translation follows the subcommentary, since the verse itself is unclear.

127. According to the subcommentator, this verse presupposes the following objection: "The reason (*hetu*) is established for you [Jñānagarbha], but not for us [the objector]" (*Sa* 43a/5). "The faults" are the same faults mentioned in verses 3 and 4. If the reason implies the assertion, then the reason itself cannot arise; and if the reason does not arise, the reason cannot be present in the example. The opponent makes the mistake of thinking that there is a relationship of implication (*vyāpti*) between reason and assertion. Since Jñānagarbha accepts only the reason, not the implication, he is not forced to deny the reality of the reason.

128. On the relationship of implication see the preceding note.

129. Here the opponent continues to argue that the parts of the argument are not established (*siddha*), but he turns his attention specifically to the relationship of implication (*vyāpti*) mentioned in verse 6. If ultimate non-arising is said to imply relative non-arising, then ultimate non-arising is the subject of the implication (lit. "that which is pervaded," *vyāpya*) and relative non-arising is the object of the implication (lit. "that which pervades," *vyāpaka*).

130. The verse reads *brtags pa* (conceptual[ly]) rather than *kun rdzob tu* (in a relative sense). The subcommentator, however, substitutes one for the other. The translation of the last *pāda* is conjectural and is based on the apparent connection between this *pāda* and the following verse.

131. Apparently Jñānagarbha is playing on the meaning of the term *hetu*, which can be either the *reason* in an inference or the *cause* in a relationship of cause and effect.

132. The commentary on this passage is unclear.

133. The subcommentator indicates that this is an objection (*Sa* 44b/1) in which the opponent objects to one of the central elements in Jñānagarbha's method. Jñānagarbha first accepts (*abhyupagama*) relative truth as established (*siddha*), then subjects it to rational scrutiny to see whether it is ultimately real.

134. After 26d the text of the *Kārikās* inserts an additional *pāda: brtags pa'i 'og tu khas blang gi* (acceptance comes after investigation). The *pāda* is almost certainly the interpolation that gives the text of the *Kārikās* an odd number of *pādas*. It is not mentioned in the subcommentary, and omitting it restores the regular progression of verses.

135. In a rare ranking of the two means of valid cognition (*pramāṇa*), the subcommentator identifies "corresponding to appearances" (*yathādarśana*) as perception (*pratyakṣa*) and valid cognition (*pramāṇa*) as inference (*anumāna*).

136. The meaning of this paragraph is unclear. Jñānagarbha seems to be saying that the opponent cannot win either way. If the opponent accepts the validity of his own argument (*pramāṇa*), then he can be contradicted by Jñānagarbha's argument. If he accepts no *pramāṇa* at all, he cannot make an argument.

137. "Without a means of cognition" is provided by the subcommentary (*Sa* 44b/5).

138. "The same thing in return" is explained by the subcommentary: "It is necessary to accept relative [truth], because [otherwise] there would be no conventional usage (*vyavahāra*) and so forth" (*Sa* 44b/7-45a/1). The rest of the verse is best interpreted as a restatement of the argument against the point of verse 25.

139. *nirbhāsate hi tad rūpaṃ naiva tat pratiṣidhyate / vedyamānasya na yuktaṃ kasyacit pratiṣedhanam* (quoted in *AAA*, p. 93). Note that the Tibetan presumes . . . *hi yad rūpaṃ*. . . .

140. *Subcommentary:* "'And so forth' includes . . . bad friends and . . . the primordial (*anādikālika*) traces (*vāsanā*) of false practice (*bhāvanā*)" (*Sa* 45a/3–4).

141. Jñānagarbha explains what he means by "contradict oneself" in the commentary that follows. Note how close he comes to holding the position of mind-only (*citta-mātra*) from the relative perspective, the distinguishing feature in Tibetan literature of a Yogācāra-Svātantrika-Madhyamaka. Jñānagarbha's argument in this passage needs only to be compared to the argument of verse 23 and 24 to see how far his treatment of cognition in its dependent (*paratantra*) aspect differs from that of Yogācāras such as Sthiramati.

142. According to the subcommentator, this verse presupposes the following objection: "It is correct to deny the real arising and so forth that are imagined (*kalpita*) when form and so forth appear. But is it not [correct to deny] the appearance of *the negation of* (?) primal matter (*pradhāna*) and so forth?" (*Sa* 45b/2–3). Jñānagarbha would normally agree with this objection, as he does in his commentary on verse 8d above. Here the verse seems to address a slightly different question. The issue is not whether the negation of primal matter appears, but whether the mistaken cognition itself appears, even though the primal matter (*pradhāna*) that it imagines does not appear. The distinction is comparable to the Yogācāra distinction between imagination (*parikalpa*) and what is imagined (*parikalpita*) in the first chapter of the *Madhyāntavibhāga*. Here Jñānagarbha takes the position (from the relative perspective) that the cognition appears, but the imagined object does not.

How then to explain the incongruity between the subcommentator's introduction and the verse itself? It is possible that the text itself is at fault, since the change of *dgag pa* ("the negation of") to *rtog pa* ("the cognition of") would bring the subcommentary into harmony with the verse. The Peking and Derge agree, however, in reading *dgag pa.*

143. The subcommentator again introduces the verse with an objection: "Some say that the phrase 'in a real sense' in the statement 'condition-

ed things do not arise in a real sense' is a qualifier of the negation (*pratiṣedha-viśeṣa*), in which case the statement 'conditioned things do not arise in a real sense' would mean that the only truth is that nothing arises. If this were the case, we could also say '[conditioned things] do not even arise in a relative sense.' This would result in the fault of contradicting something that you already accept" (*Sa* 45b/4–5).

The objector is arguing that, if the qualifier "in a real sense" modifies the whole phrase "conditioned things do not arise," there is no room to back up and say that conditioned things do arise in a relative sense. (Jñānagarbha made a similar point in the commentary on verse 21cd above.) Jñānagarbha's response is to link "in a real sense" to "arising" rather than to the whole negation. The sentence then means only that things do not arise in a real sense, not that they do not arise at all.

144. Here Jñānagarbha begins a brief section in which he uses scriptural quotations to summarize his position on relative truth. "This" refers to the whole preceding argument, both to the claim that relative truth arises dependently and to the claim that it does not arise ultimately.

145. *nāsti vai kalpito bhāvaḥ paratantraś ca vidyate samāropāpavādaṃ hi vikalpanto vinaśyati* (Vaidya edition, p. 54).

146. *parikalpitaṃ svabhāvena sarvadharmā ajānakāḥ / paratantraṃ samāśritya vikalpo bhramate nṛṇām* (Vaidya edition, p. 117).

147. *Subcommentary:* "In other words, [an objector may argue that] action (*karma*) and its result (*phala*) cannot exist in a way that is consistent with appearances (*yathādarśana*), because they are not objects of the senses" (*Sa* 46a/7).

148. The use of honorific vocabulary in the Tibetan of this section is inconsistent. The text of the commentary says only that the Buddha teaches action and results "as they appear" (*ji ltar snang ba bzhin du*). The subcommentary, however, clearly indicates that the Lord teaches action and results as they appear to *him* (*ji ltar gzigs pa de bzhin du*) (*Sa* 46b/1–2).

149. "In a way that is generally accepted" (*yathāprasiddha*) is glossed in the subcommentary as "corresponding to appearances" (*yathādarśana*) (*Sa* 47a/4).

150. The subcommentator explains that the causal sequence is one in which bondage follows passion (*rāga*) and liberation follows patience (*kṣānti*). The over-implication (*atiprasaṅga*) mentioned in the last part of the verse is one in which the causal sequence becomes confused, so that liberation follows passion and bondage follows patience (*Sa* 47b/1–4).

151. The subcommentator explains that the mention of atoms is meant to refer to the views of a realist who holds that there are external objects, and the mention of non-dual cognition is meant to refer to a Vijñānavādin who holds the view that cognition alone is real (*Sa* 47b/6).

152. The subcommentator indicates that this sentence is a response to the claim that things can be designated even though they do not appear (*Sa* 47b/7).

153. *Pāda* 35c ("because nothing can appear and nothing [can arise]") is found in the Derge and Cone text of the *Kārikās* but not in the Commentary. Since the *Kārikās* have an odd number of *pādas*, this should be considered a possible interpolation. But the extra *pāda* in verse 26 is the more likely candidate, since it poses the greatest interruption to the steady flow of the text.

154. One is tempted to add a negative particle and change "even if there were real things" to "there are no real things," but the textual evidence is firmly against it.

155. Jñānagarbha is playing on the meaning of the verb "to see" in a way that is difficult to follow in the Tibetan translation and even more difficult to convey in English. "Views" (*lta*), "insight" (*lta ba*), and "recognize" (*mthong*) are all variations of the verb "to see." "View" (*lta*) most likely corresponds to the Sanskrit *dṛṣṭi*, which refers to a mistaken philosophical view. "Insight" (*lta ba*) could be *darśana*, correct insight.

156. *ajātasya svabhāvena śāśvatocchedatā kutaḥ svabhāve hi vikalpyante dharmabhedavikalpanāḥ* (*AAA*, p. 39).

157. *pattralekhādivinyāsaḥ kenacid vyomni śakyate kartuṃ naiva tathā 'jāte dharmabhede vikalpanā* (*AAA*, p. 39).

158. The subcommentary points out that "correspond to appearances" applies both to the Buddha's cognition and to the things that arise dependently.

159. The translation of this paragraph follows the subcommentary rather than the commentary itself (*Sa* 49a/4–49b/1).

160. *Subcommentary:* "The problem of there being no omniscience is not a problem for those who hold the doctrine of Emptiness, since [for them] nothing exists" (*Sa* 49b/1).

161. The subcommentary indicates that there is a causal relationship between the elements of the sentence: "It is because the Lord's concentration

is firm that he does not get up. And why [is his concentration firm]? Because he has worshipped for many countless eons (*kalpa*) and has practiced without interruption" (*Sa* 49b/7–50a/1).

162. *Subcommentary:* "This [verse] extols the Dharma Body from the point of view of its result (*phala*)" (*Sa* 50a/4). As Jñānagarbha himself notes at the end of this section, it would far exceed the scope of this work even to begin to sketch the background of his idea of Buddhahood. But it is worth noting that Jñānagarbha follows a standard convention in Madhyamaka literature when he closes his work with an account of the Buddha. Bhāvaviveka's presentation of Madhyamaka thought in the third chapter of the *Madhyamakahṛdayakārikās* (with the accompanying commentary in the *Tarkajvālā*) ends with an extensive description of Buddhahood (verses 266–360). Candrakīrti's *Madhyamakāvatāra* follows the pattern of the bodhisattva stages (*bhūmi*) and ends with praise of the Buddha. Many of the concepts and formulas that appear in Jñānagarbha's account of Buddhahood can be found in these works of his predecessors, as well as in more specialized sources such as the ninth chapter of the *Mahāyānasūtrālaṃkāra* and the eighth chapter of the *Abhisamayālaṃkāra*, to say nothing of the hymns and sūtras that make up the corpus of Mahāyāna devotional literature. For an account of Bhāvaviveka's understanding of Buddhahood, see Malcolm David Eckel, "Gratitude to an Empty Savior: A Study of the Concept of Gratitude in Mahāyāna Buddhist Philosophy," *History of Religions* 25 (1985), pp. 57–75. For an account of the three bodies of the Buddha see Gadjin M. Nagao, "On the Theory of the Buddha-Body,' *Eastern Buddhist* 6 (1973), pp. 25–53. On the location of Dharma as a shrine and the Dharma Body as a "guide" see Edward Conze, *Buddhist Wisdom Books* (New York: Harper and Row, 1972), pp. 50, 56, and 63.

163. The Tibetan would make better sense if it read *chos thams cad kyi lus ni* to match both the grammatical structure of the subcommentary and the two subsequent sentences. The terminology suggests the element of Buddhahood (*gotra*) that pervades all living beings. See E. Obermiller, "The Doctrine of the Prajñāpāramitā as exposed in the Abhisamayālaṃkāra of Maitreya," *Acta Orientalia* 11 (1932): 1–133, and David Seyfort Ruegg, *La Théorie du Tathāgatagarbha et du gotra* (Paris: École Française d'Extrême-Orient, 1969).

164. The subcommentator indicates that "Dharma Body" is here taken as a reference to "the mass of *dharmas* (*chos rnams kyi tshogs*) and secondarily to the cause that allows the *dharmas* (or virtues) to be amassed. It is in this causal sense that the Dharma Body is the basis (*āśraya*) of ordinary and extraordinary virtues (*Sa* 50a/6–7).

165. According to the subcommentator, this sentence is added to meet an objection to the idea that the Dharma Body can serve as a cause in an active sense: "This [explanation] indicates that the term "Dharma Body" is an active term. [Objection:] But is it not the case that the [Dharma] Body is inactive? [Otherwise] how can it be the basis of inconceivable virtues? [Jñānagarbha] replies: 'It is conceived to be the basis.' Why? He says: 'Because one who attains it obtains [virtues].' That is, one who attains or understands the Dharma Element (*dharma-dhātu*) obtains ordinary and extraordinary virtues (*guṇa*)" (*Sa* 50b/1–3).

166. *Subcommentary:* "Why is [the Dharma Body] something whose nature (*svabhāva*) is discerned (*vyavasthāpita*) by reason (*nyāya*)? [Jñānagarbha] explains: 'because it is consistent with reason.' In other words, the term *dharma* refers to reason and the term *kāya* (body) refers to nature (*svabhāva*)" (*Sa* 50b/3–4).

167. *Subcommentary:* "Having given this brief account of the Dharma Body, he begins to explain the Enjoyment Body (*saṃbhoga-kāya*) by saying: 'Then concepts are absent' and so forth. 'Then' means when the Dharma Body is understood. [Objection:] If it has no concepts, how can it serve the interests of sentient beings? He explains: 'By the power of a previous,' that is, by the power of a previous vow (*praṇidhāna*). [Objection:] When, where, and in what way does it serve the interests of sentient beings? He answers: 'Always' and so forth. This [statement] means that it completely serves the needs of sentient beings, and [the statement] is a reference to 'perfection for the sake of others' (*parārtha-saṃpad*). Since perfection for the sake of others takes priority, it is mentioned first. 'Perfection for the sake of oneself' (*svārtha-saṃpad*) is the means [of obtaining] perfection for the sake of others, so it is mentioned later. The first half of the second verse refers to the perfection of knowledge (*jñāna-saṃpad*). The second half refers to the perfection of greatness (*māhātmya-saṃpad*). The first half of the third verse refers to the perfection that consists of the removal of moral hindrances (*kleśāvaraṇa*). The second half refers to the removal of cognitive hindrances (*jñeyāvaraṇa*)" (*Sa* 50b/4–51a/1).

168. *Subcommentary:* "The virtues (*guṇa*) are the superknowledges (*abhijñā*), the immeasurables (*apramāṇa*), the powers (*bala*), the eighteen special qualities of a Buddha (*āveṇika-buddha-dharma*), and so forth. The concentrations (*samādhi*) are the *śūraṃgama*, the *ākāśa-kośa,* and other *samādhis*. The trances (*dhyāna*) are the first and so forth" (*Sa* 51a/2–3).

169. *Subcommentary:* "Concepts (*kalpanā*) are the false concepts that cause defilements (*kleśa*) to arise. Traaces (*vāsanā*) are the body and speech that result from defilements" (*Sa* 51a/4).

170. *Subcommentary:* "To summarize the [first] three verses, he says: 'It contains no faults.' This refers to the perfection that consists of the removal of hindrances. 'Contains an ocean of virtues' refers to the perfection of greatness. [The last half of the verse] beginning with the term 'always' refers to the perfection for the sake of others that was expressed in the first verse" (*Sa* 51a/5–6).

171. *Subcommentary:* "'Like a wishing jewel' and so forth indicates how long [the Enjoyment Body] remains. It has no equal in its perfection for the sake of others and so forth, and it carries on as long as there is *saṃsāra.* To what is it similar in having no equal? It is like a wishing jewel . . . . To express perfection with regard to its cause, he says that it is brought about by great compassion (*mahā-karuṇā*) and is the incomparable product of inconceivable merit (*puṇya*) and knowledge (*jñāna*)" (*Sa* 51a/6–51b/1).

172. *Subcommentary:* "[The verse] beginning 'who attain true excellence' indicates to whom [the Enjoyment Body] is accessible. 'Excellence in stage [of attainment] (*bhūmi*)' refers to [the stages] that begin with the Joyful (*pramuditā*). The first *pāda* of the verse indicates that [the Buddha] possesses the prerequisite of knowledge (*jñāna-saṃbhāra*). The second [*pāda*] indicates that [the Buddha] possesses the prerequisite of merit (*puṇya-saṃbhāra*). Since [the Enjoyment Body] is inconceivable, it is only accessible to the eyes of this kind of *bodhisattva*" (*Sa* 51b/2–3).

173. *Subcommentary:* "'It' [in the phrase 'its Manifestation Body'] is the body of the Tathāgata in the form of the Enjoyment [Body]" (*Sa* 51b/6).

174. *Subcommentary:* "Some think that the manifestation does not cause its manifestation. So to specify the form of the manifestation, he says, 'the manifestation' and so forth. Why does the manifestation manifest itself? He says, 'by the power of the Lord.' 'The Lord' is the Tathāgata in the form of the Enjoyment Body. How does it act? He says, 'as if undertaking every action '" (*Sa* 51b/6–7).

175. The subcommentator explains that "and so forth" includes the bodies of Solitary Buddhas (*pratyeka-buddha*), *bodhisattvas,* and ordinary people (*Sa* 52a/2). A list of such bodies appears in the eighth chapter of the *Daśabhūmika Sūtra* in a description of the attainments of a *bodhisattva* at the eighth stage of the path. See *Daśabhūmikasūtra*, ed. P. L. Vaidya, Buddhist Sanskrit Texts No. 7 (Darbhanga: Mithila Institute, 1967), p. 45.

176. The subcommentator explains that the next three verses are spoken by an author who, "drenched by compassion," wishes to remove his opponent's anger (*Sa* 52a/4).

177. *Subcommentary*: "Why do you have no conviction? He says: 'for lack of merit.' As [the Lord] said: 'O Subhūti, the sentient beings who have even a single pure thought (*prasanna-citta*) toward this scriptural utterance have worshipped many hundreds of thousands of Buddhas and generated the roots of goodness under many hundreds of thousands of Buddhas'" (*Sa* 52b/4).

178. The final verse constitutes the transfer of merit (*Sa* 52b/6).

Part Four

The Tibetan Text

THE TIBETAN TEXT:

An Introductory Note

This edition of the Tibetan text of Jñānagarbha's *Satyadvaya-vibhaṅgavṛtti* (*Bden-gnyis-rnam-'byed-'grel-pa*) is based on the Derge (Sde-dge) edition of the Tibetan Tripiṭaka preserved in the Harvard Yenching Library.

To arrive at a critical text, the Derge copy of the *Vṛtti* was compared first with the Derge copy of the *Kārikā* (Tohoku #3881) and *Pañjikā* (Tohoku #3883), then with the copies found in the Cone (Co-ne), Peking, and Narthang (Snar-thang) editions of the canon. In the case of the Cone, comparison can be made on all three levels, the *Kārikā*, the *Vṛtti*, and the *Pañjikā*. In the Narthang and Peking only the *Pañjikā* is available. For the Cone edition of the *Kārikā, Vṛtti*, and *Pañjikā*, I used the *Cone Tanjur* (Microfiche Edition) published by The Institute for Advanced Studies of World Religions, New York (Vol. 28 [*Sa*], folios 1a–52b). For the Narthang edition of the *Pañjikā*, I used the copy found in the Harvard Yenching Library (*Sa*, folios 1a–44a). For the Peking edition of the *Pañjikā*, I used *The Tibetan Tripitaka: Peking Edition*, ed. Daisetz T. Suzuki (Tokyo: Suzuki Research Foundation, 1962), vol. 100 (*Sa*), folios 1a–48b.

To have only the *Pañjikā* in the Peking and Narthang editions means that the textual evidence for the *Vṛtti* is incomplete and necessarily inconsistent. A *Pañjikā* comments only on selected passages and does not always quote the passage verbatim. The style of commentary runs the gamut from direct quotation to paraphrase with a range of options in between. In general I have followed the more conservative option in quoting the evidence of the *Pañjikā*, limiting myself to passages where the *Pañjikā* indicates that it is quoting the text of the *Vṛtti* or where it reproduces the text so accurately that it must be based on direct quotation. As a matter of editorial method, I have followed the Derge and Cone editions of the *Vṛtti* except where the text of the *Kārikā* and *Pañjikā* agree against it, or where the grammar or the sense seem to require otherwise.

Textual variants are noted in the text in square brackets. The variant reading is normally listed first, followed by an abbreviation indicating the source. The abbreviations K, V, and P are used to indicate variants on which all available editions of the *Kārikā, Vṛtti*, or *Pañjikā* (respectively) agree. DK and CK refer to the Derge and Cone editions of the *Kārikā*. DV and CV indicate variants found in the Derge and Cone editions of the *Vṛtti.* DP, CP, PP, and NP indicate variants found in the Derge, Cone, Peking, and Narthang editions of the *Pañjikā*. In the case of variants that involve an omission or addition to the text, the omission or addition follows the reference to its source. For example [DP add *pa ma yin*] indicates that the Derge text of the *Pañjikā* adds the items "*pa ma yin*." The numbers in square brackets (for example [8a]) indicate the folio numbers of the Derge text of the *Vṛtti.*

It is hard to compare the four editions of the text and not be impressed by the remarkable homogeneity of the Tibetan canonical tradition, at least at the printed stage. There are few significant textual variants that are not attributable either to an obvious error on the part of the copyist or to a difference in the conventions of orthography. A few consistent variations show a close connection between the Derge and Cone on one side and the Peking and Narthang on the other. The Peking and Narthang, for example, consistently read *'ang* for *yang* and *bslu* for *slu*. These are seldom variants that affect the substantive interpretation of the text.

The system of romanization follows Turrell Wylie, "A Standard System of Tibetan Transcription," *Harvard Journal of Asiatic Studies* 22 (1959): 261–7.

'jam dpal gzhon nur gyur pa la phyag 'tshal lo //

gang dag dngos po'i [po P] ngo bo nyid med yang dag mkhyen gyur kyang //
thugs rjes 'khor ba ji srid bar du thub dbang sras bcas rnams //
'jig rten ma lus pa yi 'tshal ba'i dngos po bsgrub slad du //
'dir bzhugs dri med blo ldan de dag rnams la phyag 'tshal lo //

[I. Introduction]

bden pa gnyis ji lta ba bzhin du khong du chud par bya ba'i phyir / rab tu byed ['byed V] pa 'di brtsams te / gang gi phyir /

1. bden pa gnyis po rnam phye yang //
shing rta che dag rmongs nyid na //
gzhan rnams smos kyang ci dgos te //
de bas bdag gis rnam par dbye //

gzhan gyi don 'byung ba la mkhas pa bcom ldan 'das kyis skye bo blo chung du la phan gdags pa'i phyir / bden pa gnyis las mang du rnam par phye la / slob dpon klu sgrub la sogs pas kyang gsal bar mdzad du zin kyang / rang gi sde pa chen po dag kyang rmongs pa nyid yin na / de dag gi kha na las pas 'jug pa gzhan rnams lta smos kyang ci dgos /

2. bden gnyis rnam dbye shes pa dag //
thub pa'i bka' la mi rmongs te //
de dag ma lus tshogs bsags nas //
phun tshogs pha rol 'gro ba nyid //

bden pa gnyis rnam par dbye ba la mkhas pa ni / 'gro ba la phan pa 'byung ba bskyed pa'i blo dang [4a] ldan pa / bde bar gshegs pa'i bka' rab 'byam dag la shes pa'i snang ba skyes pa'i 'jig rten bsod nams dang ye shes kyi tshogs ma lus par bsgrubs pa bdag dang gzhan gyi don phun sum tshogs pa bye brag tu byar med pa'i pha rol tu nges par shin tu phyin par 'gyur ro // gzhan ni yid la bsams pa bzhin du re ba yongs su rdzogs par 'gyur ro //

3ab. kun rdzob dang ni dam pa'i don //
bden gnyis thub pas gsungs pa la //

mdo sde der zhes bya ba ni tshig gi lhag ma'l //

3cd. ji ltar snang ba 'di kho na //
kun rdzob gzhan ni cig shos yin //

don dam pa'i bden pa zhes bya ba'i tha tshig go // ji ltar ba lang rdzi mo la sogs pa yan chad kyis mthong ba de ltar kun rdzob tu bden pa rnam par gnas kyi yang dag par ni ma yin te / mthong ba dang mthun par dngos po'i don nges par 'dzin pa'i phyir ro // mthong ba ni rnam pa gnyis te rnam par rtog pa dang bcas pa dang / rnam par rtog pa med pa'o // rigs pa ji lta ba bzhin nyid ni don dam pa'i bden pa'o // ni zhes bya'i sgra ni bsnan [brnan PP NP] pa'i don to //

[II. Ultimate Truth]

[A. The Expressible Ultimate]

don dam par bden pa ni don dam pa'i bden pa ste / de ni rigs pa'i rjes su 'gro ba can gyi bden pa nyid ces bya ba'i tha tshig go // gang gi phyir /

4ab. slu [bslu PP NP] ba med pas rigs pa ni //
don dam yin te /

rigs pa'i stobs kyis don la nges pa ni slu [bslu PP NP] bar mi 'gyur te / de'i phyir tshul gsum pa'i rtags kyis bskyed pa'i rtogs pa gang yin pa de ni dam pa yang ['ang PP NP] yin la / don yang yin pas don dam pa'o // des gtan la phab pa'i don kyang don dam pa ste / mngon sum la sogs pa bzhin du brjod do //

kun rdzob min /

don dam pa ni kun rdzob kyi bden pa ma yin te / tshig tha ma khong nas dbyung ba'i phyir ro //

ci'i phyir zhe na /

4c. de ltar mi slu min phyir te /

de ji ltar shes pa'i bdag nyid la gnas pa de ltar rigs pas mi rung ba'i phyir ro //

4d. ji ltar snang ba de nyid bden //

ji ltar snang ba de nyid ni kun rdzob kyi bden pa'o zhes bshad do // zla ba gnyis pa [P om.] la sogs pa yang ji ltar snang ba kho na yin na / 'jig rten pa dag de ltar ni khas mi len te / de'i phyir yang dag pa ma yin pa'i kun rdzob ces 'og nas 'chad do //

[B. The Inexpressible Ultimate]

5. ji ltar snang ba'i dngos por ni //
rnam par gnas par mi rung ste //
shes pa'i dngos po thams cad la //
ji lta bur yang snang mi 'gyur //

don dam pa ni [4b] ji ltar snang ba bzhin du rnam par gnas pa med de / thams cad mkhyen pa'i mkhyen pa nyid la yang mi snang ba'i phyir gsungs te / ngo bo nyid mi mthing ba zhes bya ba kho nar ni de kho na mthong ba zhes gsungs so //

6ab. gal te brtags pa'i ngo bo nyid //
'ga' yang mthong ba med ce na //

brtags pa'i ngo bo nyid kyi dbang du mdzad nas 'ga' yang mthong ba med pa ni de kho na mthong ba zhes bya ba 'di gsungs par 'dod de / de ni de lta bu yin no // de lta bu [P om.] ma yin na 'ga' yang zhes ci'i phyir gsungs te / gno bo nyid mi mthong ba zhes bya ba kho nar gsung bar 'gyur ba'i rigs so zhe na / de ni mi rung ste /

6c. rang rig rigs pa ma yin [V add pa'i] phyir //

shes pa ni gnyis kyis dben pa'i ngo bo rig par byung ba yin pa dang / de med par shes par 'gyur gyi / de lta ma yin na mi rigs pa'i phyir ro // shes pa ni bdag gis [gi PP NP] bdag shes pa ma yin te / rang snang bas stong pa'i phyir shes pa gzhan bzhin no // rang snang bar khas mi [PP NP om.] len na ni tha dad par thal bar 'gyur te / sngon po dang de shes pa bzhin no //

rig pa'i ngo bo nyid yin pa'i phyir yang ma yin te / ha cang thal bar 'gyur ba'i phyir ro // gal te rang rig pa'i ngo bo yin pas de'i phyir ha cang thal bar mi 'gyur ro zhe na / de yang mi rung ste nye ba'i rgyu med pa'i phyir ro // de lta ma yin na ha cang thal ba nyid du 'gyur ro // gal te shes pa'i ngo bo nyid ni 'di 'dra ste / rang gi rgyu las skyes shing des de ltar 'gyur ro zhe na / yang mi rung ste / lan btab zin pa'i phyir ram / mi slu [bslu PP NP] ba'i tshad ma [PP om.] med pa'i phyir te / sems mi mthun pa'i [pa P] gzhan rnams ni rang gi tshul brjod pa tsam la gus par mi byed do //

shes pa rnam pa med par smra bas de skad brgal ba la / mtshan nyid dang rnam 'grel byed pa'am / gzhan yang rung gang gis yul gyi rnam pa nyid kyi tshad ma bsgrub pa ji skad brjod par bya /

6d. rgyu yi ['i V P] nus pa bkag phyir ro //

'og nas rgyu'i nus pa bkag pa'i phyir yang 'di rigs pa ma yin no // de nyid kyi phyir ngo bo nyid thams cad mi mthong ba ni de kho na mthong ba'o zhes bya bar chug na yang ['ang PP] ji ga nges par bya bar mi nus te / 'di ltar /

7. yod med dngos po mkhyen *pa po* [pa'o P] //
kun [K add mngon] mkhyen pas kyang [K om.] gang ma gzigs //
de yi [de'i PP] dngos po [PP om.] ci 'dra zhig //
shin tu zhib pa'i lta bas dpyod //

shes bya mtha' dag la khyab pa'i ye shes dang [5a] ldan pa'i phyir kun mkhyen pa ste / de mi dmigs pa ji ltar yod par 'gyur zhes bsams pa'o // de nyid kyi phyir mdo las kyang de la kun rdzob kyi bden pa gang zhe na/ji snyed 'jig rten gyi tha synad gdags pa dang / yi ge dang skad dang brda bstan pa dag go // don dam pa'i bden pa ni gang la sems rgyu ba yang ['ang PP NP] med na / yi ge rnams lta smos kyang ci dgos zhes gsungs so // 'jig rten gyi tha snyad gdags pa ni 'jig rten gyi 'jug pa ste / shes pa dang shes bya'i mtshan nyid yin gyi / rjod par byed pa'i mtshan nyid ni ma yin te / de ni 'og mas brjod pa'i phyir ro // ji snyed ces bya ba'i tshig ni mtha' dag ces bya ba'i don to // des na rnam par rtog pa med pa'i mngon sum gyi shes pas yongs su bcad pa'i ngo bo'i dngos po gzugs la sogs pa dang bde ba la sogs par rig par grub pa rnams ni kun rdzob kyi bden pa kho na yin no // de ni 'og tu yang sbyar bar bya'o // de'i phyir mdo las 'byung ba dang / yi ge dang skad dang brda bstan pa gzhan dag kyang gzung ngo //

de ni de ltar rtogs par bya ste / don dam pa'i bden pa bstan pa la / sems rgyu ba yang med [DP CP PP add de] ces gsungs pa'i phyir ro // rjod par byed pa'i mtshan nyid kho na [nar PP NP] kun rdzob kyi bden pa yin na ni / yi ge rgyu ba yang med na zhes *gsung bar* [gsungs par P] 'gyur gyi / sems zhes gsung bar ni [P om.] mi 'gyur ro // gal te ji skad gsungs pa'i go rims [rim PP NP] can de gnyis mi 'dod na ni / sems rgyu ba yang ['ang PP NP] med na yi ge rnams lta smos kyang ci dgos zhes bya bar [ba P] brjod par bya ba'i go rims [rim PP NP] ci'i phyir mdzad / rnam par rtog pa'i shes pa nyid yin par yongs su gzung [bzung CP] na ni rnam par rtog pa rgyu ba yang med na zhes *gsungs par* [gsung bar P] 'gyur te / the tshom med pa'i phyir ro // 'di la nges par byed pa'i tshad ma ni med do // spyi'i sgra yang don dang skabs la sogs pa med par bye brag tu gzhag par mi nus so //

yang na rjod par byed pa'i spyi ni rnam par rtog pa'i rjes su 'jug pa'i phyir / de brjod pas gnyis smos pa kho na yin na / ci'i phyir gnyis gsungs / de lta na ni sems rgyu ba yang med pa ni yi ge rnams rgyu ba med pa kho nar bstan pa'i phyir / yang zhes bya ba'i sgra mdzes pa ma yin pa'i phyir ro //rang gi mtshan nyid ni don [P om.] brjod [rjod P] par byed pa ma yin pa'i phyir de thugs la bzhag nas *brjod par* [rjod pa P] [5b] rung ba kho na ma yin no // don 'og ma ma brjod par yang gong ma 'dus pa nyid yin te / rjod par byed pa spyi'i rjes su nang gi brjod [rjod P] pa 'brang ba yin pa'i phyir ro // de lta bas na dngos po tsam dang mthun par byed pa'i ngang can gyi sems kyang [P om.] rgyu ba yang med ces bya ba 'di nyid yang dag par na bcom ldan 'das bzhed do // de lta na ni thams cad 'tsham mo //

de ltar gyur na /

(1) bdag nyid rig pa yin pa'i phyir //
sems kyi spyod yul gyur pa'i shes //
rnam par dag pa'ang yang dag tu //
rigs sam 'on te min zhes soms //

bar skabs kyi tshigs su bad pa'o //

[III. Relative Truth]

kun rdzob de ni yang dag pa dang yang dag pa ma yin pa'i bye brag gis rnam pa gnyis te / de la

8abc. brtags pa'i don gyis dben gyur pa //
dngos tsam brten nas gang [K om.] skyes [K add pa] te //
yang dag kun rdzob shes par bya //

brtags pa'i don ni yang dag par skye ba la sogs pa dang / rnam par shes pa snang ba dang / gtso bo dang 'byung ba'i yongs su 'gyur ba la sogs pa ste / de dag gis dben pa'o // dngos po tsam gang yin pa ni ji ltar snang ba bzhin du don byed nus pa'i phyir ro // rgyu dang rkyen rnams la brten nas skyes pa de ni yang dag pa'i kun rdzob kyi bden pa yin par shes par bya ste / 'di ltar byis pa yan chad kyi shes pa la mthun par don ji snyed rgyu las snang ba de ni yang dag pa'i kun rdzob yin par rigs te / shes pa la snang ba dang mthun par dngos po gnas pa'i phyir ro //

[A. Relative Truth is Not Confused With Anything that is Imagined]

yang dag par skye ba la sogs pa ni mi snang ste / ji lta bur yang [bu'ang P] rung ba'am / grub [sgrub CP] pa'i mtha' la brten nas sgro btags pa 'ba' zhig tu zad do // de lta ma yin na ni rtsod pa med par thal ba kho nar 'gyur ro // rgol ba dang phyir rgol ba'i shes pa la snang ba'i cha la ni rtsod pa su yang ['ang PP NP] med do // rtsod par byed na ni mngon sum la sogs pas gnod par 'gyur ro //

8d. yang dag *min ni* [ma yin K] kun brtags yin //

yang dag par skye ba la sogs pa gang yin pa de ni rtog [rtogs PP NP] pa'i bzos sbyar ba ste / de ni yang dag pa ma yin pa'i kun rdzob kyi bden pa'o // ni zhes bya ba ni bsnan pa'i don tam go rims bzlog pa'o //

'o na yang dag par skye ba la sogs pa bkag pa yang ci ga yang dag pa ma yin pa'i kun rdzob tu 'gyur te / de ni dngos po snang ba na yang dag par skye ba la sogs pa bzhin du mi snang ngo //

ma yin te dngos po'i [6a] ngo bo dang tha dad pa ma yin pa'i phyir ro // chos gzhan zhig yin par yongs su brtags [brtag PP NP] na ni yang dag pa ma yin pa'i kun rdzob tu yang ['ang PP NP] 'gyur ro // gang gi phyir /

9a. skye la sogs pa bkag *pa yang* [pa'ang PP NP] //

yang dag par skye ba la sogs par rtog pa'i dngos po bkag pa'i gtan tshigs kyis [PP NP om.] /

9b. yang dag pa dang mthun *phyir 'dod* [pa'i phyir P] //

don dam pa yin par kho bo cag 'dod do // gzhan dag ni yang dag pa kho nar 'dzin pas / yang zhes bya ba ni bsdu ba'i don to //

de yang rigs pas dpyad na kun rdzob kho na ste / ci'i phyir zhe na /

9cd. dgag bya yod pa ma yin pas [phyir V] //
yang dag tu na bkag med gsal [bsal DP CP] //

dgag bya med na bkag pa mi 'byung ba'i phyir te / yul med pa'i bkag pa mi rigs pa'i phyir ro //

gal te gzugs la sogs pa la skye ba la sogs par [V om.] rnam par rtog pa'i rgyu can pha rol pos dngos po yang dag pa nyid du brtags pa gang yin pa de dgag bya nyid yin no zhe na / gal te de lta na /

10ab. brtags pa'i rang gi ngo bo yi //
bkag pa brtags min ji ltar 'gyur //

dgag bya brtags pa yin du zin na / bkag pa yang ['ang PP NP] brtags pa nyid du 'gyur te / mo gsham gyi bu'i sngo bsangs [sangs PP NP] nyid la sogs pa bkag pa bzhin no // yang dag pa [par P] bkag pa med kyang skye ba la sogs pa yod par mi 'gyur te / bkag pas skye ba med pa la sogs pa la ma khyab pa'i phyir dang / de yod pa'i rigs pa med pa'i yang phyir ro //

10c. de bas 'di ['dir K] ni kun rdzob ste //

yang dag par na skye ba med ces bya ba la sogs pa'o //

10d. yang dag don yin yang dag min //

yang dag pa'i don ces [zhes P] bya bar bsnyegs [snyegs PP NP] so //
gang gi phyir zhe na /

11a. yang dag *nyid du* [tu na V] gnyis med de //

(1) de nyid phyir na de stong min //
mi stong ma yin yod med min //
mi skye ma yin skye min zhes //
de la sogs pa bcom ldan gsungs //

bar skabs kyi tshigs su bcad pa'o //
de ci'i phyir zhe na /

11b. de ni spros pa med pa yin //

de kho na [P add ni] rtog pa'i dra ba thams cad dang bral ba'o // de nyid kyi phyir /

11cd. 'jam dpal gyis ni yang dag dris //
rgyal ba'i sras po mi gsung bzhugs //

mdo las / de nas 'jam dpal gzhon nur gyur pas / li tstsha bi dri ma med par grags pa la 'di skad ces smras so // rigs kyi bu bdag cag gis ni rang rang gi bstan pa bshad zin na / khyod kyang gnyis [6b] su med pa'i chos kyi sgo bstan pa spobs pa mdzod cig / li tstsha bi dri ma med par grags pa cang mi smra bar gyur to // de nas 'jam dpal gzhon nur gyur pas / li tstsha bi dri ma med par grags pa la legs so zhes bya ba byin te / rigs kyi bu gang la yi ge dang skad dang / rnam par rig byed 'jug pa med pa de ni byang chub sems dpa' rnams kyi gnyis su med pa'i sgo la 'jug pa ste / legs so legs so zhes ji skad gsungs pa lta bu'o //

(1) gnyis po dag las dben pa'i dngos //
gzhan dbang dngos po yang dag na //
dris na ci phyir rgyal ba'i sras //
de ni mi gsung bzhugs par gyur //

(2) brda shes rigs pa shes pa yi //
skye bo dag ni ji ltar yang //

rang gi rtogs pa rjod byed de //
de bas mi gsung mi rigs so //

(3) de lta min na sgra rnams kyi //
rang gi mtshan nyid mthar phyin nyid //
rigs pa smra bas gang brjod de //
ji ltar rigs pa gsal bar smros //

(4) gang phyir kho na de la ni //
brjod bya'i bag kyang ci yang med //
de yi ['i PP NP] phyir na dris kyang don //
mi gsung bzhugs pas rgya cher bshad //

bar skabs kyi tshigs su bcad pa dag go //

chos rnams la chos kyi rjes su lta [blta PP NP] ba can du gnas pa'i byang chub sems dpa' des [de P] gang rten cing 'brel par 'byung ba las ma gtogs pa'i chos rdul phra rab tsam yang yang dag par rjes su mi mthong ngo zhes bya ba 'di la 'gal ba med de / chos [DP CP add zhes] smos pa'i phyir ro //

[B. Relative Truth Arises Dependently]

[1. The Distinction between Correct and Incorrect Relative Truth]

yang kun rdzob ni rnam pa gnyis su bstan te /

12. snang du 'dra yang don byed dag //
nus pa'i phyir dang mi nus phyir //
yang dag yang dag ma yin pas //
kun rdzob kyi ni dbye *ba byas* [bas PP] //

zhes bya ba'o // shes pa gsal ba'i rnam pa snang ba can du 'dra yang / ji ltar snang ba [P add de] bzhin du don byed pa la slu [bslu PP NP] ba dang mi slu [bslu PP NP] ba yin par nges par byas nas chu la sogs pa dang smig rgyu la sogs pa dag 'jig rten gyis yang dag pa dang yang dag pa ma yin par rtogs so // dngos su na [PP NP om.] gnyis ni ngo bo nyid med pa nyid du ngo bo nyid mtshungs pa kho na'o // ji ltar snang ba bzhin du ni rnam par gnas so // don byed pa la slu [bslu PP NP] ba dang mi slu [bslu PP NP] ba yang ['ang PP NP] ji ltar grags pa kho na bzhin te / de yang ngo bo nyid med pa'i phyir ro //

brten nas skyes pa don gyi bya ba byed pa dngos po tsam ni kho bo dang khyod kyis kyang khas blangs te / de la 'u bu cag bye brag ci zhig yod pa ma yin [7a] nam /

bden te /

13. gal te khyod kyang rigs min par //
ji ltar snang bzhin 'dod na ni //
'u bu cag la de mtshungs nyid //
rigs par na ni thams cad 'khrugs //

gal te ji ltar snang ba bzhin du khyod kyang 'dod na ni / 'u bu cag mtshungs pa yin te kho bo cag kyang nga rgyal ga la byed / gal te khyod 'di rigs pa'i rjes su 'gro ba can yin par khas len na ni / de kho bo cag mi 'dod do // gang gi phyir rigs par na thams cad brdas nas 'thor ba dang 'dra ba'i phyir te /

[2. It is Impossible to Know any Causal Relationship]

'di ltar rgyu dang 'bras bu'i dngos por [P add rnam par] nges pa 'di la khyod kyi thabs med pa kho na yin no // 'di ltar

(1) rnam pa med pa'i shes pa ni //
yul la 'dzin par mi rigs so //
rnam pa tshad ma min phyir dang //
mi rigs phyir na cig shos min //

(2) gang phyir sna tshogs ngo bu ru //
snang ba can gyi dngos gcig la //
rnam pa rnams bden ji ltar 'gyur //
de yi gcig nyid nyams phyir ro //

(3) de lta yin na mngon sum dang //
mi dmigs pa yi 'bras bu dang //
rgyu nyid du ni mi 'grub bo //
rnam pa gzhan zhig rnam par soms //

(4) gal te rgyu 'bras nyid blo yi //
thabs 'ga' zhig ni yod ce na //
de smros 'dud pa bdag cag la //
ser sna bya bar ga la rigs //

(5) des na thams cad mkhyen des kyang //
gzhan gyi dbang gi skad cig gi //
rgyu dang 'bras bu gsal bar ni //
cung zad tsam yang mkhyen mi spyod //

(6) sangs rgyas spyod yul bsam yas pas //
thams cad mkhyen pa kho nas mkhyen //
rigs pa'i rjes su 'gro ba la //
yug pa rkyang 'di mi rigs so //

bar skabs kyi tshigs su bcad pa dag go //

[3. NOTHING ULTIMATELY ARISES]

rgyu dang 'bras bu'i dngos po yang rigs pa ma yin te 'di ltar /

14. du mas *dngos po gcig* [gcig gi dngos K] mi byed //
du mas du ma byed ma yin //
gcig gis du ma'i dngos mi byed //
gcig gis gcig byed pa yang min //

[a. Many Do Not Produce One]

du mas gcig byed ma yin te / 'di ltar ngo bo nyid tha dad pa mig la sogs pa dag las 'bras bu tha dad pa ma yin pa 'byung na ni / rgyu'i tha dad pa ni tha dad pa byed par mi 'gyur te / de tha dad kyang tha dad pa med pa'i phyir ro // tha dad pa ma yin pa med kyang tha dad pa med par *'gyur bas* [gyur pas P] tha dad pa med pa yang tha dad pa med pa byed par mi 'gyur ro // de'i phyir tha dad pa dang tha dad pa med pa ni rgyu med pa can du 'gyur te / thams cad kyang de las [7b] gud na med pa'i phyir thams cad kyang [kun P] rgyu med pa can du 'gyur ro // de ltar gyur na rtag tu yod pa'am med pa zhig tu 'gyur ro //

[b. Many Do Not Produce Many]

de ltar [P add ni] mi 'gyur te gang gi phyir rgyu du mas du ma byed pa'i [phya'i DV] phyir ro // ci'i phyir zhe na / rang gi ngo bo nyid ji lta ba'i [bu DP CP; bu'i PP NP] bye brag gis de'i bye brag la nye bar sbyor ba'i phyir te / rgyu'i nye bar sbyor bas 'bras bu'i ngo bo nyid kyi bye brag ma 'dres pa'i phyir ro // 'di ltar mtshungs pa de ma thag pa'i rkyen gyi rnam par shes pa las ni mig gi rnam par shes pa rtogs pa'i bdag nyid du 'gyur ro // mig gi dbang po las ni rtogs pa'i bdag nyid de nyid [DP CP om.] gzugs la 'dzin nus pa nyid du so sor nges so // yul las ni de [PP om.] dang mthun pa'i ngo bo nyid [P om.] kho nar 'gyur ro // dngos su na 'bras bu tha dad pa ma yin yang [kyang PP NP] rgyu rnams kyi ngo bo nyid tha dad pa dag gis ngo bo nyid tha dad pa kho nar 'gyur te / rgyu'i [rgyu P] tha dad pas kyang 'bras bu [bu'i P] bye brag de tha dad pa med pa ni ma yin no // gzhan du yang ['ang PP NP] de bzhin du sbyar bar bya'o //

de ni rigs pa ma yin te rtogs pa'i bdag nyid la sogs pa dag phan tshun tha dad na ni / rnam par shes pa de du mar 'gyur te / de dag dang tha mi dad pa'i phyir ro // tha dad na ni rgyu med pa can du 'gyur te rgyu'i byed pa gzhan du nye bar sbyar ba byas pa'i phyir ro // de dag phan tshun tha dad pa med par yang 'gyur te / rnam par shes pa gcig las gzhan ma yin pa'i phyir ro // de lta na ni rgyu'i yul tha dad par brtags [rtogs DV] pas don ci zhig sos [gsos P] par 'gyur te / de'i phyir gnas skabs de'i nyes par 'gyur ro //

gal te 'bras bu'i bdag nyid du ma *las log* [la sogs PP NP] pa dang ldan pa'i chos rgyu dang mthun par tha dad par brtags [brtag P] pa byas na [nas P] de'i byed pa'i yul tha dad par brtag [brtags DP CP] pa byed do zhe na /

gyis shig rgyu'i byed pa de ni rtog [rtogs V] pa'i bzos sbyar ba dag la yin te / de'i phyir yang dag pa'i don du na brtags [btags V] pa [DP CP add pa] kho na yin par 'gyur ro // de lta na ni 'bras bu rgyu med pa can du 'gyur te / rgyu'i byed pa brtags pa'i bdag nyid rnams la nye bar sbyor *bar byed pa'i* [ba'i P] phyir ro //

gzhan yang gal te dngos su na 'bras bu tha dad pa ma yin yang bye brag rnams ni tha dad do zhe na / de ltar gyur na ni [yang P] chos dang chos can dngos su tha dad pa kho nar 'gyur te / tha dad pa dang tha dad pa ma yin pa'i ngo bo nyid dang ldan pa'i phyir ro // de lta na yang sngar smos [8a] pa'i nyes pa yod do //

ji ste bye brag de dag kyang brtags pa kho na yin no zhe na / de lta yin na ni rgyu'i tha dad pa'i rang bzhin rnams las bye brag tha dad pa rnams kho na 'byung ngo zhes bya ba yang rigs pa ma yin te rtog pas bkod pa'i tha dad pa ni rgyu'i byed pa la mi ltos [bltos PP NP] so //

(1) 'bras bu tha dad ma yin yang //
bye brag rnams ni tha dad dang //
gzhan min khyed 'dod de bas na //
kye ci dbang phyug gis byas sam //

(2) rtogs pa'i ngo bo las gzhan min //
de ni gzugs las skyes ma yin //
rnam pa de las gzhan min phyir //
gzugs las kyang ni skye bar 'gyur //

(3) gcig la cig car skye ba dang //
mi skye de bzhin skyed byed dang //
skyed byed ma yin yang dag par //
ci yi phyir na mi 'gal smros //

(4) kun las [nas DP CP] thams cad skye na ni //
tha dad tha dad ma yin pa //
khyed la rgyu med gsal bar 'gyur //
rigs pa'i rjes su 'brangs nas smras //

(5) gal te bye brag rkyen rnams las //
skye bar 'dod na re re ni //
skyed par byed pa ma yin 'gyur //
yin na 'bras bu rgyu med 'gyur //

(6) gal te khyod ni rkyen rnams las //
'bras bu skye bar 'dod na ni //
tha dad tha dad ma yin pa //
snga ma bzhin du rgyu med thal //

(7) ji ste de gnyis gzhan min na //
rnam par dbye ba ci phyir 'thad //
bshad zin nyes par thal 'gyur phyir //
'di ni glang chen khrus ['khrus PP NP] 'drar 'gyur //

bar skabs kyi tshigs su bcad pa dag go //

[c. One Does Not Produce Many]

gzhan yang gzhan 'di ['dir DP CP] brjod par bya ste / mig la sogs pa'i bdag nyid khyad par gang gis 'bras bu gcig skyed pa na ci de nyid kyis gzhan yang byed dam / gal te de nyid kyis so zhe na / ji ltar tha dad pa dang tha dad pa ma yin pa dag rgyu med pa can du mi 'gyur te rgyu tha dad pa med pa [P om.] bzhin du yang 'bras bu tha dad pa'i phyir ro // gal te gzhan gyis so zhe na / 'o na ni dngos po de gcig pur mi 'gyur te / bdag nyid kyi khyad par las tha dad pa med *pa ma yin* [V PP NP om.] pa'i phyir ro //

[d. One Does Not Produce One]

gal te rgyu [rgyur NP] gcig gis 'bras bu gcig kho na byed du zad mod ce [zhe PP NP] na / de lta [ltar NP] ni ma yin te / mig la sogs pa rang gi rigs dang mthun pa'i skad cig skyed par byed pa yin pa'i phyir / 'gro ba thams cad long ba dang 'on pa la sogs *pa nyid du* [pa'i dngos por P] thal bar 'gyur ba'i phyir ro // rang gi rnam par shes pa skyed par byed pa nyid yin [8b] na ni / rang gi rigs chad de / de bas na cir yang mi rung la / khas kyang mi len to //

[e. Concluding Verses]

(1) dbang phyug bzhin du gzhal bya'i phyir //
'gro ba'i byed po dbang phyug min //
de lta min na gzhal bya nyid //
la sogs ye med kho nar 'gyur //

(2) slob dpon gyis ni skye dgag 'di //
rnam pa mang po [por P] mdzad de la //
skye bo bdag nyid mi shes pas //
sun 'byin byed pa 'di 'dra smra //

(3) bdag las gzhan las zhes bya ba'i //
snyad 'dogs pa ni btags pa yin //
de bzhin skye ba 'gog byed 'di //
grub pa bsgrub pa de ma yin //

(4) *'di ltar dngos po rgyu med min*
['di ltar rgyu med dngos med pas P] //
'di yi rgyu ni dgos pas na //
de gang zheṣ ni mngon dris na //
khyod kyis 'ga' zhig mngon smra dgos //

(5) sa lu'i sa bon sogs rgyu na //
ci de gzhan nam de nyid yin //
phan tshun log pa'i lus la ni //
rnam pa gzhan dag mi srid do //

(6) brjod par mi nus zhe na yang //
mi rigs bram ze'i rgod ma bzhin //
'di ltar rigs pa shes pa yis //
lam gzhan zhig kyang bgrod na legs //

(7) tha snyad kyi ni rjes mthun par //
ji ltar bsnyad par nus pa ltar //
'di yang cung zad de bzhin gnong //
de lta min na mi smra thug //

(8) khyod phyogs gnyis las 'ga' brjod na //
de nyid [gnyis V] kho bo cag gis dgag //
de bas de lta yin na ni //
rtsod la bzo ba ga la yin //

(9) ma zhig pa las 'bras skye na //
de tshe ci phyir 'bras bu med //
zhig nas 'bras bu skye na ni //
de tshe gang las 'bras bu 'byung //

(10) de dag rnam par rtog [rtogs P] byed pa //
don med 'gyur bas yal bar dor //
lag 'gro 'o ma 'thung ba ni //
dug 'phel 'gyur ba 'ba' zhig bzhin //

(11) gcig pu byed po ma yin te //
du ma'ang byed po gang yang min //

gcig dang du ma ma gtogs pa //
gzhan gang byed po yin pa smros //

(12) gcig pu bya ba ma yin te //
du ma bya ba gang yang min //
gcig dang du ma ma gtogs pa //
gzhan ni gang zhig bya ba smros //

(13) 'di yod 'di zhes bya ba 'di [dang DP CP; te PP NP] //
tshad ma med par mi 'gyur ro //
sngar bshad *pa yi* [pa'i PP NP] rnam pa yis //
tshad ma'ang khyed [khyod P] la yod ma yin //

(14) nged kyi rkyen nyid 'di pa tsam //
ji ltar snang ba kho nar zad //
'di ltar 'di la dngos bsams na //
gnas mi rnyed pa kho na yin //

(15) nged kyang de ltar 'dod ce na //
kho bo'i dga' ston chen po ni //
dngos por 'dzin pa'i gdon babs las //
grol ba yin na 'byung bar [9a] 'gyur //

(16) rkyen nyid 'di pa [CV om.] tsam zhig ni //
yang dang yang du rjod byed de //
de bsgrub [grub P] bya la tshad ma ni //
cung zad tsam yang ston mi byed //

(17) thams cad grub par thal 'gyur phyir //
tshig gis kyang ni de mi 'grub //
bdag nyid stod par byed pa ni //
kye ma'o blo ni shin tu zhib //

bar skabs kyi tshigs su bcad pa dag go //

[4. THE ETYMOLOGY OF SAṂVṚTI]

ci ste [lta CV] kun rdzob ces bya ba 'di ci zhig yin zhe na /

15ab. gang zhig gis sam gang zhig la //
yang dag sgrib byed kun rdzob bzhed ['dod K] //

blo gang zhig gis sam blo gang zhig la yod na yang dag pa sgrib par byed pa 'jig rten na grags pa de lta bu ni kun rdzob tu bzhed de / mdo las ji skad du /

dnogs rnams skye ba kun rdzob tu //
dam pa'i don du rang bzhin med //
rang bzhin med la 'khrul pa gang //
de ni yang dag kun rdzob 'dod //

ces gsungs pa lta bu'o //

15cd. des na 'di kun *bden pa* [bde ba V] ste //
dam pa'i don du bden ma yin //

kun rdzob des na 'di kun thams cad bden pa yin no // ji ltar 'jig rten na grags pa de ltar bden no zhes bya ba'i tha tshig ste / mdo las ji skad du / rab 'byor phyin ci log ma gtogs par gang la gnas nas byis pa so so'i skye bo rnams mngon par 'du byed par 'gyur ba'i dngos po bden pa ni skra'i rtse mo'i cha shas gzugs pa'i tshad tsam yang med do zhes gsungs pa lta bu'o // phyin ci log ni 'jig rten na grags pa ste / rigs pa'i mtshan nyid gsum ji ltar 'jug pa de ltar bden no zhes bya ba'i bar du'o //

(1) kun rdzob dngos po med yin na //
skye ba dngos po yin pa'i phyir //
de tshe dngos po gcig de la //
nus dang mi nus cig car 'gyur //

(2) kun rdzob skye ba yin na yang //
kun rdzob tu skye zhes bya 'dir //
mkhas pa rnams kyi tshig don ni //
skye ba skye bar 'gyur te mtshar //

(3) 'di yi ['i P] skye ba kun rdzob ste [te PP NP] //
don dam par [pa P] ni *skye med* [ma skyes P] na //

skye ba med pas dngos po rnams //
ma skyes par ni smra na de //

(4) grub pa bsgrub pa smra 'gyur 'dis //
mi 'dod ci zhig bsgrub [bsgrubs DP CP] par 'gyur //
rigs pa'i rjes su 'brangs nas 'dis //
gnas pa la sogs de bzhin brjod //

(5) de la sogs pa ma 'brel la //
sgra don ma yin rnam rtog cing //
rgol ba kun rdzob mtshan 'di las //
nyams par khong du chud [9b] par gyis //

(6) rigs pas brtags na bden ma yin //
de las gzhan du bden pa yin //
des na gcig la bden nyid dang //
mi bden par ni ji ltar 'gal //

(7) rigs pas brtags na dngos ma yin //
de las gzhan du dngos po yin//
des na gcig la dngos po dang //
dngos po med pa ji ltar 'gal //

bar skabs kyi tshigs su bcad pa dag go //

[C. The Relativity of the Ultimate]

de ltar [lta P] yin na yang /

16. dam pa'i don du ma skyes pa //
tshig don 'di [de K] ni rigs pa yi //
rjes su 'brangs nas [na V] skye ba med //
gzhan la'ang de bzhin sbyar bar gyis //

ji ltar 'di sbyar ba de bzhin du yang dag par na med do // yang dag par na stong ngo zhes bya ba la sogs pa 'di dag la yang rigs pa'i lam kyi rjes su 'brangs na yod pa ma yin zhing de dag la stong pa nyid ma yin pa med ces bya ba la sogs pa sbyar bar bya'o //

pha rol rnams kyis dngos rnams kyi //
skye sogs rigs lam brten pa can //
'dod pa dag ni 'gog byed de //
des na 'di la ci zhig gnod //

bar skabs kyi tshigs su bcad pa dag go // de nyid kyi phyir /

17ab. kun rdzob de bzhin nyid gang yin //
de nyid dam pa'i don gyis [phyir K] bzhed //

ci'i phyir zhe na /

17c. tha dad min phyir /

kun rdzob dang don dam pa gnyis zhes bya ba lhag ma'o //

rigs de yang //
17d. ji ltar snang ba bzhin du gnas //

rigs pa yang ji ltar snang ba'i ngo bo yin pa'i phyir kun rdzob kho na yin te / rigs pa ni gzhan du mi 'jug go // 'di ltar /

18. rgol ba gnyi ga'i shes pa la //
ji tsam snang ba'i cha yod pa //
de tsam de la brten nas ni //
chos can chos la sogs par rtog //

19. de tshe rjes su dpag pa 'byung //
gang gi tshe na gzhan na min //
de bas rigs pa smra ba rnams //
de skad smra la su zhig 'gog //

rjes su dpag pa dang rjes su dpag par bya ba 'di tha snyad kyi rgol ba dang / phyir rgol ba dag gi blo'i bdag nyid la snang ba'i chos can dang chos dang dpe nyid du rnam par gzhag [bzhag PP NP] par 'byung gi / chos can dang chos la sogs pa gnyi ga [gnyis ka DP CP] la ma grub pa nyid kyis rjes su dpag pa 'byung ba mi rung ba'i phyir gzhan na ni ma yin te / gzhung lugs tha dad pa la [DP CP om.] gnas pa rnams ni gang la yang blo mtshungs pa nyid med pa'i phyir ro // chos can de lta bu la gnas pa [10a] rnams ni gtan tshigs la sogs pa de lta bu kho nas yang dag par na [P om.] yod dam med ces sems par byed par khas blang bar bya'o // de lta bas na rigs pas smra ba yang de ltar rjes su dpag pa 'byung bar byed na / su zhig 'gog par 'gyur / 'di ni mtshungs pa nyid du grub par gtan la phab pas / 'dir ni 'di'i ['di P] rgya ma bskyed do //

de nyid kyi phyir mdo las kyang rab 'byor 'jig rten gyi kun rdzob kyang gzhan la / don dam pa yang gzhan pa ni ma yin gyi / 'jig rten gyi kun rdzob kyi de bzhin nyid gang yin pa de nyid don dam pa'i de bzhin nyid yin no zhes gsungs so // yang na skye ba la sogs pa bkag pa yang 'ga' zhig gis don dam pa nyid du 'dod la / gzhan dag gis ni yang dag pa kho nar 'dod de / de lta na yang mdo'i tshig 'di legs par drangs pa kho na yin no // 'di ltar /

gzhan gyi don dam byas gang yin //
de ni gzhan gyi kun rdzob ste //
gzhan gyi mar 'dod gang yin de //
gzhan gyi chung mar 'dod pa bzhin //

zhes bshad do //

20ab. gal te rigs pa'i stobs kyis na //
kun rdzob tu yang mi skye dang //

ci ste kun rdzob tu yang snang ba dang ldan pa dang / shes pa cig shos kyis yongs su gcod par mi rung ba'i phyir snga ma bzhin du rgyu dang 'bras bu nyid nges pa med pa kho na'o // du mas dngos po gcig mi byed / ces bya ba la sogs pa gtan tshigs snga ma kho na'i phyir yang de ni rigs pa ma yin no zhes bya bar 'dod na / bshad pa /

20cd. de bden de yi phyir na 'di //
ji ltar snang bzhin yin par gsungs //

gang gi phyir / de lta yin na nyid kyi phyir // bcom ldan 'das kyis skye ba'am / gzhan yang rung ji ltar snang ba bzhin yin par /

rtag tu skye med chos ni de bzhin gshegs //
chos rnams kun kyang bde bar gshegs [P add pa] dang 'dra //
byis pa'i blo can mtshan mar 'dzin pa yis //
'jig rten na ni med pa'i chos la spyod //

ces bya ba gsungs te / 'di ltar /

[D. Relative Truth Cannot be Analyzed]

21ab. ji ltar snang bzhin ngo bo'i phyir //
'di la dpyad pa mi 'jug go //

ci ste kun rdzob ni ji ltar snang ba bzhin yin te / de la ni ji skad bshad pa'i dpyad pa'i gnas med pa nyid do // 'di ltar /

21cd. rnam par dpyod pa byed na don //
gzhan du song bas gnod par 'gyur //

kho bo [10b] cag ni 'di la dpyod par mi byed kyi / dpyod par byed pa la ni 'gog par byed do // gal te dpyad par [pa DP] byas te ma rung na ma rung du zad do // ji ltar snang ba'i ngo bo'i kun rdzob pa la brten nas de la dpyod pa byed pa ni don gzhan du 'gro ba'i phyir gnod pa 'ba' zhig tu zad do // ji skad bshad pa'i mtshan nyid ma yin pa la ni nyes pa brjod kyang kho bo cag la gnod pa ci yang med pa nyid do //

'o na gal te don dam par ma skyes pa kho na yin na de'i tshe /

22ab. ci yi phyir na rgyu 'di las //
der snang ba 'di smra bar byos //

'di yi lan glon par byed de //

22cd. 'di 'dra 'di ni rgyu 'di las //
snang ste ci zhig smra bar bya //

khyod la cha ji tsam snang ba de tsam kho bo cag [DP om.] la yang snang na de la kho bo cag la yang ci zhig dri / dris na yang kho bos de tsam kho na zhig smra bar bya'i / sngon ma byung ba ni ci yang smrar med do // de'i phyir 'dri ba 'di ni kun nas nyon mongs pa la brten pa 'ba' zhig tu zad do //

skye bo gang zhig mthong bzhin du'ang //
mi shes pa des rtsod pa yis //
grags pas gzhan la smra ba na //
mi shes ma 'phags ngan pa yin //

bar skabs kyi tshigs su bcad pa dag go //

[E. Reply to Particular Objections]

[1. THE BASIS OF RELATIVE TRUTH]

'di ni gzhi med par mi rung ngo zhes kyang brjod par mi nus te / 'di ltar /

23. brtags [btags V P] pa gzhi dang bcas pa ni //
'ga' yang gang la'ang mi snang ngo //
shing la sogs pa 'di yang ni //
gzhi la ltos pa ma yin nyid //

shing la sogs pa gdags pa'i rgyu ni yal ga la sogs pa yin la / de'i yang gzhan yin te / rim gyis rdul phra rab kyi bar du yin la / de yang phyogs tha dad pas dpyad na med pa kho na yin na / shing la sogs pa gdags pa'i rgyu dngos po yod pa de lta ga la yod / de lta bas na ji ltar snang ba 'di kho na yin gyi / gang la yang rgyu dngos po yod pa kho na la ltos nas 'jug pa ni ma yin zhes khas blang bar bya'o //

gal te kun rdzob gzhi la ni //
ltos gyur de lta yin na ni //
dngos 'gyur yang na khyod kyi gzhi //
ji [de V] ltar kun rdzob mi 'gyur te //

bar skabs kyi tshigs su bcad pa dag go //

de ni de lta yin te gang gi phyir khyod kyi ltar na yang /

24ab. 'di ltar brtags pa'i ngo bo nyid //
ci la'ang mi ltos kho na yin //

gal te med pa'i phyir mi ltos so zhe na /

mngon sum dang 'gal ba kun tu spyod de / gzung ba dang 'dzin [lla] pa ni brtags pa'i ngo bo nyid yin la / de gnyis kyang mngon sum kho nar grags pa de dag yin no //

gal te ma rig pas dkrugs pa'i rnam par shes pa nyid de ltar rtogs so zhe na /

myong ba dang 'gal ba grub pa khyod la 'gog par byed pa su zhig yod de / bdag nyid mi shes pa de lta bu de ni 'jig rten gyis thag ring po kho nar spang ngo //

gal te rmi lam la sogs pa na mthong ngo zhe na /

bden na mthong bzhin du yang mngon par zhen pa ngan pas khyod la log par snang ngo //

gang yang gzung ba dang 'dzin pa'i rnam par snang ba 'di ci zhig gzhan gyi dbang yin nam / de ni yang dag par na des dben pa'i ngo bo can yin na / ji ltar de ltar snang / ma rig pas dkrugs pa'i phyir de ltar snang bar ni chug mod kyi / de ni de'i bdag nyid ni ma yin te de'i bdag nyid ni gnyis kyis dben pa'i phyir ro // de lta yin na yang 'brel pa med pa'i phyir de snang ba na gnyis po ci'i phyir snang bar 'gyur /

gal te 'brel pa smras zin to zhe na /

24cd. gal te de lta yin na ni //
gzhan dbang nyid smros [smos P] te [de V] su bzlog [zlog P] //

cig shos kyang gzhan gyi dbang nyid du bya ba la / rgyu 'di kho nar zad la / de ni 'di la yang yod de / de bas na brtags pa med do //

gal te yang shes pa kho na rgyu dang rkyen rnams kyis skyed na / skyed la ni reg na de go ci'i phyir snang / gal te shes pa kho na de ltar snang ngo zhe na / de ni bshad zin te de dag gis ji lta bu kho nar bskyed pa de lta bu kho nar snang du zad do // gal te de lta bu kho nar bskyed do zhe na / 'o na ni gnyis kyis dben pa can gyi ngo bo ma yin te / 'di la bshad kyang zin to //

gnyis [DP CP add po] med pa'i ngo bo nyid yin [DP CP add na] yang shes pa gzhan gyis 'khrul pa'i dbang [CV add dbang] gis de ltar rtogs pa yang ma yin te / brgal zhing brtags pa mtshungs pa'i phyir ro // de'i phyir na 'di ni gyi na'o //

[2. CANDRAKĪRTI (?) ON THE NATURE OF RELATIVE TRUTH]

25. rtsod ngan grags pa kha cig ni //
yang dag par dngos ma skyes pa [pas V] //
mo gsham bu la sogs bzhin du //
kun rdzob tu yang mi skye zer //

yang dag par ma skyes pa'i ngo bo nyid gang yin pa de dag ni kun rdzob tu yang skye bar mi 'gyur te / dper na mo gsham gyi bu la sogs pa lta bu'o // gzugs la sogs pa 'di dag kyang de dang 'dra'o // de ni rigs pa ma yin te / [11b]

(1) 'jig rten gnod sogs srid pa'i phyir //
'di la bsgrub pa nyid med do //
gal te 'jig rten ma skyes phyir //
gnod pa med par khyod 'dod na //

(2) gtan tshigs la sogs med pa'i phyir //
de tshe bsgrub bya 'grub [grub P] mi 'gyur //
rang gi tshig dang 'gal ba'i phyir //
gal te de gcig ma gtogs na //

(3) 'o na des na khyod kyi ni //
ma nges nyid 'gyur bzlog par dka' //
sgrub par byed pa yod na ni //
dpe la'ang yod pa ma yin no //

(4) gal te rgyu 'di khyod la grub //
bsgrub byas khyab pa'ang [pa P] de bzhin na //
der ni bdag la nyes *med par* [pa med P] //
khyod kyis ji ltar klan ka btsal //

(5) gal te nga la tshad ma yis [yin PP] //
grub na grub ste khyod la'ang [la V] khyab //
mkhas khyod ci'i [ci P] phyir bdag nyid kyi //
nyes pa nga la 'dogs par byed //

(6) tshad mas ma grub ce na yang //
yod med skye ba bkag pa'i phyir //
yang dang yang du bsgrubs zin no [to P] //
khyab pa de yang khyod kyis smras //

(7) kho bo'i bden par ma skyes dang //
kun rdzob mi skye lhan cig tu //
khyab bya khyab byed nyid ma grub //
de lta yin na khyod kyis nyes //

(8) yang dag skye ba bkag pa yis //
yang dag par na skye med 'dod //
brtags pa mi skye de lta min //
de phyir 'di gnyis de bdag min //

(9) yang dag par na gnyis po med //
gang phyir spros dang bral ba ni //
yang dag 'dod de de phyir der //
gtan tshigs la sogs yan lag med //

(10) 'di ltar de gnyis med pa'i phyir //
rgyu dang 'bras bu med pa nyid //
'di nyid kyis ni thal bar yang //
dogs pa rnam par bzlog pa yin //

bar skabs kyi tshigs su bcad pa dag go //
gzhan yang /

26a. gal te kun rdzob mi rung na //

tshad mas so // tshad ma ma yin pa ni [la P] gzung bar bya ba ma yin pa'i phyir /

26b. rigs smra de la ci zhig gnod //

rigs pas 'ongs pa'i dngos po la rtog pa sngon du gtong ba su yang sdang bar gzo ba med pa'i phyir ro // sngar khas blangs pa'i phyir tshad mas gnod gzhin du yang dor bar mi nus so zhes kyang brjod par rigs pa ma yin no //

gang gi phyir kun rdzob khas blangs nas 'di ci rigs sam 'on te mi rigs zhes dpyod par byed pa mi mdzes pa de'i phyir 'di sngar khas ma blangs so [12a] snyam du bsams te 'di ltar /

26cd. rigs [rig K] pa shes pas dpyad [spyad CK] pa yi //
'og tu khas blangs [blang K] bya bar bshad //
brtags pa'i 'og tu khas blang gi //

khas blangs nas brtag pa 'jug pa ni ma yin no zhes bya ba'i don 'di ni tshad ma rnam par gtan la dbab pa la sogs par rab tu dpyad zin pa'i phyir ro //

27a. mngon sum la sogs 'gal zhe [ci K] na //

kun rdzob ni ji ltar snang ba bzhin yin la / de yang gal te khas mi len na mngon sum la sogs pa dang 'gal bar thal bar 'gyur bar sems na / bden na mngon sum la sogs pa dang 'gal ba /

27b. 'di ci 'di smra nyid la'am [la'ang K] //

gang gis na khyod ma gtogs par 'gyur ba khyod dang 'brel bar ma byas pa de ni med do // gal te des khyod [khyed DP CP] mi 'jigs so zhe na // de ci kho bo cag rang bzhin med par smra ba yin bzhin du yang 'jigs sam zhes bsams pa'o //

27cd. tshad mas gnod na tshad ma'i bdag //
yid brtan du ni mi rung 'gyur //

kun rdzob ni ji ltar snang ba bzhin yin la de yang gal te tshad mas mi rung na mi rung du zad do // mngon sum de la gnod pa bab ['bab P] na / tshad ma'i bdag nyid la yid brtan du mi rung bar brjod de / mtshan nyid dang ldan pa la gnod pa srid phan chad mtshan nyid sun phyung bar 'gyur ro // de'i phyir tshad ma'am tshad ma ma yin pa cir yang mi 'gyur ro // de lta na yang kun rdzob kyang dgag par mi nus pa kho na'o snyam du sems pa'o //

(1) gang zhig yang dag dngos mi 'dod //
de la kun rdzob ci zhig smos //
gal te tha snyad sogs med na //
de ci gzhan la'ang mi mtshungs sam //

(2) khyod dang de bzhin kho bos kyang //
'jig rten bzhin du bsnyad bya dgos //
de lta yin na khyod kyis ni //
bsnyad par byas pas khe ci yod //

bar skabs kyi tshigs su bcad pa dag go //
de lta bas na /

28. snang ba'i ngo bo gang yin pa //
de ni 'gog pa ma yin nyid //
nyams su myong ba gang yang ni //
dgag par rigs pa ma yin no //

mngon sum dang 'gal bar 'gyur ba'i phyir ro snyam du bsams pa yin no //

29. skye la sogs pa'i rnam pa gang //
snang ba min la de yang ni //
yang dag par zhes [shes K] bya sogs par //
gzhan gyis yongs su brtags pa 'gog //

gang yang gzugs la sogs pa snang ba dang ldan pa'i shes pa la mi snang [12b] ba'i rnam pa yang dag par skye ba dang rnam par shes pa snang ba dang / gtso bo dang yongs su 'gyur ba la sogs pa bstan bcos la sogs pa la brten nas yongs su brtags pa 'di'ba' zhig'gog par byed de // de bkag pa la mngon sum la sogs pa'i gnod pa mi 'jug pa kho na'o // sogs pa smos pa ni yod pa nyid la sogs pa yongs su bsdu ba'o //

30ab. de bas 'dir ni de lta bu'i //
brtags pa kho na dgag par rigs //

ji skad smos pa'i nyes pa med pa'i phyir ro //

30cd. brtags pa ma yin 'gog pa 'di [ni K] //
bdag la gnod 'gyur 'ba' zhig go //

gzugs la sogs pa'i lus rtog pa'i nyes pas ma sbags [spangs DP] pa gzhan gyi dbang gi bdag nyid rnam par shes pa tsam snang ba dgag par [P add bya] mi nus pa 'ba' zhig tu ma zad kyi / byed na byed pa po la mngon sum la sogs pas phyir gnod pa kho na byed do //

(1) rnam par rtog pa snang ba yi //
gtso bo la sogs yang dag par //
dngos po rnams kyi rgyur gyur par //
gzhan gyis brtags gang de 'gog go //

(2) brtags pa 'gog par byed pa la //
yang dag ces bya bkag pa yi //
bye brag min te de yi phyir //
kun rdzob ji ltar med par 'gyur //

bar skabs kyi tshigs su bcad pa dag go //
de nyid kyi phyir mdo las kyang /

brtags pa'i dngos po yod ma yin //
gzhan gyi dbang ni yod pa ste //
sgro 'dogs pa dang skur 'debs pa'i //
mthar rtog [rtogs DP CP] pa ni phung bar 'gyur //

chos rnams thams cad brtags pa yi //
ngo bo nyid kyis ma skyes so //
mi rnams gzhan gyi dbang la ni //
brten nas rnam par rtog pa skye //

zhes gsungs te / de ltar byas na / rab 'byor gzugs ni gzugs med pa'i ngo bo nyid yin no [P om.] zhes rgyas par 'byung ba dang / tshe dang ldan pa sha ri'i bu 'di ltar gzugs ni rang bzhin gyis stong ngo // gang yang rang bzhin gyis stong pa de la ni skye ba med 'jig pa med do // gang yang skye ba med 'jig pa med pa de la ni gzhan du 'gyur bar mi mngon te / tshor ba nas rnam par shes pa'i bar du yang de dang 'dra'o zhes rgyas par 'byung ba 'di yang grub pa yin no //

[IV. Karma, Transmigration, and Buddhahood]

[A. Action and its Result]

gal te dngos po ji ltar snang ba bzhin kho nar gnas par zad na las dang 'bras bu dag ji lta bu snyam pa la /

31. mthong ba po yi ['i V P] lta ba la [13a] //
las 'bras ji ltar snang ba dag //
de ltar des bshad de yi phyir //
thams cad ji ltar snang [rang K] bzhin gnas //

ston pa'i gzigs pa snang ba thogs pa mi mnga' ba can gyis mkhyen pa'i bdag nyid la las dang 'bras bu dag bye brag tu ji ltar snang ba de bzhin du 'gro ba la phan par bzhed pa thugs rje'i rang bzhin can des bye brag tu rab tu bshad de / gang gi phyir de lta yin pa de'i phyir dbang po'i yul du ma gyur pa thams cad kyang ji ltar snang ba bzhin kho nar gnas so //

32. thugs rje'i bdag nyid de nyid kyis //
rtog pas bcings pa gzigs nas ni //
sems tsam la sogs bye brag gis //
bcings pa thar pa bstan pa [par K] mdzad //

bcom ldan 'das las dang 'bras bu mkhyen pa [pa'i DP CP] thugs rje'i rang bzhin [P add can] gyi sku can de nyid kyis 'khor ba'i btson rar 'gro ba rtog pa'i lcags sgrog gis bcings pa la gzigs nas / bsam pa ji lta ba bzhin du phung po dang khams dang skye mched dang / sems tsam dang / chos thams cad bdag med par bstan pa'i rim gyis dngos por 'dzin pa ma lus par sel bar mdzad cing / 'gro ba la [P om.] bcings pa dang [P om.] thar pa bstan [brtan PP NP] pa mdzad do //

ji ste rtog [rtogs DP CP] pa zhes bya ba 'di ci yin zhe na /

33ab. sems dang sems byung khams gsum pa //
sgro btags rnam pa [P om.] can rtog [P add pa] yin //

khams gsum pa'i sems dang sems las byung ba'i sgro btags pa'i rnam pa can du 'byung ba'i rnam pa ni rtog pa yin no //

33cd. de dag 'ching ba'i rgyu nyid du //
ji ltar gzigs pa de bzhin gsungs [gsung K] //

de dag kyang de bzhin gshegs pas rnam pa gang gis kyang 'ching ba'i rgyu nyid du gzigs pa de kho na bzhin du gsungs kyi yang dag par ni ma yin te / 'di ltar /

34ab. med pa rnams kyi nus pa yang //
ji ltar *snang ba* [brtags pa K] bzhin du 'dod //

med pa rnams kyang ji ltar grags pa bzhin du 'ching ba la sogs pa'i *bya ba* [don P] byed par mi 'gal ba kho na'o // yang dag par na 'ching ba dang / 'ching [bcing P] bar bya ba dag kyang med do //

34cd. yod pa rnams kyi nus pa ni //
ji lta bur yang mi mthong ngo //

yod pa rnams don byed par nus pa ni sangs rgyas rnams kyis kyang gzigs par mi spyod de / shes pa rnam pa med pa dang / rnam pa dang bcas pas yongs [13b] su gcod pa mi srid pa'i phyir la / yongs su gcod par byed pa gzhan yang mi rung ba'i phyir ro //

gang las gang zhig yod gzigs pa //
de yod na ni de nges yod //
de med na ni de med nyid //
de phyir ha cang thal mi 'gyur //

bar skabs kyi tshigs su bcad pa dag go //

35ab. gzhan la dngos po ji bzhin du //
tha snyad rung ba ma yin no //

tha snyad thams cad ji ltar snang ba kho na bzhin du [P om.] 'jug go zhes bya ba de ni de lta yin no zhes bya bar shes par bya ste / 'di ltar dngos por smra ba'i lta ba la yang ['ang PP NP; DP CP om.] / dngos po ji lta ba bzhin tha snyad gdags su ni mi snang ba'i [PP NP om.] phyir / rigs pas mi rung ngo // shes pa'i bdag nyid la ni rdul phra rab dag dang / gnyis su med pa'i dngos po'i ngo bo mi snang ngo // mi snang ba la ni tha snyad med do // snang ba gang yin pa de yang dngos po'i ngo bo kho na ma yin te / 'dus pa dang gnyis kyang dngos po ma yin pa'i phyir ro // tha snyad ni 'di gnyis las yin na / 'di gnyis kyang dngos po ma yin pa kho na'o //

gal te snang bzhin du yang de nges par mi zin to snyam na /

des na ci de lta bu la ni tha snyad med do // snang ba [P om.] zhes bya ba yang yid ches pa med pa'i phyir mna' chu btung dgos so //

tshad ma med pa'i phyir dang / tshad mas gnod pa'i phyir yang / dngos po'i ngo bo mi rung ba'i phyir ro // de ji ltar snyam pa la /

35cd. *mi snang phyir dang mi rung phyir* [V om.] //
rigs pa'i rjes su 'brangs nas bshad //

ces bya ba smos te / de lta bas na dngos po'i ngo bo yod du zin kyang ji ltar snang ba bzhin tha snyad 'dogs pas de la mngon par zhen pa ni cir yang mi dgos so //

(1) rang lta chags pas ci zhig bya //
skye bo reng bur skyes 'gyur zhing //
yon tan nyes pa ma mthong la //
rang gi lta ba ci zhig yod //

(2) rang gi lta la chags por te //
rigs pa nyid la 'jug par gyis //
gang tshe rigs stobs las 'ongs pa'i //
dngos po yang dag nyid zung shig //

bar skabs kyi tshigs su bcad pa dag go //

lta [P add ba] 'di la chad par thal bar 'gyur ba yang ma yin te /

36. gang phyir rgyu las byung de'i phyir //
'di [de K] ni ci phyir chad par 'gyur //
de log na ni log [ldog K] pa la //
ci [ci'i P] phyir rtag [brtags K] pa nyid *yin smros* [smras so K] //

gang gi tshe dngos po 'di ji ltar snang ba bzhin las dang nyon mongs pa'i dbang [14a] gis 'khor ba ji srid par 'jug pa de'i tshe / 'di chad par ji ltar 'gyur te 'gro ba brgyud [rgyud PP NP] pa [pas P] 'khor ba'i rjes su 'gro ba kho na la ni chad par rigs pa ma yin no // gang gi tshe 'phags pa'i bden pa mthong ba'i mes / las dang nyon mongs pa mtha' dag bsregs pa can mya ngan las 'das pa'i grong khyer na gnas pa de'i tshe / 'di ji ltar rtag par 'gyur / de bas de ltar na kun rdzob kyi dngos po med pa'i bdag nyid la yang rtag pa dang chad pa'i chos nyid thag ring po kho nar gnas so // don dam pa la lta ba'i gnas mi thod pa kho na ste / 'di ltar /

(1) ma skyes ngo bo nyid la ni //
rtag dang chad nyid ga la zhig //
chos kyi bye brag rnam rtog pa //
ngo bo nyid la rtog par byed //

(2) ji ltar sus kyang nam mkha' la //
yig sogs dgod par mi nus ltar //
dngos po rnams ni ma skyes la //
chos su rnam rtog de bzhin no //

bar skabs kyi tshigs su bcad pa dag go //

37. brtags pa'i ngo bos [bo K] bden pa yi [pa'i DP CP] //
ji ltar [lta K] snang [K om.] ba 'di kho na [K add la] //
brten [rten K] te [nas P] skyes pa thams cad ni //
thams cad mkhyen pas mngon sum gzigs //

dngos po rnams ngo bo nyid med bzhin du yang ji ltar snang ba la yang dag par skye ba la sogs pas dben pa brten nas skyes pa kho na'i dngos po thams cad rnam pa thams cad du cig car mngon sum du mkhyen pas na / thams cad mkhyen pa zhes bya'o //

38. gang la don gzhan yongs gcod [spyod K] pa'i [pa P] //
shes pa cung zad kyang med pas [pa K] //
de yi thams cad mkhyen pa 'dir //
brtags yin cung zad *'gal ba med* ['dir mi gal K] //

shes bya nang gi yin par smra ba'i ltar na / thams cad mkhyen pa brtags pa kho na yin par 'gyur te / blo rnam pa dang bcas pa dang cig shos kyis yongs su gcod pa mi rung ba'i phyir ro // rgyud gzhan la yod pa'i dngos po yongs su mi gcod pa'i phyir te / rang gi rgyud la yod pa yang de dang 'dra'o // ngo bo nyid med par smra ba'i ltar na ni / ji ltar grags pa bzhin du yongs su gcod pa'i phyir nyes pa med do //

[B. The Bodies of the Buddha]

[1. THE DHARMA BODY]

gang gi tshe yang dag par skye ba la sogs par rtog [rtogs P] pa bkag pa'i ngo bo nyid kyis chos rnams ma skyes so zhes bya ba la sogs pa yang brtags pa'i bdag nyid [V add yang] dag yin no zhes bya bar khong du chud par byas nas / dngos po'i rang gi ngo bo dpyod par byed [14b] cing cung zad kyang mi mthong ba de'i tshe ni [DP CP om.] de kho na bzhin gnas te / 'di ltar /

39. gang tshe *shes dang* [PP NP om.] shes bya dang //
bdag nyid rjes su mi mthong ba [ba na PP NP;
na DP CP] //
de ni [tshe K] mtshan ma mi 'byung ['gyur K] phyir //
gnas pa brtan phyir mi bzhengs so //

bcom ldan 'das 'di rtog pa'i sa bon *mtha' dag* [thams cad P] bag chags dang bcas te / rtsad [rtsa P] nas bton pa nyid kyi phyir / mtshan ma mi 'byung na bzhengs pa lta ga la yod / bskal pa grangs med pa du mar gus par mdzad de / bar chad med par legs par bsgoms pas ting nge 'dzin brtan pa'i yang phyir ro //

40. gang la bzhugs na bsam mi khyab //
yon tan kun gyi gnas [rten du DP] 'gyur [gyur K]
dang //
mtshungs med phyag gnas 'dren gyur pa'i //
gnas skabs 'ga' de bsam mi khyab //

41. chos rnams kun gyi lus yin phyir //
yon tan bsam yas kun rten phyir //
rigs [rig K] pa'i rjes 'brang ngo bo'i phyir //
skyob pa rnams kyi chos sku yin //

rnam pa gsum gyis chos kyi sku // zhes bya ste / chos thams cad kyi lus kyi 'gro ba thams cad de bzhin gshegs pa'i ngo bo nyid las mi 'da' ba'i phyir ro // 'jig rten pa dang 'jig rten las 'das pa'i yon tan thams cad kyi rten lus ni tshogs yin pa'i phyir ram / yang na 'dir chos rnams sgrogs pa'i phyir ro // rten gyi dngos po ni de la 'jug pa thob pas kun brtags pa'o // chos kyi sku ni rigs pas rnam par gnas pa'i ngo bo nyid ces bya ba'i tha tshig go // de nyid rigs pa dang ldan pa'i phyir ro //

[2. THE ENJOYMENT BODY]

(1) de tshe rnam rtog med de yi //
sngon gyi shugs kyis sems can don //
rtag tu phyogs rnams thams cad du //
rnam pa kun tu thams cad 'byung //

(2) mkhyen pa'i skad cig gcig gis ni //
shes bya [bya'i P] dkyil 'khor kun khyab can //
yon tan rin chen 'tshogs ting 'dzin //
bsam gtan bsam mi khyab pa'i rten //

(3) rtog pa dang ni nyon mongs dang //
bag chags ma lus gtan bcad can //
shes bya'i yul la mi shes pa'i //
tshogs ni mtha' dag rnam spangs can //

(4) nyes pa kun gyi sa ma yin //
yon tan rgya mtsho kun gyi sa //
rtag tu 'gro ba thams cad kyi //
'dod pa rnam pa kun du sgrub //

(5) yid bzhin nor bu bzhin du ni //
mtshungs med 'khor ba srid du 'jug //
thugs rje ches bsgrubs bsam mi khyab //
bsod nams ye shes [15a] mtshungs med 'byung //

(6) yang dag *pa yi* [pa'i DP PP NP] mchog thob cing //
bsod nams rab che'i las mnga' ba //
byang chub sems dpa' rnams mig gi //
yul du bsam gyis mi khyab 'gyur //

(7) de las byang chub sems dpa' rnams //
gang gis chos kyi longs spyod ni //
ji ltar 'dod bzhin nyer spyod pas //
sku ni longs spyod rdzogs par 'dod //

[3. THE MANIFESTATION BODY]

(8) sems can so so'i 'dod pa'i don //
dus bzhin rab tu 'grub pa'i phyir //
de las 'sprul pa'i sprin gyi rgyun //
kun du rab tu 'byung bar 'gyur //

(9) rnam pa gang dang gang gis na //
gang dang gang na gang gang tshe //
skal ldan skye bo gang dang gang //
de de yongs su smin bya bar //

(10) rnam pa de des de dang der //
de yi tshe dang de yi tshe //
thub pa'i spu yi khung sogs nas //
sprul pa gdon [gnod CV] mi za bar 'byin //

(11) rgyal bas 'jig rten ma lus pa'i //
bya ba dag la gang gis mdzad //
de ni de yi sprul sku ste //
'gro ba dbugs 'byin mdzad pa yin //

(12) khyab bdag shugs kyi mthu yis ni //
sprul pa yis ni sprul pa yang //
ji ltar bzhed bzhin mdzad nyid de //
mdzad pa kun la 'jug pa bzhin //

bar skabs kyi tshigs su bcad pa dag go //

bcom ldan 'das kyi sku 'di ni shin tu mdor bsdus nas rnam pa gsum du bshad kyi / rnam pa thams cad du ma lus par brjod par ni / ye shes dang ldan pa thams cad mkhyen pas kyang mi spyod na bdag 'dra bas lta smos kyang ci dgos // phyogs 'dis nyan thos la sogs pa'i lus kyi rnam par dbye ba yang shes par bya'o //

[V. Conclusion]

42. de ltar bden gnyis rnam phye 'dir //
ci nyes yod dam 'on te med //
phyogs 'dzin pa yis dkrugs pa'i yid //
legs par bor la dpyad par gyis //

43. mi yang shin tu thob par dka' //
blo sbyangs [sbyang P] nyam yang rab tu chung //
'khor ba'i dgon pa bgrod par dka' //
srog kyang shin tu g.yo ba yin //

44. bshes gnyen bzang po [po'ang P] rnyed dka' na //
rab tu sdang ba gang du dgos //
mos pa med du zin na yang //
de ni 'ga' la bsod nams kyis //

45. goms par byas la rim gyis ni //
'di ni re zhig gcig [cig V] na [la K] 'gyur //
sdang bas tshig pa khyod la ni //
dal ba 'byor ba'ang ring bar gsal //

46. bden pa gnyis ni rnam phye bas //
dge ba bdag nyid [gis K] thob pa gang //
des ni 'gro [15b] ba ma lus pa //
ye shes snying por [po K] bskyed par shog //

bden gnyis rnam par gtan la dbab pa / yang dag pa mthong bar brtson pa slob dpon ye shes snying pos mdzad pa rdzogs so // paṇḍita śīlendrabodhi dang bande ye shes sde'i 'gyur //

Appendix.

The Blockprints of the Derge Edition of the Tibetan Text

To make it possible for a reader to follow the text in Tibetan script and compare the edited and romanized version with the Tibetan original we have included a reproduction of the blockprints of the Derge edition.

The blockprints include the Verses (folios 1a-3b) as well as the Commentary itself (folios 3b-15b). The folio numbers of the Commentary correspond to the numbers in brackets in the edited and romanized version of the text found in Part Four of this book.

This reproduction is made from the copy of the Derge Tibetan Tripiṭaka preserved in the Harvard Yenching Library, Cambridge, Massachusetts. Our thanks to the Harvard Yenching Library and Mr. Eugene Wu, Librarian, for permission to copy the text.

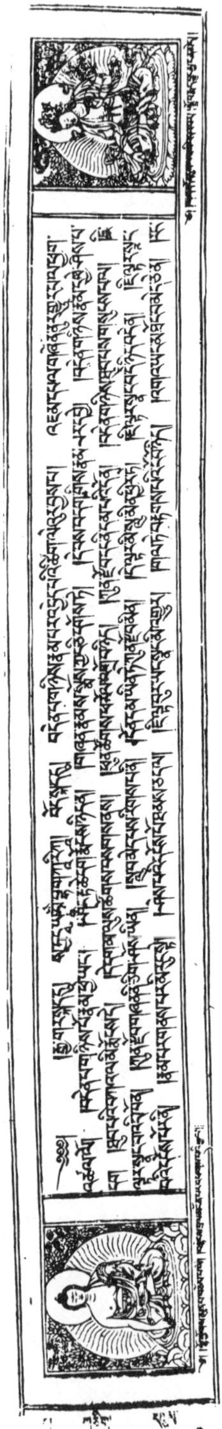

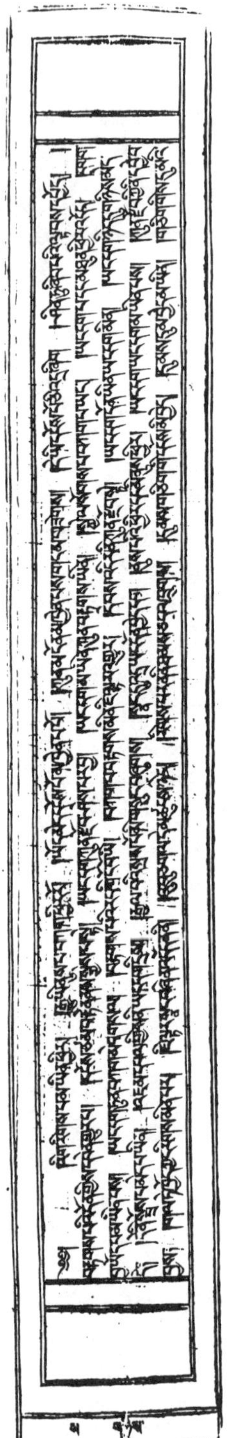

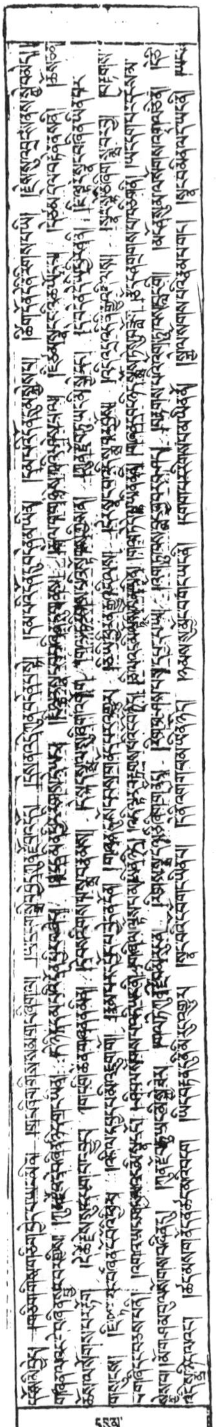

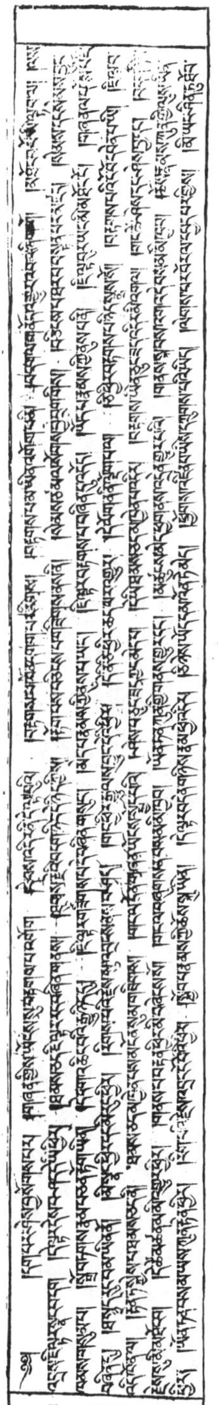

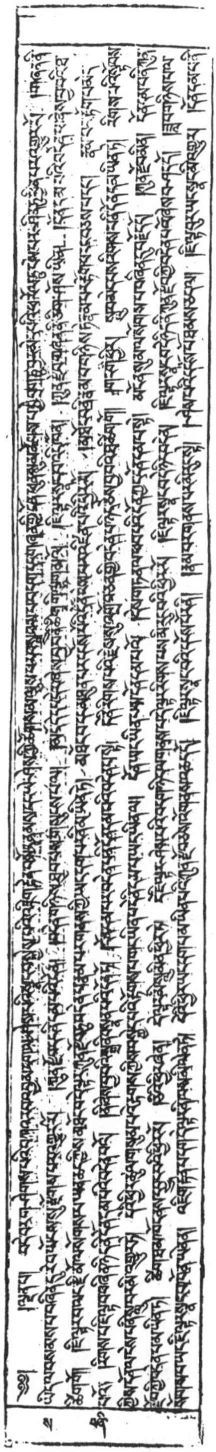

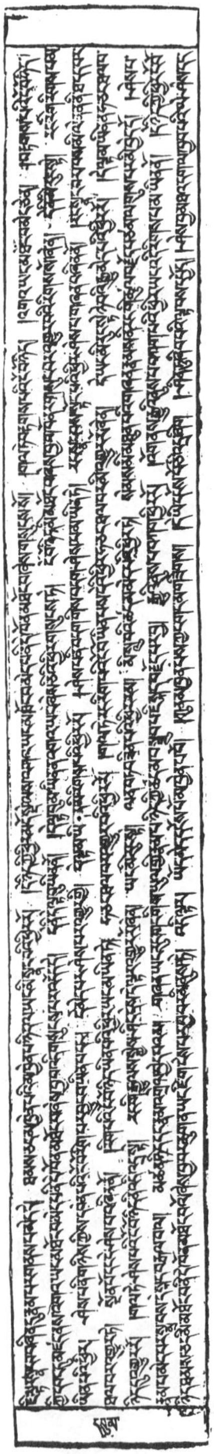

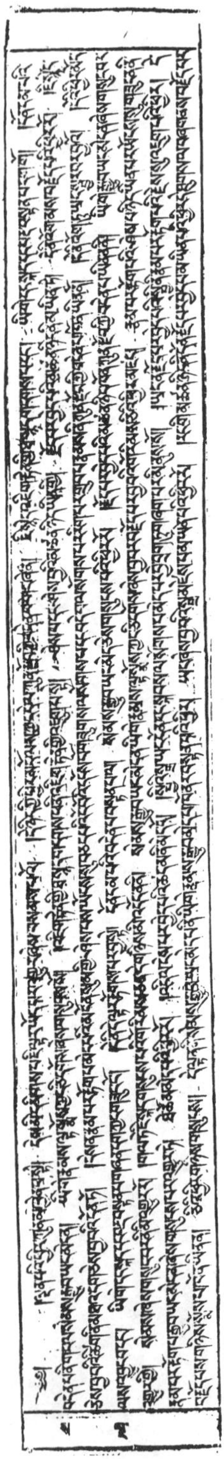

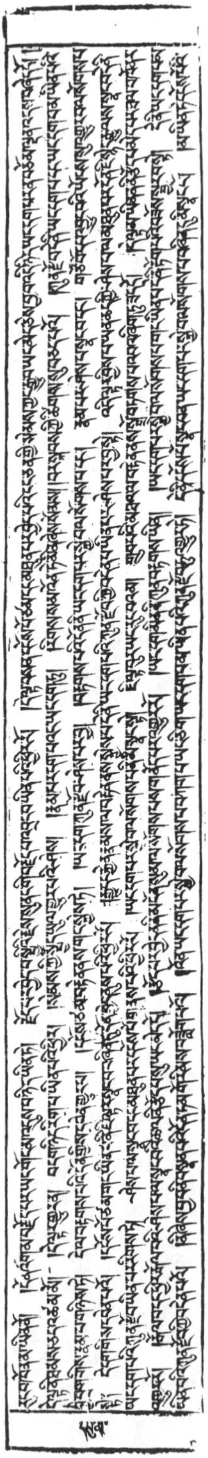

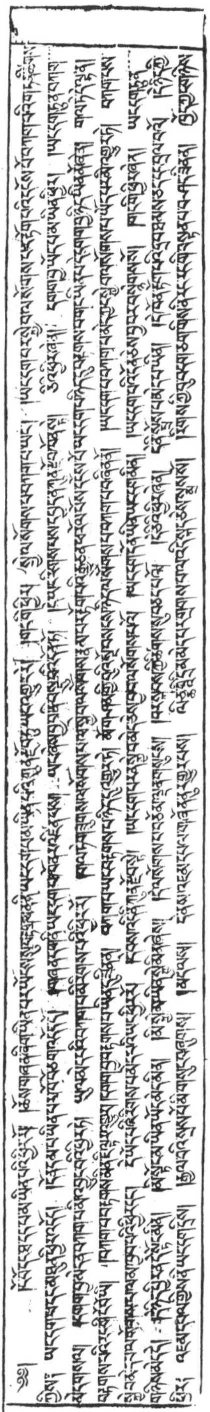

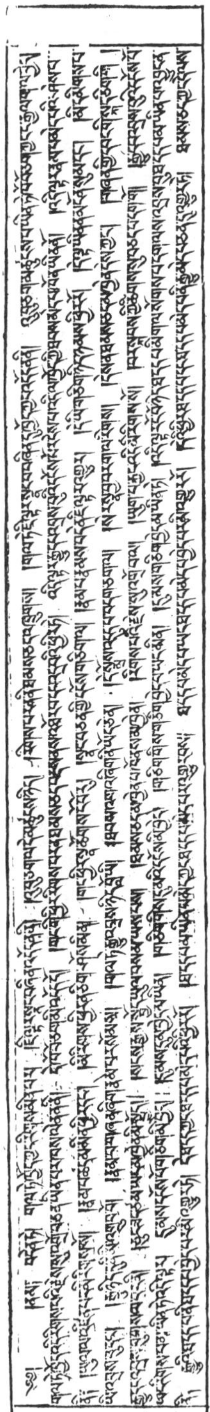

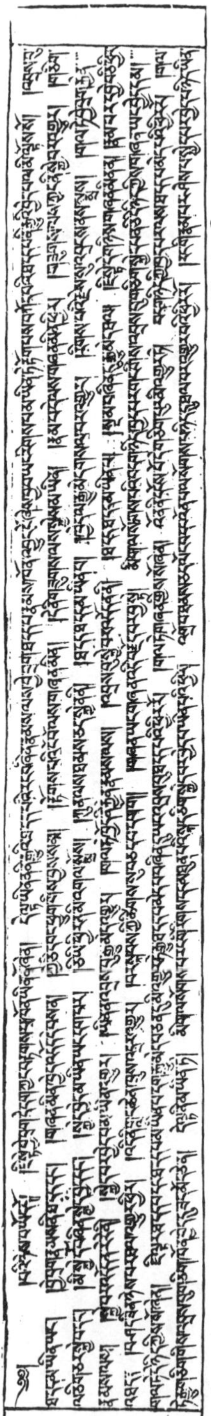

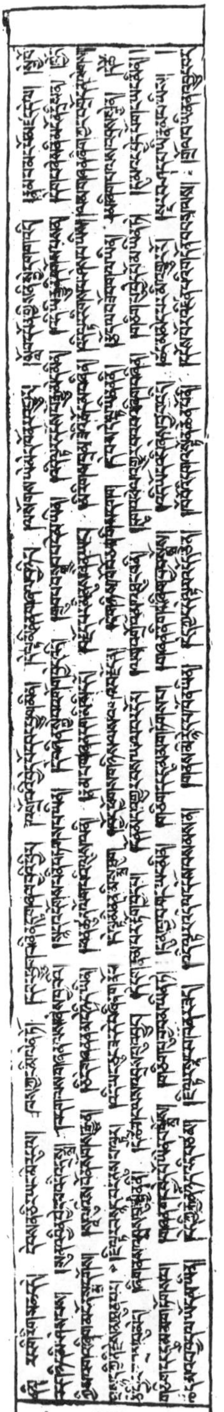

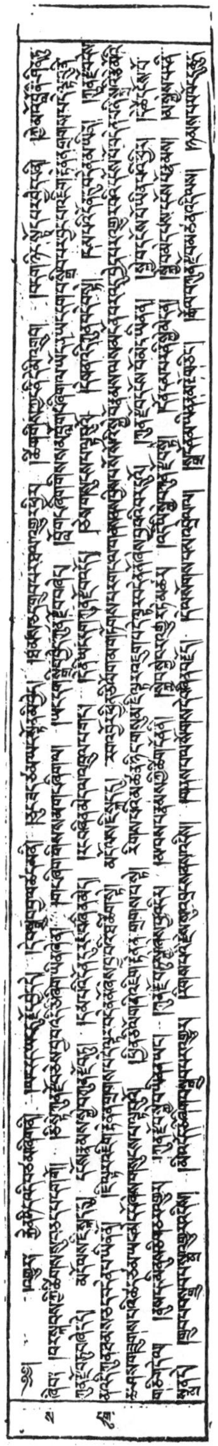

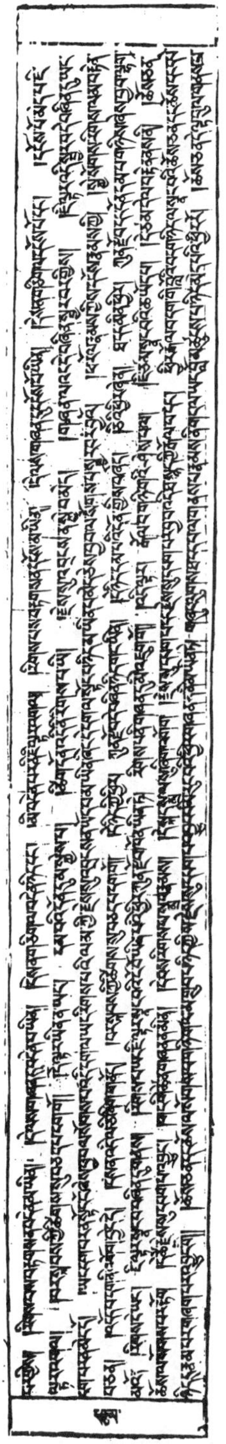

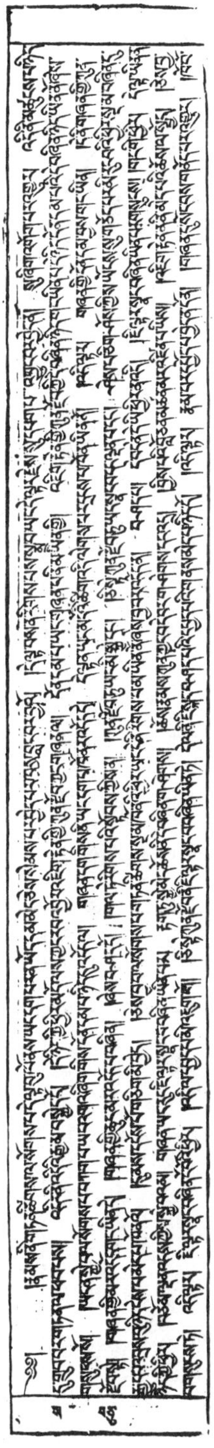

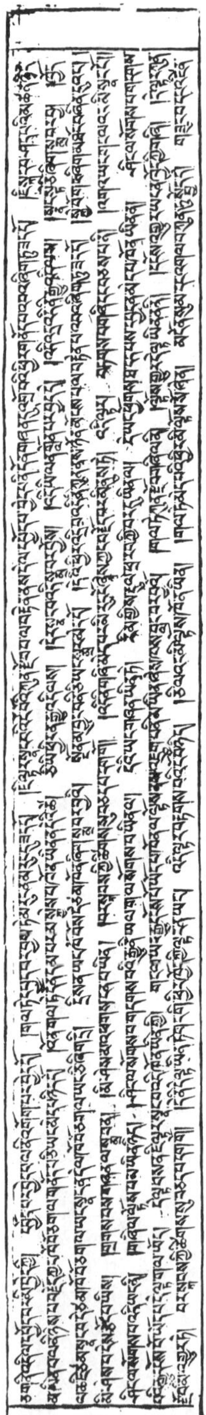

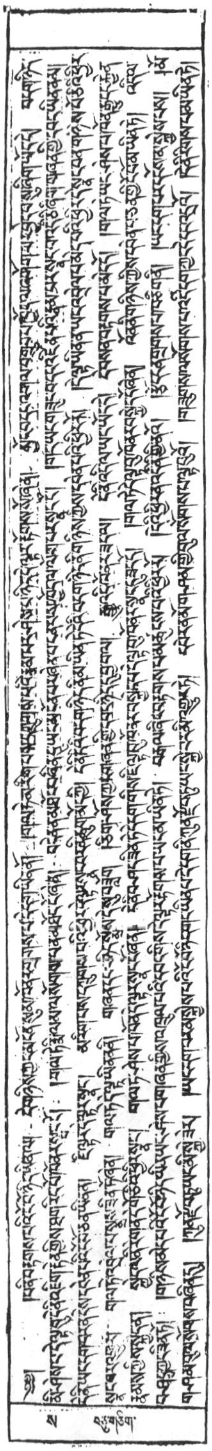

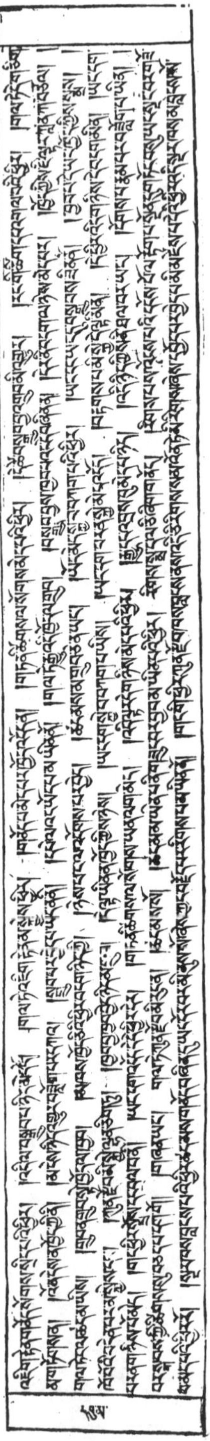

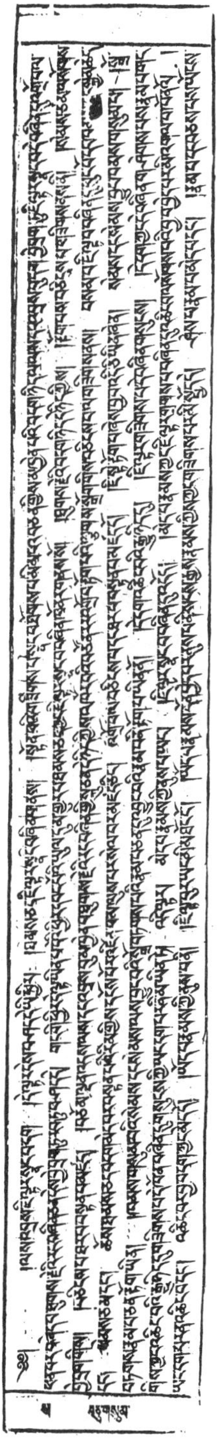

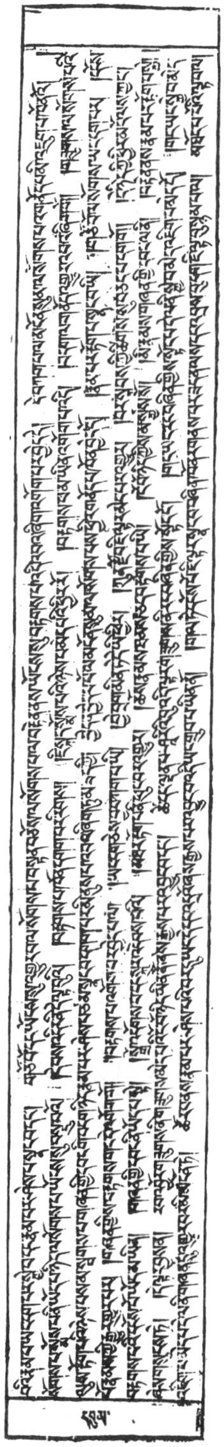

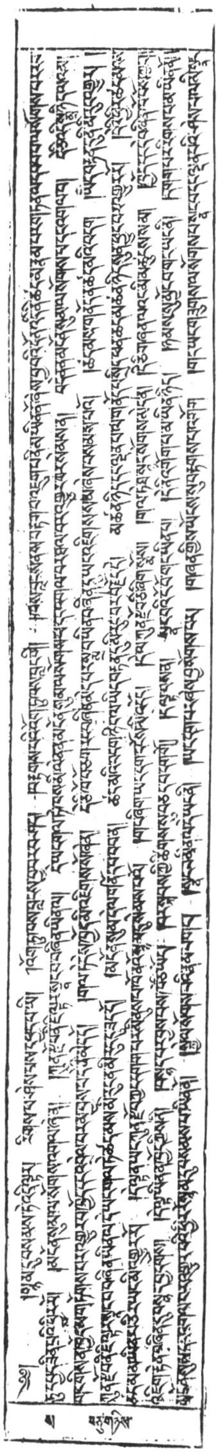

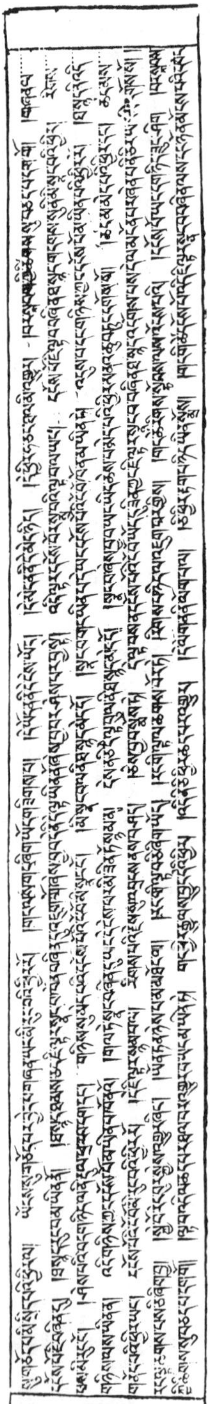

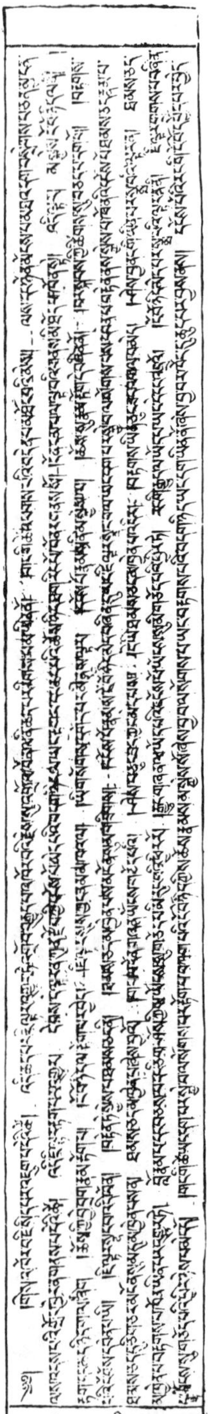

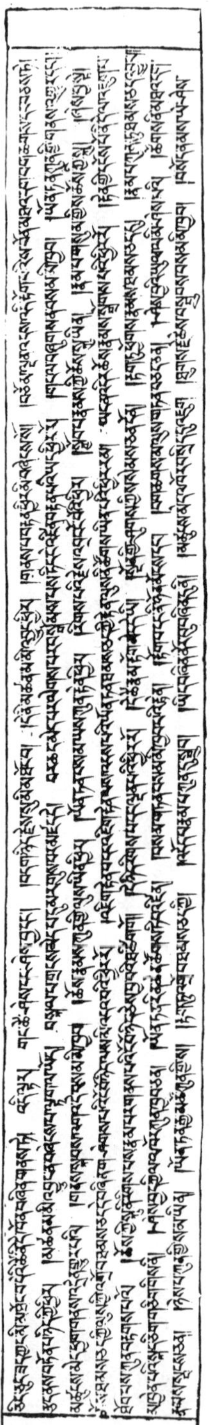

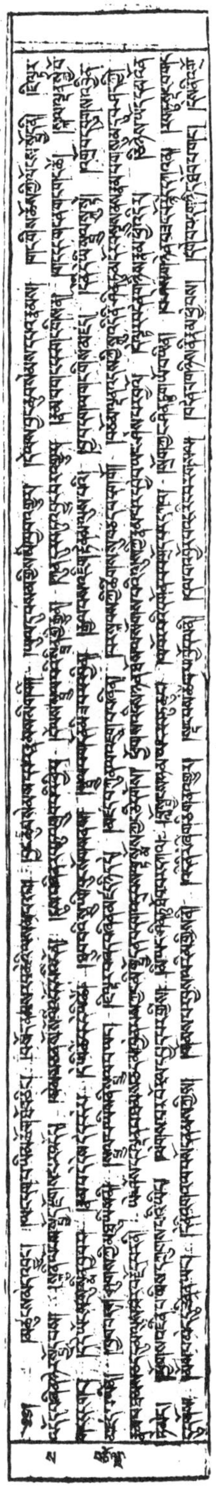

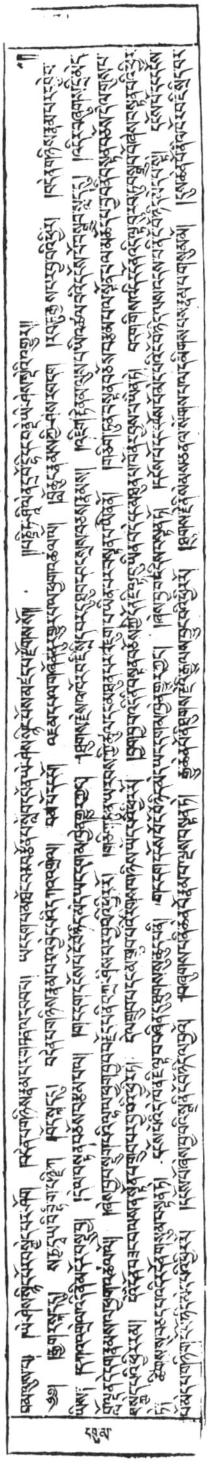

Bibliography

I. Reference Works

Apte, V. S. *Sanskrit-English Dictionary*. 2 vols. Poona: Prasad Prakashan, 1957.

A Critical Pali Dictionary. Begun by V. Trenckner, revised, continued, and edited by Dines Anderson, Helmer Smith, and Hans Hendriksen. Copenhagen: Royal Danish Academy of Sciences and Letters, 1924–.

Conze, Edward. *Materials for a Dictionary of the Prajñāpāramitā Literature*. Tokyo: Suzuki Research Foundation, 1973.

Das, Sarat Chandra. *A Tibetan-English Dictionary with Sanskrit Synonyms*. Reprint ed., Delhi: Motilal Banarsidass, 1970.

Edgerton, Franklin. *Buddhist Hybrid Sanskrit Grammar and Dictionary*. 2 vols. New Haven: Yale University Press, 1953; reprint ed., Delhi: Motilal Banarsidass, 1972.

Hirano, Takashi. *An Index to the Bodhicaryāvatāra Pañjikā Chapter IX*. Tokyo: Suzuki Research Foundation, 1966.

Jäschke, H.A. *A Tibetan-English Dictionary*. London: Routledge & Kegan Paul, 1958; reprint ed., Delhi: Motilal Banarsidass, 1975.

Miyasaka, Yūsho. "An Index to the *Pramāṇavārttika-kārikā*," Part I (Sanskrit-Tibetan Section). *Acta Indologica* III (1973–5): 1–157; Part II (Tibetan-Sanskrit Section). *Acta Indologica* IV (1976–9): 1–179.

Obermiller, E. *Indices Verborum Sanscrit-Tibetan and Tibetan-Sanscrit to the Nyāyabindu of Dharmakīrti and the Nyāyabinduṭīkā of Dharmottara*. Osnabruck: Biblio Verlag, 1970.

Sakaki, R., ed. *Mahāvyutpatti*. 2 vols. Suzuki Research Foundation Reprint Series, no. 1. Tokyo: Suzuki Research Foundation, 1962.

Steinkellner, Ernst. *Verse-Index of Dharmakīrti's Works* (Tibetan Versions). Vienna: Arbeitskreis Für Tibetische und Buddhistische Studien Universität Wien, 1977.

Yamaguchi, Susumu. *Index to the Prasannapadā Madhyamaka-vṛtti.* 2 vols. Kyoto: Heirakuji-Shoten, 1974.

II. Primary Sources: Pāli and Sanskrit

Bhāvaviveka. *Madhyamakahṛdayakārikā.* Chapter 3.1–136 edited by Shotaro Iida, *Reason and Emptiness: A Study in Logic and Mysticism.* Tokyo: Hokuseido, 1980.

———. The remainder of chapter 3 is edited by Y. Ejima, *Development of Mādhyamika Philosophy in India: Studies on Bhāvaviveka* (in Japanese). Tokyo, 1981.

Candrakīrti. *Prasannapadā Madhyamakavṛtti.* Ed. L. de La Vallée Poussin, Bibliotheca Buddhica IV. St. Petersburg, 1903–13.

Daśabhūmikasūtra. Ed. P.L. Vaidya. Buddhist Sanskrit Texts Series No. 7. Darbhanga: The Mithila Institute, 1967.

Dharmakīrti. *Nyāya-bindu.* Ed. with Dharmottara's *Ṭīkā* by Th. Stcherbatsky. Bibliotheca Buddhica VII. St. Petersburg, 1918.

———. *Nyāya-bindu* with Dharmottara's *Ṭīkā* and Paṇḍita Durveka Miśra's *Dharmottarapradīpa.* Ed. Paṇḍita Dalsukhbhai Malvania. Tibetan Sanskrit Works Series, Vol. 2. Patna: Jayaswal Research Institute, 1971.

———. *Pramāṇa-vārttika with a Commentary by Manorathanandin.* Ed. Rāhula Sāṃkṛityāna. *Journal of the Bihar and Orissa Research Society* (1938–40).

———. *The Pramāṇavārttikam of Dharmakīrti: The First Chapter with the Autocommentary.* Ed. Raniero Gnoli. Serie Orientale Roma XXIII. Rome, 1960.

———. *Pramāṇaviniścaya.* Sanskrit fragments of Chapter 1 (*Pratyakṣa*) edited with the Tibetan text and German translation by Tilmann Vetter. Vienna: Österreichische Akademie der Wissenschaften, 1966.

———. *Pramāṇaviniścaya.* Chapter 2 (*svārthānumāna*) edited with Tibetan text, German translation and notes by Ernst Steinkellner. Vienna: Österreichische Akademie der Wissenschaften, 1973–9.

———. *Vādamyāya*. Ed. Rāhula Sāṃkṛtyāyana. *Journal of the Bihar and Orissa Research Society* 21–22 (1935).

Haribhadra. *Abhisamayālaṃkārālokā Prajñāpāramitāvyākhyā*. Ed. Unrai Wogihara. Tokyo: The Toyo Bunko, 1932–5.

Kamalaśīla. *Tattva-saṃgraha-pañjikā*. See Śāntarakṣita.

———. *Bhāvanākrama*. The first and third *Bhāvanākrama* Ed. Giuseppe Tucci. *Minor Buddhist Texts* II. Serie Orientale Roma IX, 1958. *Minor Buddhist Texts* III. Serie Orientale Roma XLIII, 1971.

Mādhava. *Sarva-darśana-saṃgraha*. Ed. V.S. Abhyankar. 3rd Edition. Poona: Bhandarkar Institute, 1978.

Maitreyanātha. *Madhyāntavibhāga*. See Vasubandhu.

Milindapañho. Ed. V. Trenckner. London: Williams and Norgate, 1880.

Nāgārjuna. *Mūlamadhyamakakārikās*. Ed. J.W. de Jong. Adyar Library Series 109. Madras: Adyar Library, 1977.

———. *Ratnāvalī*. Sanskrit, Tibetan and Chinese texts ed. Michael Hahn. Bonn, 1982.

———. *Vigrahavyāvartanī*. Ed. E.H. Johnton and A. Kunst. *Mêlanges chinois et bouddhiques* 9 (1948–51): 99–152.

Prajñākaramati. *Bodhicaryāvatārapañjikā*. See Śāntideva.

Saddharmalaṅkāvatārasūtra. Ed. P.L. Vaidya. Buddhist Sanskrit Texts Series, Vol. 3. Darbhanga: The Mithila Institute, 1963.

Śaṅkara. *Brahmasūtraśaṅkarabhāṣyam*. Ed. J.L. Shastri, Delhi: Motilal Banarsidass, 1980.

Śāntarakṣita. *Tattva-saṃgraha*. Edited with Kamalaśīla's *pañjikā* by E. Krishnamacharya. Gaekwad's Oriental Series 30–31. Baroda, 1926.

Śantideva. *Bodhicaryāvatāra*. Ed. P.L. Vaidya. Buddhist Sanskrit Texts, Vol. 12. Darbhanga: The Mithila Institute, 1960.

———. *Śikṣāsamuccaya*. Ed. P.L. Vaidya. Buddhist Sanskrit Texts Series, Vol. 11. Darbhanga: The Mithila Institute, 1961.

Vasubandhu. *Madhyānta-vibhāga-bhāṣya*. Ed. Gadjin M. Nagao. Tokyo: Suzuki Research Foundation, 1964.

———. *Triṃśikā*. Edited with Sthiramati's commentary and Vasubandhu's *Viṃśatikā* by Sylvain Lévi. Paris, 1925.

III. Primary Sources, Tibetan.

Candrakīrti. *Yuktiṣaṣṭikāvṛtti*. (*Rigs-pa-drug-cu-pa'i-'grel-pa*) *PTT* (Otani #5265).

———. *Madhyamakāvatāra* (*Dbu-ma-la-'jug-pa*). Ed. Louis de La Vallée Poussin. Bibliotheca Buddhica IX. Reprint ed., Osnabruck: Biblio Verlag, 1970.

Devendrabuddhi. *Pramāṇavārttikaṭīkā*. (*Tshad-ma-rnam-'grel-gyi-dka'-'grel*) *DTT* (Tohoku #4217).

Dignāga. *Ālambana-parīkṣā*. Edited with translation and notes by E. Frauwallner, *WZKM* 37 (1930): 174–94.

———. *Pramāṇa-samuccaya*. Tibetan of *pratyakṣa* chapter edited by Masaaki Hattori in *Dignāga, on Perception*. Cambridge: Harvard University Press, 1968.

lCang-skya. *Grub-pa'i-mtha'-rnam-par-gzhag-pa*. Partially edited by Donald Lopez. "The Svātantrika-Mādhyamika School of Mahāyāna Buddhism." Ph.D. Dissertation: University of Virginia, 1982.

Śāntarakṣita. *Madhyamakālaṃkāra*. (*Dbu-ma'i-rgyan-gyi-tshig-le'ur-byas-pa*) *PTT* (Otani #5284).

Śrīgupta. *Tattvāvatāra*. (*De-kho-na-la-'jug-pa'i-'grel-pa*) *PTT* (Otani #5292).

Tsong-kha-pa. *Drang-nges-legs-bshad-snying-po*. Sarnath: Gelugpa Students' Welfare Committee, 1973.

IV. Secondary Sources and Translations

Bapat, P.V. "*Vohāra: Vyāhāra: Vyavahāra*." *Sanskrit and Indological Studies: Dr. V. Raghavan Felicitation Volume*. Ed. R.N. Dandekar et al. Delhi: Motilal Barnarsidass, 1975, pp.27–33.

Bareau, André. "Trois traités sur les sectes bouddhiques attribués à Vasumitra, Bhavya, et Vinītadeva." *Journal Asiatique* 244 (1956): 167–200.

Bhattacharya, Kamaleswar. "Mādhyamika et Vaitaṇḍika." *Journal Asiatique* 263 (1975): 99–102.

Booth, Wayne. *A Rhetoric of Irony*. Chicago: University of Chicago Press, 1974.

Chandra, Lokesh. *Materials for a History of Tibetan Literature*. Śatapiṭaka Series, vols. 28–30. New Delhi: International Academy of Indian Culture, 1963.

Chattopadhyaya, Debiprasad. *Tāranātha's History of Buddhism in India*. Simla: Indian Institute of Advanced Study, 1970.

Conze, Edward. "The Ontology of the *Prajñāpāramitā*." *PEW* 3 (1953): 117–29.

———. *Buddhist Thought in India*. Ann Arbor: University of Michigan Press, 1967.

Dayal, Har. *The Bodhisattva Doctrine in Buddhist Sanskrit Literature*. London: Routledge and Kegan Paul, 1932; reprint ed., Delhi: Motilal Banarsidass, 1970.

de Jong, Jan. "The Problem of the Absolute in the Madhyamaka School." *JIP* 2 (1972): 1–6.

———. "Emptiness." *JIP* 2 (1972): 7–15.

———. "A Brief History of Buddhist Studies in Europe and America." *The Eastern Buddhist*. NS 7, no. 1 (1974), pp. 55–106; no. 2 (1974), pp. 49–82.

———. "Textcritical Notes on the Prasannapadā." *IIJ* 20 (1978): 25–59.

de La Vallée Poussin, Louis. "Madhyamaka," "Nihilism (Buddhist)," "Nirvana," and "Scepticism (Buddhist)." *The Encyclopedia of Religion and Ethics*, ed. James Hastings. New York: Charles Scribner's Sons, 1917.

———. "Madhyamaka." *Mélanges chinois et bouddhiques* 2 (1932–3): 1–146.

———. "Le Petit traité de Vasubandhu-Nāgārjuna sur les trois natures." *Mélanges chinois et bouddhiques* 2 (1932–3): 147–61.

———. "Buddhica." *Harvard Journal of Asiatic Studies* 3 (1938): 137–60.

Demiéville, Paul. *Le Concile de Lhasa*. Paris, 1952.

Eckel, Malcolm David. "Bhāvaviveka and the Early Mādhyamika Theories of Language." *PEW* 28 (1978): 323–37.

———. "A Question of Nihilism: Bhāvaviveka's Response to the Fundamental Problems of Mādhyamika Philosophy." Ph.D. Diss.: Harvard University, 1980.

———. "Gratitude to an Empty Savior: A Study of the Concept of Gratitude in Mahāyāna Buddhist Philosophy." *History of Religions* 25 (1985): 57–75.

———. "Bhāvaviveka's Criticism of Yogācāra Philosophy in Chapter XXV of the Prajñāpradīpa." In *Miscellanea Buddhica*, ed. Chr. Lindtner, pp. 25–75. Copenhagen: Akademisk Forlag, 1985.

———. "The Concept of Reason in Jñānagarbha's Svātantrika Madhyamaka," in B. K. Matilal and R. D. Evans, eds., *Buddhist Logic and Epistemology* (Dordrecht: D. Reidel, 1986), pp. 265–90.

Ejima, Yasunori. *Development of Mādhyamika Philosophy in India: Studies on Bhāvaviveka* (in Japanese). Tokyo, 1981.

Frauwallner, Erich. "Die Reihenfolge und Entstehung der Werke Dharmakīrti's." *Asiatica* (Festschrift Weller). Leipzig, 1954, pp. 142–54.

Gokhale, V.V. "The Vedānta-Philosophy Described by Bhavya in his *Madhyamaka-hṛdaya*." *IIJ* 2 (1958): 165–80.

———. "Masters of Buddhism Adore the Brahman through Non-adoration." *IIJ* 5 (1961–2): 271–5.

Gokhale, V.V. and Bahulkar, S.S."Madhyamakahṛdayakārikā Tarkajvālā, Chapter I." In *Miscellanea Buddhica*, ed. Chr. Lindtner, pp. 76–108. Copenhagen: Akademisk Forlag, 1985.

Gombrich, Richard. *On Being Sanskritic*. Oxford: Clarendon Press, 1978.

Guenther, Herbert. *The Jewel Ornament of Liberation*. Berkeley: Shambala, 1971.

Hattori, Masaaki, *Dignāga, On Perception. Harvard Oriental Series*, vol. 47. Cambridge, Massachusetts: Harvard University Press, 1968.

Hopkins, Jeffrey. *Meditation on Emptiness*. London: Wisdom Publications, 1983.

Huntington, C.W. Jr. "The System of the Two Truths in the Prasannapadā and the Madhyamakāvatāra: A Study in Madhyamaka Soteriology." *JIP* 11 (1983): 77–106.

Ichigo, Masamichi. "A Synopsis of the *Madhyamakālaṃkāra* of Śāntarakṣita (1)." *IBK* 20 (1972), 989–95.

———. *Madhyamakālaṃkāra of Śantarakṣita* (in Japanese). Kyoto: Buneido, 1985.

Iida, Shotaro. "*Āgama* (Scripture) and *Yukti* (Reason) in Bhāvaviveka." *Kanakura Festschrift*. Kyoto: Heirakuji-Shoten, 1966, pp. 79–96.

———. *Reason and Emptiness: A Study in Logic and Mysticism*. Tokyo: The Hokuseido Press, 1980.

Inagaki, Hisao. "Haribhadra's Quotations from Jñānagarbha's *Anantamukha-nirhāradhāraṇīṭīkā*." *Buddhist Thought and Asian Civilization (Essays in Honor of Herbert V. Guenther on His Sixtieth Birthday)*. Ed. Leslie S. Kawamura and Keith Scott. Emeryville, California: Dharma Publishing, 1977, pp. 132–44.

Ingalls, Daniel H.H. *Materials for the Study of Navya-Nyāya Logic*. Harvard Oriental Series, vol. 40. Cambridge, Mass.: Harvard University Press, 1951.

———. "Śaṅkara's Arguments against the Buddhists." *PEW* 3 (1954).

Jacobi, Hermann. "Über den nominalen Stil des wissenschaftlichen Sanskrits." *Indogermanische Forschungen* 14 (1903): 236–51.

Jaini, P.S. "On the Sarvajñatva (Omniscience) of Mahāvīra and the Buddha." *Buddhist Studies in Honour of I.B. Horner*. Ed. L. Cousins et al. Dordrecht: Reidel, 1930, pp. 71–90.

Jha, Ganganatha. *The Tattvasaṃgraha of Śāntarakṣita with the Commentary of Kamalaśīla*. Gaekwad's Oriental Series, vol. 80. Baroda: Oriental Institute, 1937.

Kajiyama, Yuichi. "Introduction to the Logic of Svātantrika Mādhyamika Philosophy." *Nava-Nalanda Mahavihara Research Publication* 1 (1957): 291–331.

———. "Bhāvaviveka's *Prajñāpradīpa* (1 Kapitel)," WZKS 7 (1963): 37–62; 8 (1964): 100–30.

———. *An Introduction to Buddhist Philosophy: An Annotated Translation of the Tarkabhāṣā of Mokṣākaragupta*. Kyoto, 1966.

———. "Bhāvaviveka, Sthiramati and Dharmapāla." *WZKS* 12–13 (1968–9): 193–203.

———. "Three Kinds of Affirmation and Two Kinds of Negation in Buddhist Philosophy." *WZKS* 17 (1973): 161–76.

———. "Later Mādhyamikas on Epistemology and Meditation." *Mahāyāna*

Buddhist Meditation. Ed. Minoru Kiyota. Honolulu: the University Press of Hawaii, 1978, pp. 114–43.

Lamotte, Étienne. *Le Traité de la grand vertu de sagesse de Nāgārjuna* (*Mahāprajñāpāramitāśāstra*). 5 vols. Louvain: Institut Orientaliste, 1949–80.

———. "Der Verfasser des Upadeśa und seine Quellen." *Nachrichten der Akademie der Wissenschaften in Göttingen* (1973): 3–49.

———. *The Teaching of Vimalakīrti* (*Vimalakīrtinirdeśa*). Trans. Sara Boin. Sacred Books of the Buddhists 32. London: The Pali Text Society, 1976.

Lessing, F. D. and Wayman, A. *Introduction to the Buddhist Tantric Systems*. The Hague: Mouton, 1968; 2nd. edition Delhi: Motilal Banarsidass, 1978.

Lindtner, Christian. "Candrakīrti's *Pañcaskandhaprakaraṇa*." *AO* 40 (1979): 87–145.

———. "À Propos Dharmakīrti — Two New Works and a New Date." *AO* 41 (1980): 27–37.

———. "Atiśa's Introduction to the Two Truths, and its Sources." *JIP* 9 (1981): 161–214.

———. "Adversaria Buddhica." *WZKS* 26 (1982): 167–94.

———. *Nagarjuniana: Studies in the Writings and Philosophy of Nāgārjuna*. Copenhagen: Akademisk Forlag, 1982.

———. "Marginalia to Dharmakīrti's Pramāṇaviniścaya I–II." *WZKS* 28 (1984): 149–75.

———. "A Treatise on Buddhist Idealism: Kambala's Ālokamālā." In *Miscellanea Buddhica*, pp. 109–220. Copenhagen: Akademisk Forlag, 1985.

Lipman, Kennard. "A Study of Śāntarakṣita's *Madhyamakālaṃkāra*." Ph.D. Dissertation: University of Saskatchewan, 1979.

———. "A Controversial Topic from Mi-pham's Analysis of Śāntarakṣita's Madhyamakālaṃkāra," *Wind Horse* (Proceedings of the North American Tibetological Society) 1 (1981): 40–57.

Lopez, Donald Sewell, Jr. "The Svātantrika-Mādhyamika School of Mahāyāna Buddhism." Ph.D. Dissertation: University of Virginia, 1982.

Matilal, B.K. *The Navya-Nyāya Doctrine of Negation*. Harvard Oriental Series, vol. 46. Cambridge, Mass.: Harvard University Press, 1968.

———. *Epistemology, Logic and Grammar in Indian Philosophical Analysis*. Janua Linguarum, Series Minor, 3. The Hague: Mouton, 1971.

May, Jacques. "La Philosophiue boddhique de la vacuité." *Studia Philosophica* 18 (1958): 102–11.

———. "Kant et le Mādhyamika: à propos d'un livre recent." *IIJ* 3 (1959): 102–11.

Mimaki, K. "Sur le rôle de l'*Antaraśloka* ou du *Saṃgrahaśloka*." In *Mélanges offerts à Mgr Étienne Lamotte*, pp. 233–44. Louvain-la Neuve: Institut Orientaliste, 1980.

Murti, T.R.V. *The Central Philosophy of Buddhism*. London: George Allen and Unwin, 1960.

Nagao, Gadjin M. "The Silence of the Buddha and its Madhyamic Interpretation." *Studies in Indology and Buddhology*. Ed. Gadjin M. Nagao and Josho Nozawa. Kyoto, 1955, pp. 137–51.

———. "From Mādhyamika to Yogācāra: An Analysis of MMK, XXIV.18 and MV, I.1–2." *JIABS* 2 (1979): 29–43.

———. "On the Theory of Buddha-Body." *The Eastern Buddhist* 6 (1973): 25–53.

Nagatomi, Masatoshi. "The Framework of the Pramāṇavārttika, Book One." *JAOS* 79 (1959): 263–6.

———. "*Arthakriyā*." *Adyar Library Bulletin* 31–2 (1967–8): 52–72.

———. "*Mānasa-Pratyakṣa:* A Conundrum in the Buddhist *Pramāṇa* System." *Sanskrit and Indian Studies: Essays in Honour of Daniel H.H. Ingalls*. Ed. M. Nagatomi et al. Dordrecht: D. Reidel, 1980: 243–60.

Nakamura, Hajime. "The Vedānta Thought as Referred to in the Texts of Bhavya." *Professor M. Hiriyanna Commemoration Volume*. Ed. V. Raghavan and G. Marulasiddaiah. Mysore, 1972.

———. *A History of Early Vedānta Philosophy*. Delhi: Motilal Banarsidass, 1983.

Nishitani, Keiji. *Religion and Nothingness*. Berkeley: University of California Press, 1982.

Obermiller, E. "The Doctrine of the Prajñāpāramitā as exposed in the Abhisamayālaṃkāra of Maitreya." *AO* 11 (1932): 1–133.

Potter, Karl. *Presuppositions of India's Philosophies*. Englewood Cliffs, N.J.: Prentice Hall, 1963; reprint ed., Westport, Conn.: Greenwood Press, 1972.

———. "Realism, Speech-Acts, and Truth-Gaps in Indian and Western Philosophy." *JIP* 1 (1970):

Robinson, Richard H. *Early Mādhyamika in India and China*. Madison, Wisconsin, 1967.

———. "Did Nāgārjuna Really Refute All Philosophical Views." *PEW* 22 (1972): 323–31.

Roerich, George N. *The Blue Annals*. Calcutta, 1949; reprinted: Delhi: Motilal Banarsidass, 1976.

Ruegg, David Seyfort. "Ārya and Bhadanta Vimuktisena on the Gotra-theory of the Prajñāpāramitā." *WZKS* 12–13 (1968–9): 303–17.

———. *La thèorie du tathāgatagarbha et du gotra*. Publications de l'École Française d'Extrême-Orient, no. 70. Paris: École Française d'Extrême Orient, 1969.

———. "The Uses of the Four Positions of the *Catuṣkoṭi* and the Problem of the Description of Reality in Mahāyāna Buddhism." *JIP* 5 (1977): 1–71.

———. "The Study of Tibetan Philosophy and its Indian Sources." *Proceedings of the Csoma de Korös Memorial Symposium*. Ed. Louis Ligati. *Bibliotheca Orientalis Hungarica* 23 (1978): 377–91.

———. *The Literature of the Madhyamaka School of Philosophy in India*. Wiesbaden: Otto Harrassowitz, 1981.

Schayer, Stanislaw. "Das mahāyānistische Absolutum nach der Lehre der Mādhyamikas." *Orientalistische Literatur-Zeitung* 38 (1935): 401–15.

Sherburne, Richard. *A Lamp for the Path and Commentary by Atīśa*. London: George Allen and Unwin, 1983.

Staal, J.F. "Negation and the Law of Contradiction in Indian Thought: A Comparative Study." *Bulletin of the School of Oriental and African Studies* 25 (1961): 52–71.

Stcherbatsky, Th. *Buddhist Logic*. Vol 1. Bibliotheca Buddhica, 26. Leningrad: Academy of Sciences of the USSR, ca. 1930; reprint ed. New York: Dover Publications, 1962.

———. "Die drei Richtungen in der Philosophie des Buddhismus." *Rocznik Orjentalistyczny* 10 (1934): 1–37.

———. *Madhyānta-vibhaṅga: Discourse on Discrimination between Middle and Extremes*. Reprint ed., Calcutta: Indian Studies Past and Present, 1972.

Steinkellner, Ernst. "Wirklichkeit und Begriff bei Dharmakīrti." *WZKS* 15 (1971): 179–212.

———. *Dharmakīrti's Pramāṇaviniścayaḥ: Zweites Kapitel: Svārthānumānam*. 2 vols. Vienna: Österreichische Akademie der Wissenschaften, 1973–9.

Tachikawa, Musashi. "A Logical Analysis of the *Mūlamadhyamakakārikā*." *Sanskrit and Indian Studies*. Ed. Masatoshi Nagatomi et al. Boston: D. Reidel, 1980.

Tauscher, Helmut. *Candrakīrti: Madhyamakāvatāraḥ und Madhyamakāvatārabhāṣyam (Kapitel VI, Vers 166–226)*. Wiener Studien zur Tibetologie und Buddhismuskunde. Vol. 5. Vienna: Arbeitskreis für Tibetische und Buddhistische Studien Universität Wien, 1981.

Thurman, Robert A.F. *The Holy Teaching of Vimalakīrti*. University Park: Pennsylvania State University Press, 1976.

———. "Buddhist Hermeneutics." *Journal of the American Academy of Religion* 46 (1978): 19–39.

———, *Tsong Khapa's Speech of Gold in the Essence of True Eloquence*. Princeton: Princeton University Press, 1984.

Tillemans, Tom. "The 'Neither One nor Many' Argument for *Śūnyatā*, and its Tibetan Interpretations: Background Information and Source Materials." *Études de Lettres* (1982): 103–28.

———. "Two Tibetan Texts on the 'Neither One nor Many' Argument for Śūnyatā." *JIP* 12 (1984): 357–88.

Van Den Broeck, José. *La Progression dans la méditation (Bhāvanākrama de Kamalaśīla)*. Brussels: L'Institut Belge des Hautes Études Bouddhiques, 1977.

Vetter, Tilmann. *Erkenntnisprobleme bei Dharmakīrti*. Vienna: Österreichische Akademie der Wissenschaften, 1964.

———. *Dharmakīrti's Pramāṇaviniścayaḥ: 1. Kapitel: Pratyakṣam*. Vienna: Österreichische Akademie der Wissenschaften, 1966.

———. "Die Lehre Nāgārjunas in den Mūla-Madhyamaka-Kārikās." In *Epiphanie des Heiles*. Ed. Gerhard Oberhammer. Vienna, 1982, pp. 87–108.

———. *Der Buddha und seine Lehre in Dharmakīrtis Pramāṇavārttika*. Vienna: Arbeitskreis für Tibetische und Buddhistische Studien Universität Wien, 1984.

Vidyabhusana, Satis Chandra. *A History of Indian Logic*. Delhi: Motilal Banarsidass, 1971.

Warder, A.K. "The Concept of a Concept." *JIP* 1 (1971): 181–96.

Williams, Paul. "Some Aspects of Language and Construction in the Madhyamaka." *JIP* 8 (1980): 1–45.

Index of Sanskrit Terms and Phrases

Index of Proper Names